IT'S ALL CONNECTED

A COMPREHENSIVE GUIDE TO GLOBAL ISSUES AND SUSTAINABLE SOLUTIONS

FACING THE FUTURE:
PEOPLE AND THE PLANET

By Benjamin Wheeler, M.A.; Gilda Wheeler, M.Ed.; and Wendy Church, Ph.D.

IT'S ALL CONNECTED

A COMPREHENSIVE
GUIDE TO GLOBAL ISSUES
AND SUSTAINABLE SOLUTIONS

By Benjamin Wheeler, M.A.; Gilda Wheeler, M.Ed.; and Wendy Church, Ph.D.

ISBN 0-9711005-4-3

Design and layout by Amy Marchegiani, Graf X design

Copy editing by Kris Fulsaas

Front and back cover photo credits:
Tanzanian woman with solar cooker, photo © Sarah Bones, courtesy of CARE;
San Francisco, California, © Djordje Zlatanovic; Kosovar man with cows, © 2002 Alan Gignoux, courtesy of CARE;
Yellowstone National Park, courtesy of National Park Service;
Bangladesh mother and daughter, © 2000 Billy Howard, courtesy of CARE;
Volunteers, photo courtesy of FEMA;
African women with fuel wood, photo © Sarah Bones, courtesy of CARE.

Printed on recycled paper

Facing the Future: People and the Planet
is a nonprofit organization providing resources and action opportunities
on global issues and sustainability for teachers, students, and the public.
For more information about *Facing the Future: People and the Planet*
and to order copies of this book, visit our website at
www.facingthefuture.org or contact us at:

FACING THE FUTURE: PEOPLE AND THE PLANET
811 First Avenue, Suite 454
Seattle, WA 98104
(206) 264-1503
Email: office@facingthefuture.org
www.facingthefuture.org

ACKNOWLEDGMENTS

This book could not have been created without the input of many organizations and individuals. We would like to thank each of the following for their time and expertise in making this book accurate and engaging for students.

CONTENT REVIEWERS

Char Alkire, science supervisor, Teacher Education Program, University of Washington

James Bennett, research scientist, School of Oceanography, University of Washington

Dr. Louise Chawla, professor, Whitney Young School of Honors and Liberal Studies, Kentucky State University

Maura Clevenger, technology education consultant

John DeGraaf, filmmaker and author of *Affluenza: The All-Consuming Epidemic*

Dee Dickinson, CEO and founder of New Horizons for Learning

Dr. Thomas J. Edwards, managing consultant, Telecommunications and Contact Center Optimization

Ara K. Erickson, forestry research consultant, Rural Technology Initiative, University of Washington

Alden M. Garrett, family law attorney and mediator

Árni Ísaksson, director, Freshwater Fisheries, Reykjavík, Iceland

William C. Jacobs, president and CEO, Middleton Foundation for Ethical Studies, Olympia, Washington

Terry L. Leitzell, general counsel, Icicle Seafoods, Inc.

Susan Reba McIntyre, PhD, Leadership Charters, LLC

Joseph F. Murray, forester, Merrill and Ring Timber and Land Management Company

Population Reference Bureau staff

Jennifer Potter, director, Initiative for Global Development

Jacqueline Sherris, PhD, program leader, Reproductive Health, Program for Appropriate Technology in Health (PATH)

Dr. Debra Sullivan, director, Praxis Institute for Early Childhood Education

Verna Swanljung, international business instructor, North Seattle Community College

Dr. Stephen G. Warren, professor, Department of Atmospheric Sciences, University of Washington

Dr. Anand Yang, director, Jackson School of International Development, University of Washington

TEACHER REVIEWERS

Bekki Brown-Winkels, Mariner High School, Everett, Washington

Cindy Chang, English Language Program, University of Washington, Seattle, Washington

Chris Fontana, Global Studies Academy, Cleveland High School, Seattle, Washington

Robert Ford, Ridgefield High School, Ridgefield, Washington

Chris Koester, Moses Lake High School, Moses Lake, Washington

Bob Mazelow, Lakeside High School, Seattle, Washington

Larry Steele, Franklin High School, Seattle, Washington

John Wiley, Shawnee Mission West High School, Overlake Park, Kansas

We would like to thank the students of Bob Mazelow's global studies class at Lakeside High School and Chris Fontana's global studies class at Cleveland High School for their reviews and comments.

Thank you also to Kim Rakow Bernier, Heidi Radenovic, Leah Barrett, Ellie Mazzarella, and Alicia Robbins for their assistance in research, editing, and production.

We dedicate this book to the late Dr. Alexander Bill,
whose founding vision continues to inspire the organization,
and to Lee Minto and Dr. Jack Leversee, whose longstanding
commitment on our board sustains us.

IT'S ALL CONNECTED
A Comprehensive Guide to Global Issues and Sustainable Solutions

It's All Connected can to be used as a stand-alone text for a global issues course or as a supplemental text for other classes, including social studies (history, civics, economics, and geography), science, environmental studies, mathematics, English as a second language, and language arts. Ideally, this book will be used in tandem with the curriculum guide *Facing the Future: People and the Planet—Classroom Activities for Teaching About Global Issues and Solutions*, which features engaging hands-on activities, thought-provoking discussion questions, in-depth research assignments, easy-to-use, standards-based lesson plans, reproducible handouts, and additional resources to add depth to classroom discussions.

It's All Connected provides a thorough overview of a full range of global issues, as well as in-depth explorations of particular topics, debates, and solutions. Each unit contains thematically related chapters. Unit 1 includes an introduction to global issues and sustainability as well as definitions for some important concepts. Units 2–6 address specific global issues, such as food, water, forests, oceans, poverty, culture, education, health, and conflict. The book concludes with a final unit on ideas and tools for addressing global issues, including a curriculum activity for students to study a particular global issue or region. Units can be read separately, sequentially, or in any order to fit particular curriculum needs.

Each unit begins with an introductory chapter that frames the scope and purpose of that unit. Introductory chapters include **Essential Questions** on issues and concepts that are explored in the unit, a relevant **Story from the World**, and a **Youth in Action!** feature highlighting the creativity and enthusiasm of young people taking action. Subsequent chapters within each unit address specific global issues and include definitions, concepts, challenges, and sustainable solutions. Important terms are introduced in **bold print** and are defined in the **Glossary** at the back of the book.

It's All Connected combines information, concepts, and inspiring real-world examples. Alongside the main portion of the text, numerous **Features** emphasize interesting and important aspects of global issues. In addition to the essential questions at the beginning of each unit, **Curriculum Connections** offer topical explorations in math, literature, science, and technology. Each unit concludes with suggestions for *Facing the Future* **Activities** linked to the unit and a **Further Information** listing of relevant texts, websites, and videos. Extensive **Endnote** references for each unit can be found in the back of the book.

FACING THE FUTURE: PEOPLE AND THE PLANET

Facing the Future: People and the Planet is a nonprofit organization that brings global issues and sustainability education to middle and high schools. The organization researches and writes curriculum materials that promote critical thinking and meet national education standards; provides professional development training to teachers on global issues, sustainability, and service learning; and consults with schools to integrate global sustainability issues across their curricula.

Facing the Future curriculum and publications
are available through the website **www.facingthefuture.org**,
which also offers extensive opportunities for student
service learning and action projects.

UNIT 1
GETTING STARTED WITH GLOBAL ISSUES

The essence of global issues is a recognition that the people of the world are inexorably linked and that, in today's world, that which touches some touches us all.

—Paula J. Dobriansky
(U.S. Undersecretary of State
for Global Affairs, 2002)

Essential Questions

- **What are global issues?**

- **What is sustainability?**

- **What is a global perspective?**

- **How can youth be involved in global issues and sustainable solutions?**

- **What concepts and tools can help people understand and work toward sustainable solutions?**

Chapter 1. Introduction

We are living in an increasingly interconnected world, especially since the advent of the computer age in the twentieth century. This interconnection and integration among people, **economies***, and societies throughout the world is commonly called **globalization**.

Human beings around the world, now more than ever, are connected to each other. Coca-Cola markets its products all over the world; information about political movements, **terrorism**, and war spread almost instantly via the Internet. Epidemics of disease can spread quickly around the globe via air travel. In many cases, as human beings change the environment in their own communities, they affect the environment of people in other countries. Because of this, it is more important than ever for people to understand some of the basic concepts about global issues and learn how to develop a global perspective.

* *Glossary words appear in **bold** the first time they occur in each unit.*

This book discusses a number of global issues—issues that affect nearly everyone on the planet. A good place to start is to first define what global issues are and also to define some other important concepts that are important in understanding global issues. Then we will explore some of the most important global issues facing us today, including what kinds of solutions exist that can make life better for people and the planet.

What Are Global Issues?

Global issues are significant issues relating to or involving most or all of the Earth. An issue is likely to be global if it:
- persists or is long-acting
- is **transnational** or **transboundary**
- affects large numbers of people
- is an underlying cause of events
- is connected to other issues that meet these criteria

Global warming serves as a good example of a global issue that meets these criteria. Global warming occurs when **greenhouse gasses** such as **carbon dioxide** (which can result from the

GLOBAL ISSUES MOBILE

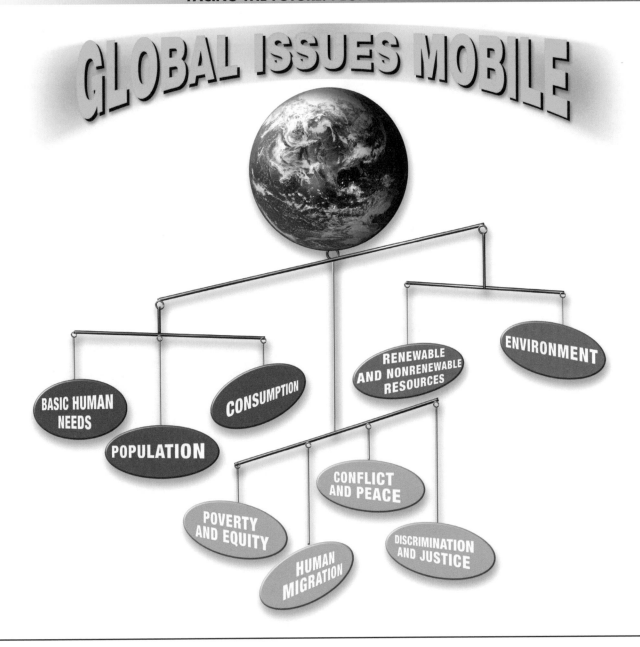

burning of **fossil fuels** including coal, oil, and natural gas) build up in the atmosphere and trap heat from the sun. Global warming is *persistent and long-acting* in that it may take years or even decades to be fully felt, and it may require similar time frames to be resolved. Global warming has proven to be *transnational*, meaning that its effects are felt well beyond the borders of countries responsible for creating it. Global warming can *significantly affect millions of people* and is an *underlying cause* of many events such as **desertification** (spreading of desert areas), crop failure, and diminished water supplies.[1] Last, global warming is *interconnected* to many other issues: efforts to slow global warming could in turn positively impact a number of other issues such as food security and **refugee** issues tied to climate change; these efforts could also affect economies, for better or worse.

Under the criteria listed above, many issues could be considered "global." This book focuses on some of the most pressing global issues recognized today by experts and the public.

Interconnections

A useful metaphor that shows the interconnectedness of global issues is that of a mobile. Although a mobile's component parts are separate and unique and may move in different directions, they are linked to one another by strings or wires. A force exerted on one part of a mobile will affect all of its other parts—in ways major or minor, sometimes predictable, and sometimes surprising.

A mobile serves as a model of the interconnectedness that is inherent in natural environments, wherein each individual organism is part of an elaborate web of life. Human-made systems and environments also mirror mobiles. For example, a great many of the items consumed in **developed countries** such as the United States are produced in **developing countries**. The production of these consumer goods plays a key role in those countries' economies, the lives of people there, and the natural environment. The Earth itself is one large, interconnected "system" that may be thought of as a remarkably complex mobile, wherein changes in one part of the system cause changes elsewhere.

Desertification in Darfur contributes to dust storms and resource scarcity

Photo © CARE Evelyn Hockstein

The conflict in Darfur in western Sudan serves as a good example of the global issues mobile. The most recent conflict there began in an arid and impoverished region early in 2003 after a rebel group began attacking **government** targets. The rebels asserted that the government oppressed black Africans in favor of Arabs. As of 2004, it is estimated that as a direct result of this conflict, up to 300,000 Darfur residents died and more than 1.2 million were displaced from their homes.

The region has long suffered from **scarcity** of wood, food, and water, stemming in part from desertification—which many experts believe is caused by human-induced climate change. This resource scarcity created fierce competition for diminishing water and **arable land** between Arab nomadic herders and African farmers. The combination of a high **fertility rate** of about six or seven children per woman and resource scarcity contributed to increased poverty and hunger in the region. The people of Darfur also lacked services, especially those of education, health care, and transportation. The desertification fueled **migration** from rural to urban centers because of a loss of animal resources and crops, as well as due to a lack of job opportunities and services in rural areas.[2]

The issues underlying the Darfur conflict—resource scarcity, lack of services and education, rapid population growth, migration, and environmental degradation—are interconnected (that is, connected to each other). Like a mobile, a change in one issue (whether positive or negative) clearly affects the other issues.

How might this interconnected mobile reflect other past and present situations around the world?

Imagining a Future that People Want

So why should people care about global issues? One reason is that global issues will, to a large extent, determine what the world will be like in the future. Think for a moment about what future you want.

Most people in the world would agree that they want to enjoy a **good quality of life**. Quality of life means different things to different people, depending on their circumstances and their **culture**. We know that everyone wants good food, clean water, good health, and shelter to stay warm and comfortable. Most people also want to enjoy their friends and family and be part of a community. They don't want to worry about war or some other crisis disrupting their lives.

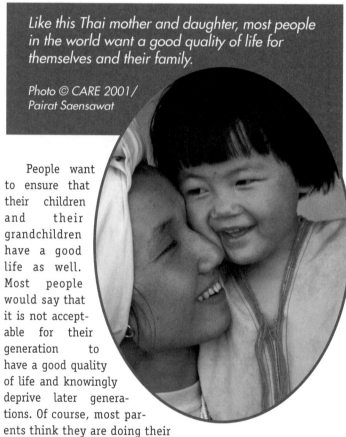

Like this Thai mother and daughter, most people in the world want a good quality of life for themselves and their family.

Photo © CARE 2001/ Pairat Saensawat

People want to ensure that their children and their grandchildren have a good life as well. Most people would say that it is not acceptable for their generation to have a good quality of life and knowingly deprive later generations. Of course, most parents think they are doing their best for their children. But sometimes doing their best for their family and their community can have a negative impact on others and the Earth's long-term ability to support their descendants. And these days, with the global reach of national economies, what people do locally can have an impact on the happiness and well-being of people around the world. As you begin this exploration of global issues, it is important to keep in mind the future you want for yourself, your family, and future generations—at home and around the world.

What is your vision for the future?

Youth in Action!
Claim a Cause, Find Your Voice, and Vote (Portions excepted from *YES!* magazine, www.yesmagazine.org[3])

One way you can begin to address global issues is through civic engagement, whether by simply exercising your right as a citizen to vote or by working to engage others to participate in their community. Among the many ways to address global issues, here is what one inspired young person did in his community to promote **civic engagement**.

Motivated by his concern for the struggle of homeless people in his native San Francisco, William Upski Wimsatt founded the League of Hip-Hop Voters, a grassroots campaign to register young voters and inform them of pressing ballot issues. Wimsatt was concerned that many eighteen-year-old high school students are not even aware that they are of voting age. Wimsatt's organization collaborated through the Internet and meetings to implement voter education programs. These programs are aimed at organizing voters to agree on issues and candidates and at holding elected officials accountable to their campaign promises—and the interests of young citizens.

In the United States, only 36 percent of voters between the ages of eighteen and twenty-four turned out for the 2000 presidential election. (During the 2004 presidential election, 10.5 million eighteen- to twenty-four-year-olds voted, raising their estimated turnout to 42 percent.) These low numbers motivate young leaders like Wimsatt to organize and advocate for active citizenship. His efforts are reflected and amplified by numerous other voter registration groups aimed at young people, such as *Rock the Vote* and the *Hip-Hop Summit Action Network*, founded in 2001 by Def Jam Records.

Registering voters on a college campus.
Photo by Leah Barrett

Smaller, more local grassroots organizations also play an important role in educating and inspiring youth to take action at the local level. One example is the Rhythmic Forward Movement, whose founding Blue Scholars group offers these lyrics:[4]

I'm a blue scholar worker studying the art of labor to create
flavor to relate to listeners, alleviate
the danger associated with strangers
Isn't it strange how we estrange ourselves from our neighbor?
Enables us thru music to connect
releasing fluids in our neck
with the rhythmic forward movement of our heads and back again
Indeed as we succeed the pioneers
maybe give back all that we been taking thru the years
I bleed for what I believe to be the truth
nurturing the seed planted in the fertile youth.

Now is a good time to begin thinking about global issues and what actions young citizens can take on the local level to create a better world.

Developed and Developing Countries: What's in a Name?

When talking about economic conditions and quality of life in countries around the world, people use many different terms.

Some people use the terms *developed* and *developing* to refer to the differences in levels of wealth and standard of living between different countries around the world. Developed countries have higher average per capita (per-person) incomes; Japan, Canada, the United States, Australia, New Zealand, and countries in Western Europe are considered developed countries. Virtually all other countries are considered to be developing.[5]

The World Bank classifies countries based on per capita gross national income. In 2004, low-income countries were defined as those with a per capita income of $735 or less per year—this means that, on average, each person's income for one year was $735 or less. Middle-income countries include those with a yearly per capita income ranging from $736 to $9,075. High-income countries are those with a yearly per capita income of $9,076 or more.[6] This book sometimes refers to low-income countries as poor and high-income countries as rich.

Other terms used by people to describe relative level of development and wealth in different countries are *first, second,* and *third world*; *global north* and *global south*; and *high-consuming* and *low-consuming countries*.

Some of these terms can be misleading. For example, some countries that are considered to be developing are not actually experiencing economic growth at all, while many developed countries have economies that continue to grow. In addition, these terms could imply that all countries should try to become developed. In fact, many experts and people in developing countries think some developed countries are actually "over-developed" and need to reduce their use of resources. Finally, categorization of a country as *rich* or *poor* doesn't acknowledge the other factors that might make those people perceive a high quality of life for themselves, such as richness or poverty of culture, tradition, family life, and countless other factors.

Although none of these terms are perfect, this book most often uses the terms developed/developing and rich/poor when highlighting differences between countries' economic status.

Chapter 2. Understanding Sustainability and Resources

This chapter explores some concepts that are important to the study of global issues, including sustainability, **carrying capacity**, and quality of life.

What Is Sustainability?

Sustainability means that we meet our own needs without limiting the ability of future generations to meet their needs. The "seventh generation" viewpoint of the Native American Iroquois Confederacy presents a good example of the concept of sustainability. This viewpoint requires that tribal leaders consider the effects of their actions on their descendants through the next seven generations.[7]

Sustainable solutions to problems that people are facing today not only deal with present challenges, but also include provisions for the well-being of future generations.[8] The key to sustainability is first knowing what is sufficient for a happy life, then figuring out how most people can have that and also determining how future generations can have it as well. Of course, we can't know how people in the future will define happiness, but we can do our best to ensure that they have the opportunities and resources to figure that out for themselves.

Sustainability means that we meet our own needs without limiting the ability of future generations to meet their needs.

Photo by FAO

A measure of sustainability considers the areas of environment, economy, and society

SOCIETY

ENVIRONMENT   ECONOMY

An assessment of sustainability considers three broad areas: environment, economy, and society—each of which must be healthy and viable over time. For example, a sustainable solution to meeting humanity's energy needs would require that energy resources not be used faster than they can be replaced, or substituted for, and that their use not damage the environment. A sustainable solution should ensure that people's livelihoods are not compromised and that the livelihoods of future generations are also not compromised. Finally, a sustainable solution should not threaten the cultural traditions or social institutions of present or future generations.

In this book, progress toward sustainability is sometimes called **sustainable development**. This refers to efforts made by nations and organizations that enable people of the world to lead healthy, fulfilling, and economically secure lives without destroying the environment and without endangering the future welfare of people and the planet. One underlying assumption of sustainable development is that economic development alone is not necessarily equated with positive or sustainable growth. Environmental balance and people's well-being are also important.[9]

It is important to keep in mind that sustainability is not a finished product but a work in progress. Every step we take in our lives takes us closer to or farther away from a sustainable world. It's up to each of us to decide what steps we are ready and willing to take on the road to sustainability.

Resources and Carrying Capacity

The environment is one component of sustainability because Earth's resources supply the necessities of a healthy and fulfilling life, and how people use natural resources affects the present and future supply of these resources.

Some of Earth's resources are **renewable**, meaning they can be restored or replenished at basically the same rate they are consumed. Forests and fish are examples of living resources that may be renewed through natural processes, careful management, and conservation. Wind, water, tides, and solar radiation are examples of nonliving renewable resources.

Other resources are **nonrenewable**, meaning they exist in fixed amounts and cannot be quickly renewed or restored by natural or human processes. Nonrenewable resources include metals, minerals, and fossil fuels such as oil, gas, and coal. Resources such as soil and water may be termed either nonrenewable or renewable, depending on circumstances. For example, some underground water reservoirs (**aquifers**) replenish so slowly (over thousands of years), such as the Ogallala Aquifer in the southwestern United States, that they are effectively nonrenewable.

Wind is one form of renewable energy.

The availability and use, or **consumption**, of renewable and nonrenewable resources are important because they largely determine how many people the Earth can support now and into the future. Earth has an overall carrying capacity, a concept from ecology that refers to the population that an area can support without undergoing environmental deterioration.[10] The Earth's carrying capacity for humans is the maximum number of people the planet can support without causing permanent ecological damage or using up the resources that future generations will need to survive.

The twentieth-century agricultural revolution, in which food production was greatly increased, is an example of how Earth's carrying capacity can be *enhanced* through improved agricultural technology. Population growth, higher levels of resource use by people, pollution, and habitat destruction are examples of some ways that humans *reduce* Earth's carrying capacity.

Resource Distribution and Scarcity

Resources are not naturally distributed equally over the planet. Some places have more or less of a given resource. Fresh water serves as a good example of this. People near a mountain lake might have more than enough water to meet their needs, whereas people in a desert or on an island in the ocean might have very little fresh water. When a particular geographic area has a limited amount of a resource, that area faces **environmental scarcity**.

To deal with environmental scarcities, people have developed systems to redistribute resources. These have led first to local and then to global economies that channel and exchange resources and goods all over the world. However, economies don't always ensure a fair distribution of resources and goods. Unequal distribution is is an example of a **structural scarcity**, since it depends on how particular economies are structured.

Working toward sustainability involves understanding how resources are distributed, how they are used, and how they renew. Sustainability involves understanding the types and causes of scarcity and determining how they can be best addressed to equitably meet the needs of all people.

Sometimes a community of people overruns the available resources in their area. Some scientists believe that the original people who lived on Easter Island around 400 CE did this as their tribal culture consumed all the timber upon which their seafaring lifestyle depended. Eventually, this Polynesian culture collapsed as the people found themselves trapped on an island without resources to leave to future generations.[11]

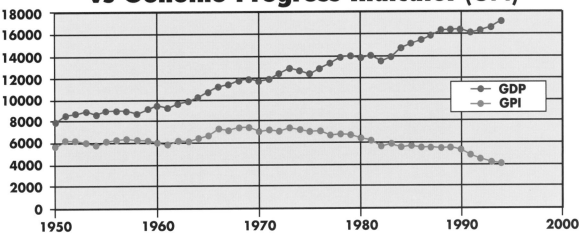

U.S. Gross Domestic Product (GDP) vs Genuine Progress Indicator (GPI)

This graph compares the Gross Domestic Product (GDP) with the Genuine Progress Indicator (GPI) over a 50 year period.

Quality of Life—How Do We Measure It?

In exploring the environmental, economic, and social aspects of sustainability, it is important to consider the well-being or quality of life of people around the world. A number of factors contribute to an individual's quality of life, some of which can be measured or tracked. These include a person's income and his or her access to education, health care, goods, and services. Other contributors to quality of life are harder to measure, such as happiness, creative expression, religious or spiritual involvement, and the relative degree of freedom and justice enjoyed by an individual. One important question to think about when considering global issues is how all of these, and other diverse qualities of the human experience, can be measured.

In trying to assess quality of life, experts have developed **quality of life indicators** to measure the extent to which people have met their needs and wants. Many countries use the **gross domestic product (GDP)**, which quantifies economic production, as a measure for quality of life. GDP is a calculation of the total monetary value of goods and services produced annually in a country.[12] GDP increases with any kind of economic growth, even if that growth results from a disaster (such as a hurricane) or negative events (such as when people get cancer).

Whereas GDP measures a country's economic production, other indicators can help people measure aspects of well-being and quality of life that are not captured in the GDP. For example, the **Genuine Progress Indicator (GPI)**, developed by the nonprofit organization Redefining Progress, is a measurement that adds the value of nonmaterial services, such as paid and volunteer work, but subtracts negative things such as crime, pollution, and divorce. The Genuine Progress Indicator quantifies the value of housework, caring for children and the elderly, volunteerism, and the hours spent on free time or family and community activities—all of which can be viewed as good for the economy, despite no money changing hands.[13] New quality of life

indicators can help people figure out what behaviors and actions are environmentally, economically, and socially sustainable.

How would you measure progress in your own community and country?

Happiness means different things to different people
© Andy Singer, 2003

Chapter 3. Sustainable Solutions: New Ways of Thinking

We can't solve problems by using the same level of thinking we used when we created them.

—Albert Einstein
(twentieth-century
German physicist and
Nobel laureate)

The preceding two chapters cover some concepts that are important to the study of global issues. Now this chapter frames an approach to sustainable solutions and offers some effective tools and ways of thinking about global issues.

Personal and Structural Solutions

Throughout this book we help identify some **personal solutions** that individuals can take to increase sustainability. We also discuss **structural solutions** that address the underlying cause of problems and often require action by governments and nations. Structural solutions usually occur when governments enact policies and laws that encourage or discourage certain behaviors by large segments of the population.

Both types of solutions are important because, as with the global issues mobile, solutions to many of the issues facing us today are interconnected. For example, you may not be able to recycle (a personal solution to resource scarcity) if there is no **infrastructure** in your community to support it. You can, however, encourage local governments to build that infrastructure (a structural solution).

In some cases, this book suggests personal and structural solutions, but it is also important for you to think about other solutions to address global issues.

Personal solutions for sustainability include individual actions, such as recycling.

Photo by G. Wheeler

Policies and Sustainability

In some ways, sustainability is about making choices as an individual. The choices we make as individuals influence the choices that we make as a society. And the choices we make as a society can have a global impact.

Structural solutions primarily occur through government decisions and policies. All governments, regardless of their type, set policies that encourage or discourage certain economic and social behaviors in their populations and their neighbor nations. For example, governments set policies on land use, borders, and access to rivers, coasts, and raw resources (such as minerals and forests). Governments also control rights to transportation routes (air, land, and sea), trade, communication (radio and television airwaves), utilities (power and water), and processes and inventions via patents. They impose or grant relief from taxes on transactions, grant **subsidies** (money given to businesses to encourage something the government believes is desirable) for investing in certain products and services, and regulate how businesses operate. Governments also typically control the management of retirement funds, social welfare programs, and health services for citizens. They also grant citizenship to **immigrants**, which allows them to participate in the country's society and economy.

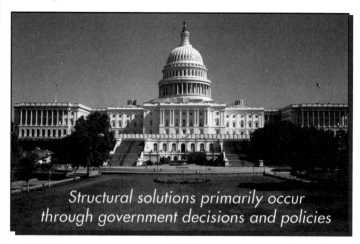

Structural solutions primarily occur through government decisions and policies

Policies are set at all levels of government: local, state, and federal. In a **representative government**, the interests of different groups are weighed by the government, typically through a legislative body, which is lobbied by **stakeholders** to have their interests recognized. Once enacted, policies are enforced, depending on the type government, by force of law or force of arms.

Government policies have large effects, because policies influence what jobs or businesses are available to people, what education people have for those jobs, and how much people and businesses will be taxed. These policies structure a country's economic life. Changing policies to reflect more sustainable behaviors can effect a structural change in a country and in some cases in the world. This book looks at some past, present, and potential future policies and their effects on global issues and solutions.

Systems Thinking:
A Framework for the Future

Systems thinking takes a comprehensive approach to problem solving that is well suited to global issues. It is a field of study that looks carefully at all the important components of a system and how they interrelate. Systems thinking offers a particular perspective, a specialized language, and a set of tools that can be use to address problems. It has been an important tool for many businesses and is a useful way to address global issues.

A *system* is a group of interrelated components that form a complex and unified whole. Systems are everywhere. For example, your school and classroom, the circulatory system in your body, and the predator/prey relationships in nature are all systems.

This organic fair trade coffee farm in Jinotega, Nicaragua is one example of a dynamic system which depends on and is affected by the interactions of people and the environment.

Photo © 2002 April Pojman, Courtesy of Photoshare

Ecological systems and human social systems are living systems; human-made systems such as cars and washing machines are nonliving systems. Most systems thinkers focus their attention on living systems, especially human social systems. Other systems thinkers are also interested in how human social systems affect the larger ecological systems of our planet.

Suppose a landfill in a city becomes full, leaving the citizens with nowhere to put their garbage. A nonsystems approach to this problem might be to build another landfill or find a landfill in another city that would take the garbage for a fee. A systems thinking approach would look not only at these two options, but also at other aspects to this problem and ask a number of questions: Where does the garbage come from? What's in the garbage? Is there a way to reduce the amount of garbage produced? Is there a use for the garbage? Answering these questions could give the city a number of alternatives, including starting or expanding a recycling program, raising fees for garbage disposal as an incentive for citizens to create less garbage, or working with manufacturers to produce less packaging for their products, thus leaving fewer materials to throw out.

A systems thinking approach can help structure the study and analysis of global issues in such a way as to account for the interconnections between environment, economy, and society. This greatly improves the chance of achieving sustainable solutions. Systems thinking can help people seek out underlying causes and address them in solutions, rather than merely responding to surface events and leaving the system unchanged.

Worldview

Understanding people's **worldview**—their beliefs and assumptions about how the world works—is a key component of systems thinking. People's worldviews are influenced by major cultural forces in their lives, such as history, family, politics, religion, and education. It is a powerful force in what people do and believe—even, and often, when they are not aware of it.

Worldview is often what some people believe to be true about the world, but other people in the world may not believe it to be true. For example, if you visited India you might be surprised to see cows wandering around freely. That's because in many countries, cows are owned by farmers and ranchers and kept in pens or otherwise fenced in, but in India cows are considered sacred and are often seen roaming freely. So for many people, their worldview about cows would be that they are owned by people and live in enclosures, whereas the worldview of a person in India regarding cows would be different.

As you study global issues and explore solutions, it is important to keep in mind how different worldviews affect problems and their solutions.

The Iceberg Model

One model that is helpful for understanding global issues is the iceberg model often used in systems thinking. We know that an iceberg has only 10 percent of its total mass above the water while 90 percent of it is underwater. But that 90 percent is what the ocean currents act on and what creates the iceberg's behavior at its tip. Global issues can be looked at in this same way. If we apply the iceberg model to global issues, we would say that at the tip, above the water, are *events*, or things that we see or hear about happening in the world, such as a bomb blast in Iraq, a catastrophic flood in China, a terrorist attack in Spain, or an oil spill in Alaska. The events that we hear about in the news represent the iceberg tip.

If we look just below the water line, we often start to see *patterns*, or the recurrence of events. This might be multiple terrorist attacks around the world or recurring oil spills. Patterns are important to identify because they indicate that an event is not an isolated incident.

Like the different levels of an iceberg, deep beneath the patterns are the *underlying structures* or root causes that create or drive those patterns. For example, the underlying structure of a problem such as recurring oil spills might be our dependence on fossil fuels. If you looked only at the event, you might think that we should just build stronger tankers and better pipelines. But if you look at the root cause of such spills, you can start to understand and address long-term, sustainable solutions such as developing energy sources that do not rely on oil transportation.

Finally, at the very base of the iceberg are the *assumptions* and *worldviews* that have created or sustained the structures that are in place. The important thing to understand is that in solving problems, the greatest leverage is in changing the structure—applying deep ocean currents to move the iceberg, which will change the events at its tip.

An example of the iceberg model can be seen in our own health. Catching a cold is an event, and catching colds more often when we are tired is a *pattern*. The *systemic structures* or causes for getting tired might include overwork, unhealthy diet, or insufficient rest. We tend to get lost in the immediate event of suffering from a cold, forgetting that it is part of a pattern of events that is caused by the underlying structures of our lifestyle.[14] If we take a systems thinking approach to solving the problem of frequent colds, we would try to find ways to make ourselves less overtired, rather than just focusing on the immediate relief (in the form of aspirin or other medicine) that solves the problem of the current cold.

What global issues might the iceberg model help us analyze?

ICEBERG MODEL

The iceberg model can be a helpful way to understand global issues by looking for the patterns and structures that drive events.

"WATERLINE"

EVENTS

PATTERNS

STRUCTURES

Seeing From Multiple Perspectives and Thinking Critically

Another useful tool in the study of global issues is being able to look at an issue from **multiple perspectives**. This refers to valuing cultural and intellectual diversity and promoting healthy competition and sharing of ideas. This is in contrast to viewing and considering global issues solely from the perspective of one particular group, belief system, or worldview.

The study of history provides a good example of using a multiple perspectives approach. To enrich the writing of history, historians draw not only from the biographies of famous figures, but also from the multiple perspectives of everyday working people, as well as people of various ethnic and religious backgrounds. Just as a thorough grasp of history must include the many different voices from the past, the study of global issues and sustainable solutions deserves an airing of many viewpoints.

How might different groups of people perceive, understand, and begin to solve a particular global issue?

Critical thinking is another important concept and tool for a student of global issues. Critical thinking is the process of acquiring information and evaluating it to reach a logical conclusion or answer. Critical thinking requires thinking carefully and deeply, with concern for accurate evidence to support generalizations, arguments, and ideas. The study of global issues requires us to constantly make connections between the environment, economy, and society. It requires the analysis of competing arguments around difficult and relatively new topics, such as carrying capacity and sustainability. Critical thinking means asking questions, both small and large. For example, a critical thinker might ask:

- **Is there any evidence for a particular position?**
- **Is the evidence credible (believable)?**
- **What are other positions?**
- **Does the range of positions account for the scope of the issue or problem?**
- **Are positions solution-oriented?**
- **Does the solution meet the standard of sustainability?**

Worldview: How U.S. Citizens View Their Role in the World

Youth volunteering after a tornado. *Photo courtesy of FEMA*

Research has shown that there are a number of positive values that hold an important place in the worldview of many U.S. citizens. These values together constitute a vision that many hold for how the United States should act in the world and for how U.S. citizens would like to be perceived by the world.

Some of these commonly held values have origins in personal, cultural, and national history and include being pragmatic (practical and realistic), smart, farsighted, trustworthy, collaborative, and principled (wanting to "do the right thing"). Studies reveal that U.S. citizens are interested in international issues, want to see the United States act as a respectful citizen in the world community, and are eager for strong leadership in the United States' role in world affairs.[15]

While these general values might lead one U.S. citizen to be an "interventionist" (favoring American involvement in foreign affairs) and another U.S. citizen to be an "isolationist" (favoring minimal U.S. involvement in other nations' issues), they nonetheless constitute a worldview of shared values through which new ideas and information are filtered and prioritized. Understanding these commonly held values can be a powerful starting point for solving problems.

TECHNOLOGY CONNECTION:

NAVIGATING THE GLOBAL ISSUES NET

The Internet is a defining trait of globalization, an electronic highway of information that connects the world. Some think of the Internet as one large book that the world is writing. How can someone navigating this huge resource know whether it is a reliable source of information?

On one hand, the Internet is an essential and remarkably productive tool for exploring global issues, especially because it can provide up-to-date information from a range of sources, including governmental, commercial, and nongovernmental websites. The Internet was an essential resource in creating this book, and readers should refer frequently to endnote references to trace the origins of borrowed information.

On the other hand, the "global issues net" is huge and uneven in both quality and reliability. In addition to being immensely time consuming, "surfing the net" can be overwhelming—and even misleading, if done recklessly or uncritically. Below are some tips for getting the greatest return from your Internet access.

Internet User Guidelines

To find out if an Internet site you are visiting is a reliable source of information, ask the questions below before you start paraphrasing or quoting it, downloading files, or printing out information. Of course, there is no guarantee that a good website will pass every test on this list; however, an unreliable website will usually fail to meet several of these criteria.

1. What is the address or Universal Resource Locator (URL) for the site? What does this indicate about the type of organization that has produced the site? (.edu is an educational institution, .org is a nonprofit or other nongovernmental organization, .gov is a governmental body, and .com is a corporation or company.) Is this a permanent address that you can confidently cite in a paper or project, or is it a temporary page?

2. Who is the author or sponsor of the material? Does the website clearly indicate who wrote the information or what organization is responsible for its content? Be wary of personal websites that are not affiliated with an organization. They tend to be less accountable and less reliable.

3. Who is the audience for this website? Is it intended for scholarly use? Popular use? Entertainment? Is the site primarily commercial in nature? Is the site designed to educate or to sell a product or point of view?

4. What are the scholarly standards and reputation of the sponsoring organization or individual? Is there any indication that the site has been reviewed? Has it won any educational awards or commendations?

5. What was the original source of the material? In other words, how does the site know what it knows? What was the process for digitizing material? Was any information lost in that process? Can you still access the original copy, if necessary, at an archive or library?

6. Is the site complete or a work in progress? How might additions or corrections affect the claims you wish to make? How might this make proper source citation difficult?

7. Are the documents a selection from a larger collection? What were the criteria for selection? Who selected this material for posting on the Internet?

8. Are graphics, sound, and other multimedia features provided to give you information for your research? Are these features relevant to the information on the site?

9. How long has the site been in existence? When was the last time material on the page was updated? How long will the material remain on-line?

10. Is there a recommended way to cite material from this collection? When you borrow information by paraphrasing or direct quotations, always give the authors or sponsors full credit in your references.

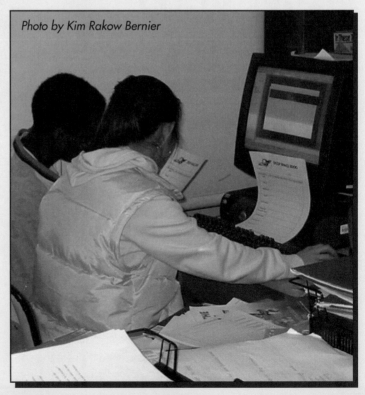

Photo by Kim Rakow Bernier

Global Issues on the Internet: Useful Starting Points

Another way to help make sense of the Internet is to write an annotated bibliography (a brief description and evaluation of the source) for websites you visit, similar to what is offered below. Include a citation with the website name and URL address on the first line, followed by a paragraph that summarizes the website's content and its usefulness for different audiences. The following are examples of governmental, intergovernmental, and nongovernmental websites:

The CIA World Factbook, http://www.cia.gov/cia/publications/factbook/

Drawing on the considerable information-gathering ability of the U.S. Central Intelligence Agency, the U.S. government has made a wealth of information about every nation in the world available to the public, free of charge, on this governmental website. The CIA World Factbook is limited to "finished intelligence," or "the final product of the Intelligence Cycle ready to be delivered to the policymaker." The entire factbook is updated at least annually, with much of it updated more frequently. The central feature of the factbook is its simple main page, with a pull-down menu to "Select a Country" (listed alphabetically). This takes the viewer to that nation's title page, with a flag and map, followed by detailed, to-the-point information on these major topics: historical background, geography, people, government, economy, communications,

Map of the internet showing worldwide network connections on a single day in 2003.

Map created by the OPTI Project.

transportation, military, and transnational issues. For a starting point to research a country or compare countries, The CIA World Factbook is a powerful and easily navigated resource.

United Nations, http://www.un.org/english/

The United Nations (UN) website is probably one of the largest intergovernmental Internet sources available. These are just some of the topical links offered from the UN home page: news center; daily briefing; media; documentation and maps; publications, stamps, and databases; peace and security; economic and social development; human rights; humanitarian affairs; and international law. The home page offers options for both keyword searching and for a detailed subject index. Because of the sheer size of the UN website, the viewer may have the best luck by first reviewing the index for a desired subject. In terms of understanding the UN's goals for global issues, the UN Millennium Development Goals link is especially important, as are the full economic and human development reports, issued annually.

Wikipedia—The Free Encyclopedia, http://en.wikipedia.org/

One efficient way to explore global issues and expand global issues **literacy** is through the free on-line encyclopedia Wikipedia. Wikipedia is written collaboratively by its readers, with the goal of creating "a reliable and free encyclopedia—indeed, the largest encyclopedia in history, in both breadth and depth." The purpose of Wikipedia—to reach out to the entire planet to build a multilanguage dictionary—is its blessing and its curse. Wikipedia seeks submissions with a neutral point of view and has a process for editing and revision. The results are impressive, and the site is easily searched by keyword(s) from the main page, taking the viewer directly to articles that not only "define," but also "explain" the query, offering valuable history, context, debate, and links to other related topics. Given the diverse origins of Wikipedia content, it is a good idea to start there, then cross-reference with another source.

Facing the Future: People and the Planet, www.facingthefuture.org

The publisher of this book is a nonprofit organization. The extensive references (endnotes) listed at the back of this book for each unit in the book provide examples of the numerous nonprofit and **nongovernmental organizations** (NGOs) of all types and sizes that provide essential services and information around global issues, ranging from political lobbying and activism to education and research. Facing the Future's mission is to provide "teachers, students, and the public with sustainability and global issues educational materials and action opportunities to shape our future." Facing the Future's programs address the "interconnected issues of population, poverty, consumption, peace and conflict, and the environment." Used by students, teachers, and the public at large, Facing the Future provides information, links, and resources on global issues, sustainability, and service learning. This website is navigated through a series of interconnected websites and links.

UNIT 1
FACING THE FUTURE ACTIVITIES

- **From Issue to Opportunity**
  (defining and exploring global issues)

- **Creating Our Future**
  (envisioning and taking action for a future that people want)

- **What's in the News**
  (using the iceberg model to analyze the news)

- **Worldview Mingle**
  (understanding how our worldview affects us and others)

To download activities visit http://www.facingthefuture.org

UNIT 1
FURTHER INFORMATION

For in-depth information about sustainability and sustainable development, visit http://www.iisd.org/, the website of the International Institute for Sustainable Development.

For explanation of Genuine Progress Indicator, visit Redefining Progress at http://www.redefiningprogress.org.

For a brief, reader-friendly explanation of systems thinking, read the book, Introduction to Systems Thinking, by Daniel H. Kim, Pegasus Communications, Inc., 1999.

UNIT 2
UNDERSTANDING POPULATION AND CARRYING CAPACITY: HISTORY, TRENDS, AND POSSIBILITIES

Slower global population growth will relieve pressure on the environment and other problems and grant time to find solutions. There are many actions that must be taken to alleviate poverty, improve food supply, end malnutrition, and provide adequate housing. The first is to achieve balanced population growth.

—Dr. Nafis Sadik
(Under-Secretary General,
United Nations Population Fund, 2004)

Essential Questions

- What drives population growth?

- What is the Earth's carrying capacity for human population?

- How is population connected to other global issues?

- What are personal and structural approaches to population growth and carrying capacity issues?

Chapter 1. Introduction

It might be argued that without the pressure of population, none of the issues facing humanity today would be of sufficient magnitude to qualify as global. Population growth and human consumption patterns are two critical and interconected global issues.

About fifty years ago, in 1950, there were 2.5 billion people living on Earth. It took nearly all of human history—from prehistoric time until after World War II—for human population to reach that level. Now that number has more than doubled to 6.5 billion people, with about 80 million people added to the planet each year.[1] That's like adding another Germany every year or another San Francisco every three and a half days.[2] Demographers, who study population growth and other human statistics, project that by 2050 there will be about 9 billion people living in the area where 6.5 billion of us live now.[3]

Population is increasing by about 80 million people per year. That's like adding another San Francisco every three and a half days!

Photo © Djordje Zlatanovic

The larger question surrounding population growth is not only the number of people living on the planet, but also what their collective impact is—whether positive or negative. This unit explores the issues, varying opinions, and potential solutions surrounding population growth.

Stories from the World:
Bringing a New Future to 22-Year-Old Minya Mother[4]

Organizers conduct activities for the Minya Initiative, a collaborative effort to increase family planning awareness in Egypt.
Photo © 1993 Bushra Jabre/ CCP, courtesy of Photoshare

One way to begin to understand the many implications and issues of population growth is by looking at how population is connected to individual people's lives. One day, while riding on a local bus in Minya, Egypt, Aleya heard a voice over a loudspeaker that changed her life. A 22-year-old Egyptian woman, Aleya had already borne three children and had two miscarriages. The tape-recorded message asked people to think before having another child. The message invited women to attend a community meeting with an imam (religious leader) from the local mosque and the village health clinic's female doctor to learn how family planning could help them.

Aleya had dropped out of school at 12, married at 14, and was now exhausted from caring for her family, working in the fields, and recovering from her numerous pregnancies. But she was afraid of family planning. Village rumors implied that family planning harmed women or was against Islam.

Because the meeting was at the local mosque with the imam and the local female doctor would be there, Aleya decided to attend with her sister. There they found other women from the village, giving them all some comfort in a situation that was new and uncharted for this extremely close-knit and traditional society.

Encouraged by the presence of friends and relatives, the women of Minya began asking about family planning. They were told it was perfectly safe and not against Islam. Aleya left the meeting with a pamphlet telling her where the nearest family planning clinic was located. The following day she went there to ask about the best contraceptive method for her. With the case of Aleya, we can see that population is connected not only to family planning, but also to society, education, religion, and personal values.

Youth in Action!
When the Students Become the Teachers

Cleveland High School IRC Voices student speakers.
Photo by David White-Espin

Pressures resulting from population growth are often tied to **refugee** issues. One way that a classroom of students studied and helped to address this issue can be seen in the following example.

David White-Espin teaches global communications at Cleveland High School in Seattle, Washington. Refugees from Southeast Asia and East Africa are among the students in his class. Wanting to capture the attention and interest of his diverse group of students, White-Espin had the class study international and domestic refugee issues. The students created a video for other student audiences about refugee issues and facts, blending their own personal experiences with newfound knowledge.

White-Espin then coordinated with the International Rescue Committee (IRC) to create a unique service-learning project for his students: a refugee speakers bureau called "IRC Voices."[5] The IRC's mission is to help newly arrived refugees achieve **self-sufficiency** by providing initial resettlement along with other support services to help them succeed in their new environment.[6] White-Espin's students helped the IRC by visiting local middle and high schools to present their video and talk about their refugee experiences.

Some of the IRC Voices student speakers had spent nearly a decade of their childhoods in refugee camps waiting to gain **asylum** (protection in a foreign country that would accept their refugee status). Camp conditions are often harsh, marked by limited food, water, and medical care. The plight of refugees is linked to high rates of population growth, where competition for scarce food and water resources can create conflict or intensify existing rivalries, often between different ethnic and religious groups.[7]

The middle school students who heard from the IRC Voices student speakers were often struck by the differences between their own relatively comfortable and predictable childhood and the trauma experienced by many refugees, including violent discrimination, dislocation, escape, and long periods of waiting or even detention. Student audiences were also impressed by the multiple languages spoken by the student refugees, in addition to their near mastery of English, a new language for them. They were stirred by the IRC Voices speakers' sense of personal dignity, cultural pride, and dedication to family, school, and a professional future.

The IRC Voices speakers valued the experience as well. One student said, "I learned a lot of things about myself. I had to ask my parents about the civil war (in our home country of Somalia). I learned that we can correct the misconceptions that young people have about refugees by telling them about our lives as refugees." As they adapt to a new language and their new lives, White-Espin's "students as teachers" provide invaluable insight into the dire situation faced by the world's estimated 9.7 million refugees.[8] They also offer a beacon of hope by living reclaimed lives and a call to action for refugee relief work.

Chapter 2. Population Throughout History

Prehistory and the Growth of Civilizations

For most of human history, population growth was low and slow. Living in small tribes as hunter-gatherers, early humans (about 50,000 years ago) followed the migrations of animals and the seasonal growth of plants. Population during this time remained stable, with almost as many people dying every year as were born. Some historians estimate that there were fewer than 1 million people on the planet by the late Paleolithic era (about 15,000 years ago).

During the Neolithic era, about 8000 **BCE (Before Common Era)**, human existence and population growth rates were radically altered as people learned to domesticate plants and animals. By the dawn of agriculture, the population of the world was approximately 5 million people.[9] Farming can produce up to 100 times as much food as will grow wild on the same amount of land. When food is plentiful, a population tends to grow. As people became farmers rather than nomads, they learned how to build walls and large buildings, which allowed them to store and protect their extra food. During the Neolithic era, regional populations around the world grew rapidly and were increasingly concentrated in towns and villages.

These Neolithic civilizations (people living together in communities) started in areas rich in natural resources, such as fertile soil in which to grow crops, abundant fresh water, and forests that provided wood for building and fuel. Availability of those resources led to not only prosperity and growing populations, but also sometimes resource **scarcity**.

The societies that arose in the Fertile Crescent (a part of the Middle East from the Nile to the Tigris and Euphrates Rivers) prospered at first, but over time the forests that once covered much of the region were cleared for agriculture or harvested for firewood or timber. The area's limited rainfall meant that vegetation didn't grow quickly, so goats and other livestock easily overgrazed the fragile environment. This caused erosion and limited the agricultural production that had enabled the population of the area to become denser. Eventually, political power and population shifted from the Fertile Crescent to societies farther west, where more rainfall ensured that crops grew more quickly.[10]

By the year 1 **CE (Common Era)**, there were about 250 million people on the entire Earth—fewer than the number of people who live in the United States today. As towns and cities grew, more food was required to feed the expanding population. When food became available, the population grew even more, and the cycle of increased food supplies and swelling populations continued.

Still, for centuries worldwide population remained low because many people died at a young age from disease, war, or hunger. With people living closely together in cities, diseases such as measles, smallpox, and bubonic plague broke out, and millions of people died. It is estimated that the population of Europe was cut in half by a plague in the sixth century CE.[11] When the "Black Death" plague returned in the fourteenth century CE, it killed one-third of the people in Europe.[12] **Famines** also killed many people, and when bad weather or crop diseases lowered food production, many people starved. Despite these setbacks, overall population continued to grow slowly as more people were born each year than died. At the beginning of the sixteenth century, world population had doubled since 1 CE, from 250 million to 500 million people.

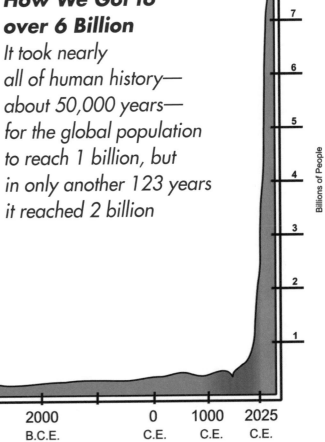

Population Through the Centuries: How We Got to over 6 Billion

It took nearly all of human history— about 50,000 years— for the global population to reach 1 billion, but in only another 123 years it reached 2 billion

Billions of People

| 2-5 million years | 6000 B.C.E. | 4000 B.C.E. | 2000 B.C.E. | 0 C.E. | 1000 C.E. | 2025 C.E. |

Rise and Fall of the Vikings
—Winning and Losing with Technology[13]

Around the year 1000 CE, North America was visited by Vikings from Greenland, who attempted to settle what they called "Vinland." Historians have hypothesized that Viking raids and exploration in the New World may have been driven by overpopulation and scarcity of land and food of Scandinavia in the Old World. This overpopulation may have been caused by advances in technology, especially the development of iron, which improved the Scandinavians' capacity for farming, hunting, and fishing. Also, Viking long ships provided the ideal marine technology for rapid travel, hit-and-run attacks, and navigation of shallow shorelines and rivers.

However, though the Vikings' technology could fuel population growth and expansion, their technology could not overcome climate change. At the height of the Viking expansion, the northern hemisphere entered a period of unusual and persistent cold lasting for several hundred years. This miniature ice age decimated the agriculture of the Greenland colonies and ended the Vikings' westward expansion. The Greenland colony vanished completely because the Vikings did not adopt the hunting and fishing **economy** of the local Inuit, who did survive this climate change. The Vikings were, in a sense, trapped by their **worldview** and cultural practices which included not eating fish!

Technology and worldview may have contributed to both the rise and the fall of the Viking empire. What implications about worldview and technology might this have for people today?

Population Growth and Colonization

During the sixteenth century, with growing populations and rapidly expanding demands for goods, in addition to political and religious motivations, European countries began to establish colonies in Asia, Africa, and the Americas. This brought a flood of new resources to the European continent. Gold, silver, and spices from the colonies made some nations rich, while many of the colonized countries remained poor. Some of the plants the colonists brought back, such as potatoes and corn, grew well in European climates. This resulted in an increase in food supplies for European countries. The increase in food supply and improvement in **sanitation** (clean water and sewage waste disposal) in Europe triggered another burst of population growth. In the 250 years between 1500 and 1750 CE, Europe's population grew as much as it had in the previous 1,500 years.

Between 1600 and 1870 CE, the colonies brought new resources to Europe, but they also relieved population pressures in European countries. Many people migrated to the colonies in North America, Africa, and Asia because of crowding, famine, and a scarcity of farmland in Europe, in addition to a desire to pursue religious freedom and economic opportunity.

Colonial times were often violent, as European colonists used force against native peoples. Across North and South America and Africa, native peoples were often pushed out of their homes by colonizers and were sometimes enslaved or murdered in the process. European colonists also unknowingly brought diseases with them. These diseases killed millions of native peoples, who had never been exposed to them before and had little or no resistance to them.[14] So, while European population increased because of **colonization**, native populations began to decrease.

Europeans invaded Peru in the 16th century and conquered the people living in the city of Machu Picchu.
Photo © Jason Sangster courtesy of CARE

The Industrial Revolution Powers Population Growth

Beginning in the 1800s, resources extracted by Europeans in the New World (North and South America), Africa, and Asia, as well as the technological advances of the Industrial Revolution, created an economic boom. Europeans began using coal to power their industries, rather than the earlier methods of animal labor, wood fuel, or wind. Steam-powered trains and ships (fueled by coal) allowed goods and raw materials to be transported farther and more quickly than ever before. New technologies meant that fewer workers could produce even more food from the same amount of land. Increased food supplies allowed for increased populations, though not necessarily a better **quality of life**. In Ireland, importation of the potato from the New World led to rapid population growth; however, when the new food source was suddenly eliminated due to a crop disease (the infamous potato blight), poverty worsened. This precipitated a major famine and mass migration to other continents, including North America.

By 1830 CE, there were more than 1 billion people on Earth. People in Europe began to live longer, healthier lives. By the early 1900s, the discovery that germs cause disease had led to improvements in medicine and sanitation. Better water and sewer systems cut back the death toll from communicable diseases. The development of antibiotics and vaccines controlled many diseases that had been fatal in the past. The seeds for a modern population explosion had been planted.

Population Growth in the Modern Era

In the second half of the twentieth century, health and sanitation advances from the developed world were brought to **developing countries**, where 72 percent of the global population lived.[15] Because of improved medicine, sanitation, and health care, deaths from disease fell and many more children survived to adulthood. In addition, twentieth-century advances in agricultural practices, such as the use of fertilizers, pesticides, and irrigation techniques, increased food production, which in turn allowed more people to survive and thrive. The rapid fall in the **mortality rate** and increased food production created **exponential growth** of global population expansion. India and China, which already had large populations, experienced some of the biggest population increases after World War II.[16]

It took nearly all of human history—about 50,000 years—for the global population to reach 1 billion, but in only another 123 years it reached 2 billion. The third billion was added in just 33 years and the next billion in only 14 years. Presently, another billion people are added to the planet every 12 to 14 years.[17]

A small slice of a billion–this photo was taken at the busiest street in Chennai, India.
Photo © 2002 Vijay Sureshkumar, courtesy of Photoshare

MATH & TECHNOLOGY CONNECTION:
EXPONENTIAL GROWTH— LIKE LILIES GROWING IN A POND

A quantity grows exponentially when a constant rate of growth is applied to a continuously growing base. A common example of exponential growth is seen with compound interest in bank accounts. If you deposit $100 in a savings account with

Photo courtesy of NOAA

a 7 percent annual compound interest rate, your investment will double in ten years. Exponential growth also applies to populations. If a population grows at 7 percent per year, it too will double in ten years.

Consequences of the phenomenon of exponential growth are surprising. The $100 invested at a 7 percent annual return will double in ten years to approximately $200, double in another ten years to approximately $400, and double again in the next ten years to approximately $800. Significant gains can be made by simply relying on exponential growth over time. One way of saying this is that the longer you wait (on your investment), larger returns will start to come in faster.

Unfortunately, exponential growth can work against us, too. When populations continue to grow, the impact of growth becomes increasingly significant over time. In other words, because of the nature of exponential growth, when things get bad, they get bad in a hurry.

Consider a country with 1,000 people, growing at 7 percent per year. In ten years, the population will double to 2,000 people, in another ten years it will double again to 4,000 people, and ten years after that it will double again to 8,000 people.[18]

With populations, this "doubling" effect of exponential growth can go unnoticed until a doubling of startling consequences or scope occurs. A French riddle captures the surprising potential of the doubling effect:[19] Imagine a water lily growing on a pond. The plant doubles in size every day. You are told that, left unchecked, it would cover the pond in thirty days, choking out all other life forms in the pond. Because the lily plant seems so small, at first you decide you will not cut it back until it covers half the pond. On what day will that be?

ANSWER: On the twenty-ninth day, the pond is half covered. Because its growth is exponential, it will double by day thirty to cover the pond. You have just one day to save your pond! If you hadn't been warned about the doubling effect, would you have figured this out?

Chapter 3. Population Trends, Carrying Capacity, Ecological Footprint, and Migration

The Population Equation— Mortality and Fertility

Population growth is affected by both mortality rates and **fertility rates**. The mortality rate is the average number of deaths per total number of people in a given area and time (for example, 10 deaths per 1,000 people per year). The fertility rate for a certain society is the average number of children born per woman.

Mortality rates have been a key factor in limiting population growth over history. Modern advances in technology and medicine promote both food production and human health; this has generally served to lower mortality rates in human populations. **HIV/AIDS** is slowing population growth in hard-hit countries. In some cases, it is triggering population decline. Botswana had a negative growth rate in 2002 due to high rates of HIV prevalence combined with relatively low fertility rates. By 2010, Lesotho, Mozambique, South Africa, and Swaziland are projected to lose population.

Worldwide, about 136 million people are born each year and 56 million die; the difference is the increase in global population.[20] The bottom line is that the human population grows whenever more people are born in a year than die, and with population increases, exponential growth can cause population to spiral upward.

A woman uses a flip chart to discuss family planning with a group of adolescent girls, women, and young men as part of the "Come Let's Talk" campaign in India.

Photo © 1998, CCP, courtesy of Photoshare

Although many developing countries are currently experiencing high fertility rates, worldwide fertility rates have come down, from an average of 5 children per woman in 1950 to 2.8 children per woman in 2004. However, there are many more people of childbearing age today than ever before. Human population size would eventually stay constant if each family had 2 children, one to replace each parent.[21] But it takes only a slight increase in fertility rates to significantly increase population. A worldwide average of 2 children per family could stabilize world population in the next century, to around 9 billion by 2050, but if the current fertility rate remained constant, the planet's current population could grow to almost 13 billion by 2050.[22]

Population Projections for the Twenty-first Century

How and where will world population change? With roughly half of the world's population under age twenty-five, world population will increase by several billion when those 3 billion people start families over the next few decades. During the next half century, it is expected that 98 percent of population growth will occur in developing countries in Asia, Africa, and Latin America. India is expected to soon surpass China as the world's most populous country. Meanwhile, shrinking populations are predicted for some **developed countries** such as Japan, Russia, and the nations of Europe.[23]

WORLD POPULATION: 1950-2000, AND PROJECTIONS: 2000-2050

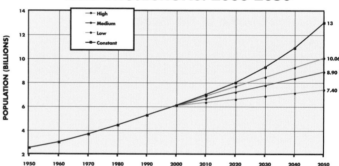

Source: United Nations Development Program. Graph by Facing the Future

Latest estimates show the global population growth rate slowing. In 1990 experts predicted there would be 8.5 billion people in 2025. In 2002 those projections were down to 7.9 billion.[24] This is because the number of children being born dropped more quickly than predicted, partly due to better access to health care and family planning services in countries around the world.[25]

Worldwide, population experts point to a **demographic** divide (demographics are the characteristics of a population, such as education level and religion) that is viewed by some in industrialized countries as an important issue. While poorer, developing regions in Africa, Asia, and Latin America have large populations of young people who will fuel population growth with families of their own, some developed countries actually face decreasing overall population and a higher percentage of elderly people. Those developed countries have fewer people of working age to maintain their country's economic productivity and contribute to the **government** tax base that funds health care and retirement benefits for the elderly. The United States, for example, has a large number of aging adults whose retirement will require greater support needs and provide less tax contribution.

Unlike many other developed nations, the United States has high **immigration** rates that provide a seemingly inexhaustible labor supply. Other industrialized nations have begun to consider ways to boost their decreasing numbers, in some cases by allowing more immigration and offering incentives for larger families.[26]

POPULATION GROWTH IN MORE DEVELOPED AND LESS DEVELOPED COUNTRIES

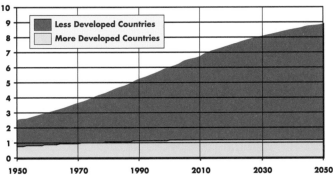

Most of the projected population growth over the next 50 years will take place in less developed countries.
Graph Source: United Nations, World Population Prospects: The 2002 Revision (medium scenario), 2003.

These population statistics and trends have important consequences, especially when combined with other global issues such as poverty. Of the 5.2 billion people living in developing countries, nearly 60 percent do not have basic sanitation, and one-quarter lack proper housing. Twenty percent do not have access to modern health services, and 20 percent of children do not attend school through grade five.[27] Given these harsh realities, people in poorer countries may rely on large extended families to make a living and to care for the elderly. For example, in rural areas people need help to gather cooking fuel, haul water, grow their food, and tend their livestock. Yet because disease and **malnutrition** (inadequate or unbalanced nutrition) kill many children before they grow up, large families are often seen as a necessity. This tends to keep fertility and population growth rates up, which can have the effect of perpetuating poverty, illness, and conflict over scarce resources.

Carrying Capacity— How Many People Can the Earth Support?

An important concept in looking at population growth is that of the Earth's **carrying capacity**. Carrying capacity is the number of people the Earth can support without using resources faster than the planet can reproduce them. Experts disagree on this number because carrying capacity depends on a number of debatable factors: the type and quantity of available resources, how these resources are distributed, how much of the resource each person uses, and people's relative quality of life. People often disagree over what constitutes good quality of life. Some would argue that families should be able to enjoy multiple cars and a diet rich in meat, whereas others contend that such a lifestyle creates an unacceptably large impact that results in resource depletion and pollution and is thus generally unsustainable.

Another variable in determining carrying capacity is whether or not people believe that areas need to be left for plant and wildlife species, in addition to providing for humans and their immediate needs.

Photo © Derek Beauchemin

Because of different assumptions used in determining the Earth's carrying capacity, estimates range from as low as 1 billion people to as high as 40 billion. At the lower estimate of 1 billion, the current world population of more than 6 billion obviously puts us well over carrying capacity and into *resource debt*, which means we are depleting food, water, and other resources much faster than they can be renewed by human or natural processes.[28]

Some people believe that Earth can support many more people than are currently living on the planet. The late economist Julian Simon is perhaps the most well-known advocate for seemingly unlimited carrying capacity. Simon opposed government-sponsored family planning measures, arguing that greater numbers of humans are in fact essential for survival. He reasoned that freedom and **democracy** empower people to develop their talents for their own sake. This ultimately benefits others because such efforts cause economic growth. Each generation creates a little bit more than it uses and is richer than the previous generation. Simon believed that our very survival depends on all that humans can imagine and do and that more people will lead to greater cumulative human intelligence and productivity on the planet.[29]

Although Simon was an economist and argued that economic growth will ultimately compensate for any negative effects of population growth, virtually all scientists and many development experts agree that the Earth does in fact have limits and cannot support unchecked population growth. Scientists and other experts base their assessments of population growth and carrying capacity on scientific research and data as they monitor the state of the environment.

Ecological Footprint

The concept of the **ecological footprint** is useful when analyzing the Earth's carrying capacity, because it allows people to quantify human impacts. An ecological footprint calculation determines the amount of productive land and water area it takes to provide the resources consumed by an individual or a population.[30] This includes farmland, pasturage, and fishing grounds to provide food, as well as forested area for lumber and paper. It takes into account lakes, rivers, and **aquifers** to meet fresh-water needs. It includes all the area necessary to provide energy and jobs and dispose of wastes (including **carbon dioxide**), and it also includes all the area needed to support the **infrastructure** of our lives, such as homes, highways, hospitals, schools, and shopping malls.

Although population is not growing as fast in rich countries as it is in poor countries, the average person in a wealthy country consumes many more resources than the average person in a poor country and thus has a much larger ecological footprint. Ecological footprints are measured in acres; 1 acre is about the size of a football field. Experts calculate that the average person in India has an ecological footprint of less than 2 acres. By comparison, the average ecological footprint in Mexico is about 6 acres; in France, 14 acres; and in the United States, 24 acres.[31]

If the average level of worldwide resource consumption increases, or if population grows, the total human ecological footprint on Earth also increases. If both population *and* average resource consumption increase—as is the case today—the total human ecological footprint on Earth can potentially grow at an exponential rate. Remember the lily pond?

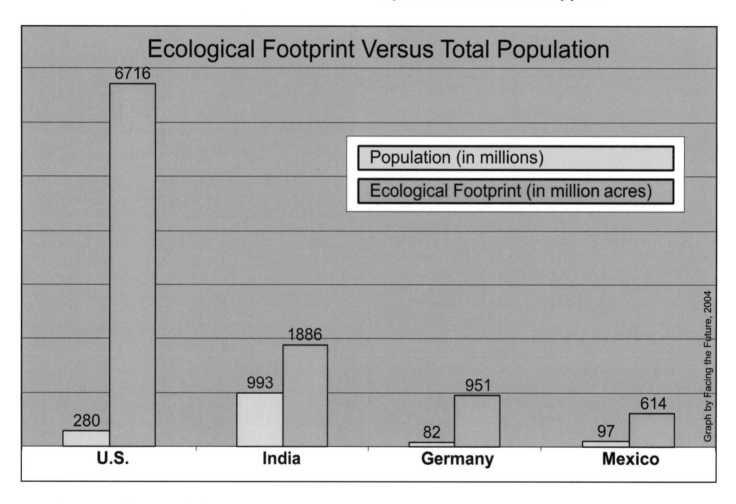

Ecological Footprint Versus Total Population

Population (in millions)
Ecological Footprint (in million acres)

U.S.: 280, 6716
India: 993, 1886
Germany: 82, 951
Mexico: 97, 614

Graph by Facing the Future, 2004

The ecological footprint concept is one that can help individuals, societies, and nations stay within Earth's carrying capacity by becoming aware of resource use and lifestyle impacts. It is an important "big picture" consideration in global issues that can help people be aware of the combined impacts of population growth and resource consumption.

Population and Migration—People on the Move

The concepts of carrying capacity and ecological footprint may help people in the developed world reduce resource use and plan for a sustainable future, but many of the Earth's people have the opposite problem. They lack sufficient resources or the security to have a decent quality of life. Their ecological footprint is insufficient to meet even basic needs such as having enough food and water to survive. When this is the case, people are often forced to move or migrate in search of more resources to meet their basic needs or safety for themselves and their families.

A refugee is someone who has fled his or her country because he or she fears persecution based on race, religion, nationality, social group, or political opinion.[32] This definition is sometimes expanded to include people fleeing war or other armed conflict. Refugees seek asylum status outside of their native country, meaning that a host country accepts them and will process them as refugees either for resettlement in a new country or for repatriation (return to their native country). In 2004 there were 9.7 million refugees worldwide.

The combination of increased population, competition for resources, and resource scarcity has helped fuel more than 150 armed conflicts since the end of World War II and driven tens of millions of people from their homes as economic migrants or refugees. Many security analysts expect conflict over essential resources such as fresh water, farmland, and **fisheries** to intensify as shortages of them reach critical levels.[34]

There is cause for optimism. The United Nations refugee agency reports that because of increased international efforts to help internationally uprooted people, the number of worldwide refugees in 2004 dropped to its lowest number (9.7 million) in a decade. Record numbers of refugees (more than 5 million people in the preceding few years) were able to return to their homes or find asylum in a new homeland.[35] Concerted international efforts to address poverty, resource scarcity, and conflict—the root causes of massive movements of people around the globe—are examples of **structural solutions** to the problems leading to refugees and immigration.

Girls practice writing at the Kakuma Refugee Camp in Kenya.
Photo © 2000, Kathryn Wolford, courtesy of Photoshare

The United Nations Ukwimi refugee camp in Zambia shelters refugees from Burundi, Angola, and Rwanda. In this photo, a Peace Corps volunteer assigned to the camp poses alongside Sport for Life coaches. Sport for Life is a regional health program that recruits prominent soccer players to become role models within their peer networks and communities.

Photo © 2004 Ian Oliver/ Kirk Friedrich/SFL/ Grassroot Soccer, courtesy of Photoshare

Another group of people on the move are **internally displaced persons**, who move about their own country (as opposed to moving to another country) in search of safety. It is estimated that in 2004 there were about 25 million internally displaced persons worldwide.[33]

While refugees leave their country for safety, **emigrants** leave their native countries and **migrants** move within their homelands seeking food, water, land, or work. Poverty and resource scarcity drive legal and illegal immigration into the United States and other developed nations, as people struggle to survive and support their families.

Chapter 4. Sustainable Solutions: Stabilizing Population and Reducing Consumption

Population growth and the associated demand for resources bring urgency to other pressing global issues such as poverty, conflict, and environmental degradation. Stabilizing population growth would allow humans to live within Earth's carrying capacity and improve quality of life for many people. Given that people in wealthier countries on average have large ecological footprints, reducing footprints in these countries is another important way to live within the carrying capacity of the planet.

There are both personal and structural ways to address population growth and resource consumption. Some of these solutions are discussed below.

Personal Solutions
Consider Your Own Family Size

At some time in their lives, most people will need to make a decision about family size. Family planning is perhaps the most important **personal solution** to population growth and carrying capacity. Questions each person can ask when making important decisions about family size include:

- What family size will I be able to economically support?
- What family, friends, community support, and health care are available as I raise children?
- How will I reconcile decisions about family size with my religious or spiritual beliefs?
- What is a responsible decision in terms of the size of the ecological footprint my family will likely have on Earth?

Reduce Your Ecological Footprint

There are many pathways toward **sustainability** and plenty of good first steps. According to scientists who study human impact, the five specific actions below are the most important steps that people can take to shrink their ecological footprint:[36]

1. Your Family Car—If you or your family are going to buy a new car, consider getting one that is fuel-efficient and minimally polluting.

2. Alternative Transportation—Whenever you can, use your feet, a bicycle, a skateboard, or a bus to get around.

3. Low-Impact Foods—Production of meat requires many more resources than production of nonmeat sources of protein. If you want to shrink your ecological footprint, choosing to eat one fewer meal with meat each week can have an impact.

4. Organic Food—Buying food that is produced organically (or growing your own organic food) can reduce your ecological footprint because organic food is grown without pesticides or fertilizers, which are sources of water and soil contamination.

5. An Energy-Efficient House—Make energy-efficient changes in your home when possible. Begin by looking for places to install compact fluorescent light bulbs. When replacing a big appliance such as a refrigerator, water heater, washing machine, or clothes dryer, consider purchasing one that is energy efficient.

What are other ways that individuals can personally address population growth and carrying capacity issues?

Organic vegetables.
Photo courtesy of Oxbox Farms, Duvall, Washington

Biodiesel bus in Telluride, Colorado.
Photo by Stanford Berryman

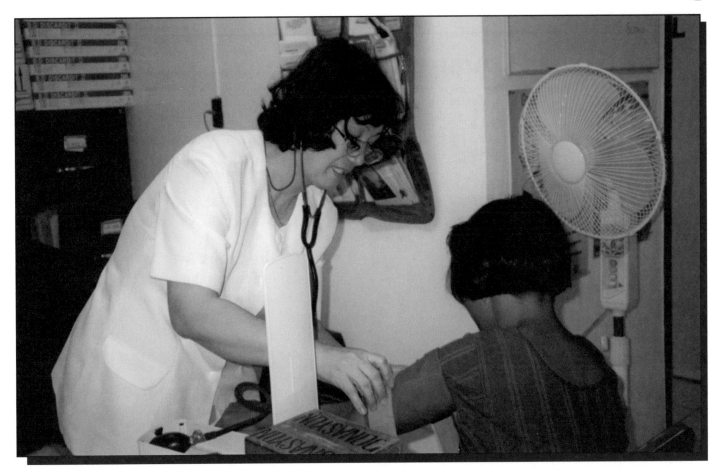

The provision of primary health care is an important structural solution to help stabilize population growth. A health worker checks the blood pressure of a client at the Catmon Health Center in Malabon, Philippines.

Photo © 1999, Jennifer Bowman, courtesy of Photoshare

Structural Solutions:
Providing Primary Health Care

Many structural actions can be taken to help stabilize human population growth. One important step is providing **primary health care** around the world, to lower infant and child mortality, increase life expectancies, and provide other essential services. In many parts of the world, infant mortality is so high that families often have more children in the hopes that at least a few will survive. If families had access to basic health care, which prevents most childhood deaths, many families would have only the number of children that they ideally want.

Reproductive health care is an important part of primary health care that allows parents to choose the number and timing of their children. The Programme of Action adopted at the 1994 United Nations International Conference on Population and Development (ICPD) was the first major international program to define the term "reproductive rights" on the international stage and to affirm the link between existing **human rights** treaties and reproductive rights. Governments endorsed the following statement at the ICPD:

"Reproductive rights embrace certain human rights that are already recognized in national laws, international laws, and international human rights documents and other consensus documents. These rights rest on the recognition of the basic right of all couples and individuals to decide freely and responsibly the number, spacing, and timing of their children and to have the information and means to do so." [37]

As our population increases, basic human needs—food, fresh water, and energy—increase proportionately. In turn, these increases place more pressure on the environment and on relations between individuals, **cultures**, religions, regions, and states. When population growth adversely pressures Earth's carrying capacity, many other global issues are affected. Alternately, when population growth is stabilized, demand for resources can be reduced. When solutions go even further, not only to reduce demand but also to achieve greater efficiency by preventing resource reduction, global issues move in positive and sustainable directions.

What are other large-scale, structural solutions that could help stabilize population and reduce the large ecological footprints of wealthier nations?

Population Policy in an Islamic Country[38]

The Muslim country of Iran is noted for having a successful population policy. In the 1980s, when Iran was at war with Iraq, the Iranian government encouraged families to have many children, in part because it was felt that a large population would be an advantage in the war. Government policies promoted large families, and doctors were told not to provide family planning. During this time, women had an average of seven children, and by the end of the 1980s, Iran began to feel the pressure of a

"Less population, more opportunities, prosperous future."

Poster from Iranian family planning program

rapidly increasing population as the economy slumped and the population became too large for its needs to be met by the country's public services. Ayatollah Khomeini, the political and religious leader of Iran at the time, decided that the country needed to address the issue of its growing population in order to prosper.

The steps taken by the Iranian government included providing free family planning services to all citizens, encouraging families to space their children's births farther apart, educating men about family planning, offering maternity leave for only the first three children per family, and using the **media** to raise awareness of population growth and family planning. Government policies also focused on lowering infant mortality rates, promoting women's education and employment, and extending social security benefits so that families wouldn't feel a need to have many children to support them in old age.

Between 1986 and 2001, the average number of children per woman in Iran dropped from six to less than three. Curbing population growth in Iran has helped its citizens in many ways. Iran already faces water scarcity and has to import grain to feed its population. A quickly growing population would have made it more difficult to provide citizens with adequate food and drinking water.

The example of Iran shows that strong leadership within the government can be an important factor in curbing a rapidly growing population and improving people's quality of life.

UNIT 2 FACING THE FUTURE ACTIVITIES

- **Watch Where You Step!**
  (Discover what makes up our ecological footprint)

- **Now Hear This!**
  (Compare two country's ecological footprints)

- **When the Chips Are Down**
  (Model exponential growth of population and resource consumption)

To download activities visit http://www.facingthefuture.org

UNIT 1 FURTHER INFORMATION

For definitions and data on population: Population Reference Bureau website http://www.prb.org/.

For an exploration of the "Demographic Divide" between developed and developing nations: "World in Balance," NOVA (video), WGBH Boston, http://www.wgbh.org.

To experience an on-line math model of exponential growth for a fixed population visit this website: http://www.hostsrv.com/webmaa/app1/MSP/webm1010/exp_growth.msp.

For information on ecological footprints and on calculating footprints: http://www.redefiningprogress.org.

For a book that follows the life cycle and product trail of everyday consumer items, such as coffee, shoes, and french fries: Stuff: the Secret Lives of Everyday Things, by John C. Ryan and Alan Durning (Seattle, WA: Northwest Environmental Watch, 1997).

For information on refugees: United States Committee for Refugees, http://www.refugees.org/, and "Uprooted: Refugees of the Global Economy" (video), National Network for Immigrant and Refugee Rights, 2001, http://www.nnirr.org/get/get_video.html.

UNIT 3
MEETING ESSENTIAL HUMAN NEEDS: FOOD, WATER, AND ENERGY

Earth provides enough to satisfy everyone's need, but not enough to satisfy everyone's greed.

—Mahatma Gandhi
(pacifist and founding father
of modern India, 1869–1948)

Essential Questions

- **How much food, water, and energy do humans need to maintain a good quality of life?**

- **What is Earth's capacity to supply food, water, and energy?**

- **How can current and future human needs be met in a sustainable manner?**

Chapter 1. Introduction

What will it take to meet the growing human population's need for food, water, and energy? The answers, like the issues, are interconnected. Meeting worldwide food needs requires addressing water supply issues in order to ensure there is enough water for growing food. Certain types of energy (such as hydroelectric power) increase demands on water supplies, and some types can compromise water quality through pollution (such as nuclear energy). Thus, energy policies and development of renewable and clean sources of energy are part of any long-term water solution and therefore must be considered when addressing long-term human needs for food.

This unit first explores the natural link between food and water and then turns to current and future energy uses. The unit concludes with sustainable solutions to meet these essential human needs.

Stories from the World:
Bringing Food to Brazilian Families[1]

Brazil provides an inspiring example of the topics of hunger, poverty, and hope. In 2003 Brazilian President Luiz Inácio Lula da Silva launched the Fome Zero (Zero Hunger) Program to fight poverty and end hunger in Brazil. The program's goal is simple: to give each Brazilian citizen the opportunity to have at least three meals a day.

In the remote farming town of Guaribas, Brazil, a rail-thin man named Isais opens a grimy sack to take out his most valuable possession: a yellow identity card entitling him to 50 *reals* ($17 U.S.) every month for food.

The sixty-one-year-old farmer was among the first to benefit from Brazil's Zero Hunger Program. Isais used the money to buy rice, soybean oil, dried beef, coffee, and sugar for his wife and two children. The family also bought chicken, something not seen for months on the rough-hewn wooden table in their tiny, mud-brick home. ``Fifty *reals* may not sound like a lot, but to buy basic things for a family of four, it's OK," Isais said.

The Zero Hunger Program is made up of dozens of integrated actions to eradicate hunger, the aim being to establish a standing policy that will provide food security to the millions of Brazilians who lack sufficient income to obtain adequate nourishment. The program includes two types of policies: one is a policy with more immediate effects, which aims to increase access to nourishment for those living below the poverty line; the other includes longer-term structural policies aimed to help people move out of poverty and become **self-sufficient**. By the end of 2004, it is expected that 5 million families will have received benefits from the program.[2]

Youth in Action!

Urban Los Angeles Mothers and Youth Become Ambassadors for a Wild California Lake[3] (excerpted from *YES! magazine,* www.yesmagazine.org)

Mono Lake, California. Photo courtesy of Mono Lake Committee.

For most of the twentieth century, a system of aqueducts delivered water from Mono Lake, located east of the Sierra Nevadas, to thirsty Los Angeles, 350 miles across the desert. Northern California's Mono Lake is a vital habitat for more than eighty species of migrating birds and supports a unique food chain of algae, brine shrimp, and alkali flies. Los Angeles's water demands threatened the health of Mono Lake and the plants and animals that depend on it for their survival. Activists and conservation groups from the Mono Lake area petitioned the Los Angeles Department of Water and Power to stop draining Mono Lake. In 1994 the California State Water Resources Control Board ordered Los Angeles to reduce Mono Lake water diversions enough to return the lake to a healthy level. This required Los Angeles to conserve water, since the city could no longer siphon from distant Mono Lake. That left the difficult question of how people in Los Angeles could reduce their water use.

When the Department of Water and Power decided to test a pilot program of distributing low-flush toilets in Los Angeles, the then–executive director of the Santa Isabel chapter of Mothers of Los Angeles, Elsa Lopez, sent her grassroots organization's East Los Angeles members door to door, promoting and delivering the new, efficient toilets. The volunteers spread the word that by reducing water use by one-third, each toilet could save 5,000 gallons a year toward replenishing Mono Lake. Lopez inspired further enthusiasm for water conservation by organizing trips for students and adult community members to visit Mono Lake and gain appreciation for its natural beauty and ecological value. Young people rapidly became ambassadors for the cause of water conservation in Southern California's campaign to save Mono Lake.

This surprising and effective alliance of rural activists, environmental groups, and urban mothers and children resulted in Los Angeles cutting its water usage by 15 percent and lowering its demand for water to levels not seen since 1970, despite a 30 percent population increase. Thanks to the vision and commitment of this diverse group of people, Mono Lake is presently on the road to good health.

Chapter 2. Food for People and Water for Food

Well-fed people have many problems; hungry people have only one.

—Chinese proverb

Hunger, Malnutrition, and Food Security

Access by all people at all times to enough food for an active, healthy life—sometimes called "food security"—is a global issue. The United Nations World Food Program recommends a daily intake of 2,300 calories per person.[4] Worldwide food production has tripled since the 1970s, theoretically providing enough for everyone in the world to have at least 2,720 calories each day.[5] It is projected that worldwide food production will grow faster than population through 2030. However, experts believe that people will still go hungry in many parts of the world unless the problems of poverty and unequal food distribution are addressed.[6]

Hunger is defined by the United Nations as a diet consisting of less than 2,000 calories a day, 300 calories less than is recommended for good health.[7] Consider the following facts about food and hunger worldwide:

- More than 840 million people today—mostly women, children, and the elderly—are hungry.[8]
- The majority of the world's hungry are concentrated in India and sub-Saharan African countries.[9]
- **Malnutrition** (poor nutrition and calorie deficiency) causes nearly one in three people worldwide to die prematurely or be disabled.[10]
- Eleven million children five years old or younger die every year, more than half from hunger-related causes.[11]
- While U.S. citizens commonly assume that hunger is a problem only outside their borders, about 35 million U.S. citizens—including almost 13 million children—live in households that experience hunger or the risk of hunger.[12]

Malawi woman with child mixing maize flour.

Photo © 2002 Valenda Campbell, courtesy of CARE

Causes of Hunger and Malnutrition

Sometimes people go hungry when there is enough food to go around but food is not distributed equally. This is sometimes called **structural scarcity**, which can occur because of discrimination, poverty, corrupt **governments**, or **intrastate** (**civil**) **war**. In some cases, even if food is available, poor people do not have the money to buy it. In other cases, a specific ethnic group may be prohibited from accessing food resources. Sometimes governments in poor countries export the food they grow in order to pay debts to other countries instead of using it to feed their people.

Another reason for unequal food distribution is that although there are enough calories to feed everyone on the planet, some people consume a much larger percentage of those calories than others. This is primarily due to the **consumption** of high-protein, animal-based foods, requiring the indirect consumption of grain and other feed by those animals. In other words, a percentage of available food and calories is not consumed directly but, rather, is used to feed animals that are then consumed by people. To put this in perspective, it takes about 9 pounds of grain to produce 1 pound of beef; in India the average annual per capita meat consumption is about 11 pounds, while in the United States it is about 269 pounds.[13]

Average Daily Per Capita Calorie Availability, 1999

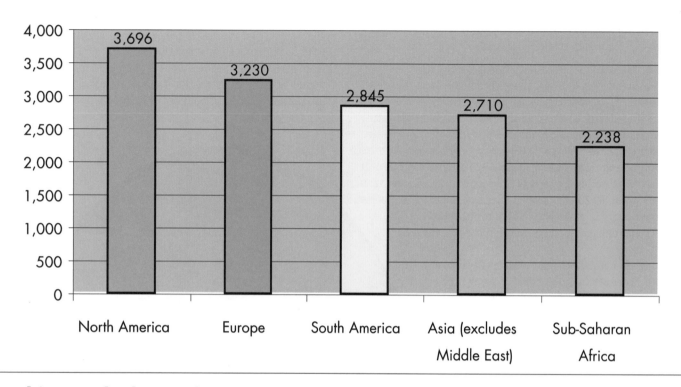

This graph shows the per-person daily average amount of food calories that are available in different regions of the world.

World Resources Institute, 2004. Graph by Facing the Future

The phenomenon of **global warming** also potentially impacts global food production and hunger. Scientists agree that global warming has resulted in higher temperatures worldwide. These higher temperatures can lower crop yields by adversely impacting photosynthesis and seed fertilization and can also reduce livestock health and productivity.[14] If global warming continues, scientists believe that these impacts are likely to be most severe in tropical and subtropical areas, where even a very slight increase in temperature can damage or kill plants that are already at the high end of their survivable temperature range.[15]

Malnutrition can be caused not only by lack of food, but also by poor-quality food. In **developing countries,** poor-quality food usually lacks sufficient nutrients, but in **developed countries** poor-quality food is usually those items high in fats, salts, and sugars. In modern times, consumption of these foods has led to the phenomenon of *development-driven obesity*, also known as "globesity."[16] Globesity is rapidly becoming a problem not only in developed countries, but also in developing countries, where unhealthy Western foods, primarily fast foods, are becoming increasingly popular.

More than 1 billion people worldwide, mostly in developed countries, now overeat to the point of being overweight or obese.[17]

In 2004 one-half of adults in the United States exceeded the upper healthy weight limit. In part, this is because about one-third of the calories consumed in the United States come from sweets, soft drinks, alcohol, salty snacks, and fruit-flavored snacks.[18] Obesity in the United States has reached epidemic proportions; nearly 59 million adults are obese. Moreover, the percentage of young people who are overweight more than doubled between 1980 and 2000. Of children and adolescents aged 6–19 years, 15 percent—about 9 million young people—are considered overweight.

We live in a toxic environment. It's like trying to treat an alcoholic in a town where there's a bar every ten feet. Bad food is cheap, heavily promoted, and engineered to taste good. Healthy food is hard to get, not promoted, and expensive.

—Kelly Brownell, director,
Yale Center for Eating
and Weight Disorders

Numerous serious health problems are associated with this obesity epidemic, which results in at least 400,000 deaths a year through increased risk for type 2 diabetes, cardiovascular disease, stroke, gallbladder disease, and some types of cancer.[19]

Increasing the Food Supply Through Technology

Food production has thus far been able to keep up with population growth due to mid-twentieth-century technological advances in agriculture, called the **Green Revolution**.[20] The Green Revolution started in 1944 when the Rockefeller Foundation formed an institute to improve the agricultural output of Mexican farms through the use of chemical fertilizers, pesticides, and herbicides; new plant varieties; and more-efficient growing techniques. By 1956 Mexico had changed from having to import half its wheat to being completely self-sufficient (supplying all its own wheat). By 1964 Mexico was actually *exporting* a half million tons of wheat per year. These new agricultural technologies of the Green Revolution quickly spread to regions all over the world, increasing crop yields at a rate that soon outpaced population growth. By the 1960s, Green Revolution monocultures (single-crop production) and heavy dependence on chemical fertilizers, pesticides, and herbicides had become the norm in agricultural production worlwide.[21]

Harvesting wheat.
Photo courtesy of USDA

Critics point to some downsides of the Green Revolution. Gains in food production came from creating more farmland by clearing forests, filling wetlands, and converting prairie land. These processes resulted in losses of plant and animal habitats. Intensive irrigation, which accelerated greatly during the Green Revolution, also had a negative impact on the environment. Small amounts of salt and other minerals found in water build up in soil when that soil is irrigated, and eventually these saltier soils are not able to produce as much food. Also, pesticides and fertilizers can run off fields and into lakes, rivers, and ground water, affecting humans, other species, and natural systems.[22]

Genetically Modified Foods

Some people see the increasing use of **genetically modified organisms (GMOs)** as the necessary successor to the original Green Revolution and the only way to feed the rapidly growing population of the developing world. Genetic modification involves the insertion of genes from one organism into another to produce altered genetic material (DNA). The technology is being used to alter certain properties of food crops—for example, to make plants resistant to disease or to delay rotting in fruits.[23] GMOs include seeds and plants that deliver higher crop yields through resistance to pests, weather, and viruses. **Genetically modified (GM)** foods are developed and marketed because there is a perceived advantage to either the producer or consumer of these foods. These advantages include lower prices and potentially greater crop durability and nutritional value.[24]

Proponents of GM foods note that their use has already increased worldwide food production. For the future, GM foods can feed people who might otherwise starve and also buy time for population growth rates to level off, which will further slow the growing demand for food.[25]

Some environmentalists, health experts, and scientists oppose the development and use of GMOs. They question the safety of GM foods for humans, citing possible toxicity, allergens, and adverse nutritional effects. One key environmental concern is the potential for GMOs to escape their agricultural setting and introduce engineered genes into wild populations.[26] In light of these concerns, in 1998 European countries implemented labeling requirements for GM foods.[27] This allows consumers to decide for themselves if they want to purchase GM foods. Finally, critics of the past Green Revolution and the modern development of GM foods assert that regardless of whether or not biotechnology is safe for humans and the environment, increasing food production will not alleviate hunger because it fails to address the underlying problems of poverty and unequal food distribution.

Whether people favor them or not, GM foods already constitute a substantial part of daily food intake. It is estimated that almost 70 percent of the processed foods in supermarkets contain at least one genetically modified ingredient, often in the form of corn syrup sweeteners or soy and vegetable oil products. In 2003 about 672 million acres of land were under cultivation worldwide, of which 25 percent grew GM foods. Since 1996, the United States has consistently planted more genetically modified crops than any other country, with about 106 million acres of GM food crops in 2003.[28]

University of California Plant Gene Expression Center's genetically engineered barley. Some bioengineered barley carries a gene that may help the plants resist attack by barley yellow dwarf virus.

Photo by Jack Dykinga, USDA

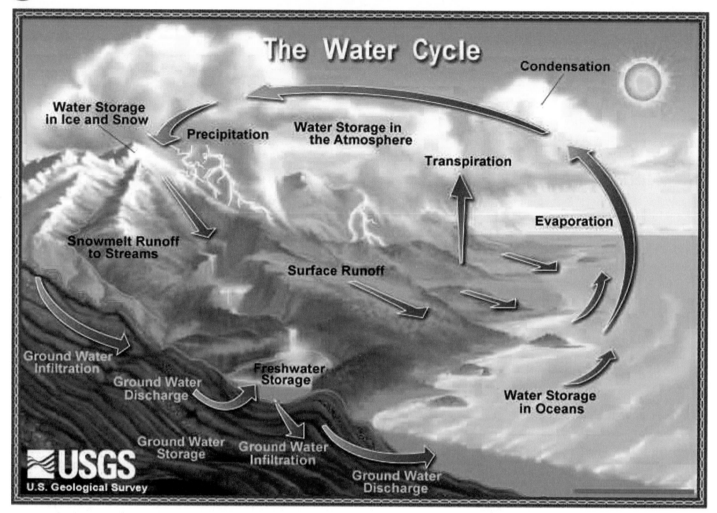

The water cycle, also called the hydrologic cycle, is the cycle by which water continuously circulates from the Earth to the atmosphere and back to the Earth. Many processes, including evaporation, condensation, transpiration, precipitation, and runoff, are involved in the hydrologic cycle.

Graph by John M. Evans, USGS, 2004

Providing Food for Today and the Future

Addressing food and hunger issues today and in the future is a sizable challenge. Some of those challenges include continuing to grow enough food for everyone, finding food technologies that are sustainable, achieving food distribution that is equitable, and when sufficient food is available, maintaining a healthy diet and a lifestyle that includes regular exercise.[29]

People facing hunger need food security, which is achieved when nations can assure that food supplies will be dependable, adequate, and evenly distributed. Here are some questions to consider: Should people focus on increasing food supplies by turning more natural habitats into farmland and producing more GM foods, or should they focus on limiting demand for food by controlling population growth and altering their diet? Will food security be attained through the higher-yield levels of GM food technology, or will these new technologies compromise food security by endangering the well-being of humans and **ecosystems**?

Fresh Water Resources

When you drink the water, remember the spring.

—Chinese proverb

The water cycle (known scientifically as the **hydrologic cycle**) involves the continuous exchange of water between the atmosphere, land, surface water, and groundwater. It includes four main phases: evaporation, precipitation, infiltration, and runoff. Water is a **renewable resource** in the sense that the Earth produces water—but it produces about the same amount of water each year, which means there is a fixed amount of water on Earth. The following are some basic facts about water on Earth: [30]

- Of all water on Earth, 97.5 percent is salt water.
- Of the remaining 2.5 percent that is fresh water, approximately 70 percent is frozen in the polar icecaps; the other 30 percent is mostly present as soil moisture or in underground aquifers.
- Less than 1 percent of the world's fresh water is readily accessible for human uses.

Fresh water is at least as important to human survival as is food, but in many parts of the world **potable water** (clean and drinkable water) is scarce. The fixed amount of water on Earth means that as population increases, demand for water grows, so the available water per capita decreases. Currently more than 1.5 billion people lack access to potable fresh water, and more than 3 million people die every year from diseases related to nonpotable (unclean) water.[31] Twenty-five countries, representing more than 600 million people, face water **scarcity**.[32] Water scarcity in many parts of the world has led to predictions that in this century, wars will be fought over who has access to water.[33]

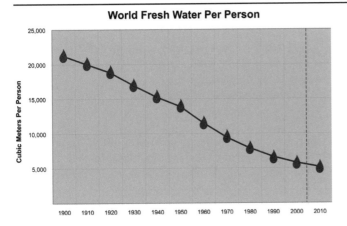

World Fresh Water Per Person

The fixed amount of water on Earth means that as population increases, the available water per capita decreases.
Graph by Facing the Future

A Critical Link: Water and Food

In the past, water shortages have forced civilizations to move or sometimes to collapse; today, water may be the ultimate cause of food shortages.[34] Since there is a fixed amount of water on Earth, as irrigation for crops increases, the amount of water available per acre decreases. Thus, there are strong links between water availability and the ability to grow enough food to feed everyone. A number of these links are discussed below.

Aquifer Depletion

Aquifers (underground water tables) and rivers are important sources of irrigation water; they are fed by rain and snowfall. Snow is a particularly important source because it stores water over time, gradually releasing it into the underground aquifers as it melts. Scientists and environmental experts believe that global warming is one cause of aquifer depletion. Research indicates that the current trend in global warming is already reducing the amount of snow accumulating on some mountains.[35]

Important aquifers for grain irrigation in the world's largest grain-producing countries—China, India, and the United States—are in danger of drying up or becoming inaccessible because of water levels dropping so low, they are too deep to reach. Aquifer depletion could result in a crisis in which

food production no longer keeps up with food demand due to a shortage of water for irrigation. Research indicates that this water and food crisis has already begun in the arena of grain production.[36]

Food Choices and Subsidies

People in the developed world consume more animal-protein foods than people in the developing world. Animal-protein foods use a large amount of water to produce. For example, it takes about thirty-seven times more water (12,000 gallons) to raise 500 calories' worth of beef than it does to grow corn that provides the same number of calories.[37]

It takes about 12,000 gallons of water to raise 500 calories' worth of beef.

Photo courtesy of USDA

One reason why people in the developed world are able to buy inexpensive, water-intensive foods is because the cost of producing beef in the United States is kept artificially low by government **subsidies**, in this case by tax breaks given to the beef industry. It is because of subsidies that U.S. citizens pay relatively cheap prices for many foods and water. People in poorer countries, however, pay on average twelve times more for their fresh water than do people in the developed world.[38]

Population Growth and Consumption

Other factors affecting water availability and food production are population growth and increases in the consumption of water-intensive foods. Population has doubled in the past half century, and demand for water, primarily to produce food, has tripled.[39]

Many scientists and environmentalists see this convergence of global warming, population growth, and high resource consumption as a recipe for a serious crisis of water and food shortages. Reducing the consumption of water and grain-intensive products will not in itself provide food for people in need. Nor will alleviating poverty in itself provide for people in need, if food is not available. The problems are interconnected, and so are the solutions. Only when people have the resources to buy food, and when food is available to people in need, can hunger and malnutrition be effectively addressed.

LITERATURE CONNECTION:

A River Runs Through It

Throughout human history, water has been a force in our stories, religion, and art. Twentieth-century American novelist and professor Norman McLean suggests some of the power and mystery that water holds for the human imagination in his novel *A River Runs Through It:*

Eventually, all things merge into one, and a river runs through it. The river was cut by the world's great flood and runs over rocks from the basement of time. On some of the rocks are timeless raindrops. Under the rocks are the words, and some of the words are theirs.

I am haunted by waters.

What do you think McLean means when he says he is "haunted by waters"?

(Excerpt from *A River Runs Through It and Other Stories* by Norman McLean, published by the University of Chicago Press. © 1976 Used with permission of the publisher.)

Chapter 3. Sustainable Solutions: Food and Water

Personal Solutions for Food and Water

There are a number of actions that individuals can take to address worldwide food and water security. Some of these are highlighted below.

Water Conservation

Residential water conservation can help address local and global water availability issues. By conserving water at home and by buying water-efficient appliances and fixtures, not only are individuals directly saving water in their local communities, but they are also supporting the development and distribution of technologies that could be used on a larger scale.

Consumption: Food for Water and Health

One key to water conservation is growing food that requires less water to produce. By adopting healthier diets, people in the developed world can help reduce the overall amount of water used to produce food. Lowering intake of foods rich in sugar, simple carbohydrates, and fats not only helps curb the obesity epidemic, it also relieves pressure on water use. If people consume healthy foods that require less water to produce, there will be more water left to irrigate crops for those who suffer from hunger or malnutrition.

Support Hunger Alleviation and Fresh Water Projects

Another level of personal involvement is to support hunger-related causes, ranging from volunteering at local food banks and contributing to food drives to backing international organizations in their efforts to reduce hunger and malnutrition. There are also many international organizations committed to improving access to safe water supplies in developing countries. Supporting these organizations is an important way in which individuals can help address the pressing issue of food and water security now and in the future.

More than 200 million hours are spent each day by women and girls collecting water from distant, often polluted sources
Photo courtesy of WaterPartners International

What other personal measures can you take to help address the world's food and water needs?

Structural Solutions for Food and Water Productivity

In addition to personal steps that individuals can take, there are many structural measures that can help meet the world's food and water needs.

Water: Reducing Demand and Increasing Efficiency

Because the amount of water on Earth is finite, sustainable water solutions should address demand for and efficient use of water. An impressive range of innovations for conserving water and increasing water productivity are supported by many water experts and are already being implemented and tested around the world:[40]

1. **Improve irrigation water productivity.** Proven technologies can be used to make irrigation more efficient: low-pressure/low-elevation overhead sprinklers to reduce evaporation; drip irrigation to water the root zone directly; and laser leveling of farmland to reduce runoff.
2. **Raise crop yields.** This can be achieved by planting more water-efficient grains such as wheat rather than rice.
3. **Collect and harvest rainwater runoff.** Simple, existing technology such as terraces and local earthen dams can be used to collect runoff. This also serves to recharge aquifers.
4. **Replace water-based sewage systems.** Technology for composting toilets can be instituted and improved to replace water-based sewage systems, which require large volumes of water to "wash" waste away.
5. **Phase out nuclear and fossil fuel energy.** Types of energy facilities that have extensive water needs for cooling can be replaced by renewable wind, solar, and geothermal energy facilities that require much less water to operate. For instance, nuclear and fossil fuel energy currently comprise 39 percent of U.S. water use.

Food—Efficient Production

The steps outlined above toward meeting water needs would help ensure adequate water for crop irrigation, but achieving sustainable food supplies also involves rethinking land productivity (the amount of food that can be produced on a certain quantity of land). Several proven and available measures could be implemented to increase land productivity and maintain an adequate food supply:[41]

1. **Produce more grain-efficient animal protein.** Producing animal protein that uses less grain than beef (such as pork, poultry, and fish) can increase food supplies, because currently 75 percent of the world's grain harvest goes toward producing animal protein.
2. **Conserve arable land** (land that can sustain food crops). Current technologies such as terracing, contour farming, and conservation tillage (which reduces or eliminates plowing) can help combat erosion and **desertification**.
3. **Limit conversion of arable land.** Adopting urban boundaries to halt suburban sprawl and building mass transit as an alternative to paving roads, which consumes farmland, can help preserve arable land.

Mangoes are the most consumed fruit in the world. This woman is sorting and drying mangoes in Guinea.
Photo courtesy of UN FAO

Progress with these structural measures for meeting humans' food and water needs requires cooperation between citizens, organizations, and governments. The technology and knowledge exist, but individual and collective human will are the ingredients that will allow people to provide food and potable water sustainably for everyone on the planet.

United Nations Equity Programme
—Polytunnel Farming in Sri Lanka[42]

In South Central Sri Lanka, the country's poorest province is making significant steps forward with assistance from the Area-Based Growth with Equity Programme of the United Nations. In a region where 50 percent of the people are dependent on government welfare and 98 percent are employed in agriculture, innovative technologies have been introduced to increase land productivity and economic growth. These technologies include improved seed varieties and technical and material assistance.

One new technology is the "Polytunnel," a long plastic tube that protects crops from heavy rains and winds. This relatively inexpensive technology allows for year-long harvest of high-yield and high-value crops such as bell peppers and tomatoes. A variety of other enterprises have also improved the **quality of life** for Sri Lankans in the area, including freshwater fish farming of tilapia and carp, a loan program for small to medium-sized business projects, a community-based hydroelectric project, and a community radio station.

WaterPartners International
—A Safe Drink of Water for Everyone[43]

Photo courtesy of WaterPartners International

WaterPartners International works to provide clean drinking water for communities in developing countries. Since 1990, WaterPartners has helped more than 30,000 people in 63 communities develop accessible, sustainable, community-organized and managed water supplies. WaterPartners addresses the social, economic, and environmental sustainability of water supply and delivery systems.

Gualcinse, Honduras, is the site of the largest WaterPartners project in Central America, involving six Honduran communities that now share a water source and a central water transmission pipe. Before construction of their water project, the 2,200 people of these communities obtained water for domestic use from rivers and holes in the ground where rainwater collected. During the dry season, families walked for up to two hours on steep paths to collect water. Upstream pollution, the presence of farm animals near water sources, and open sewage contaminated the available water sources and caused health problems such as intestinal parasites leading to diarrhea and malnutrition. Because of the work of WaterPartners, the people of Gualcinse, Honduras can now have a safe drink of water.

To learn more about the work of WaterPartners International visit their website at: www.water.org.

Working for Food Solutions
—Organizations Large and Small

A great many organizations are dedicated to dealing with world hunger. Some are large intergovernmental organizations, such as the United Nations World Food Programme (WFP), which provides relief for regions facing acute hunger crises and long-term **famines**. WFP addresses the structural, root causes of hunger, such as poverty, population, and conflict. WFP does this through programs that boost **economic development**, agricultural production, and food security. In 2003 alone, WFP fed 104 million people in eighty-one countries—including most of the world's **refugees** and **internally displaced people**.[44]

Chicken is served only on special occasions in this Senegalese woman's home. Photo © Elizabeth Benedict Huttman

A large number of smaller **nongovernmental organizations (NGOs)** also are pursuing a range of solutions to hunger. One such organization is Heifer International, whose programs provide livestock and training in livestock care to people in need around the world. International donors sponsor gifts of breeding pairs of domestic animals, such as goats, cows, or chickens, to poor communities; residents are then trained to care for their animals and harvest their milk or eggs. With Heifer gifts, children receive vital sources of protein; families earn income for school, health care, and better housing; communities go beyond meeting immediate needs; and farmers learn sustainable, environmentally sound agricultural techniques.[45] Heifer International requires livestock recipients to donate their livestock offspring to other community members, thus ensuring the expansion and sustainability of the program. Recipients are also encouraged to develop local control and accountability by deciding what type of animals and training are most needed. Heifer International pursues a **structural solution** focusing on the local level to break the cycle of poverty.

Chapter 4. Energy— Fossil Fuel Issues and Impacts

Electric power is present everywhere in unlimited quantities and can drive the world's machinery without the need of coal, oil, gas, or any other of the common fuels.

—Nikola Tesla (nineteenth-century Serbian-American inventor and scientist)

Energy: A Basic Human Need

After food and water, energy is the most basic human need. We use energy to cook, to heat our homes, and to move from place to place in cars, trains, boats, and airplanes. Energy impacts virtually every aspect of our life, whether we microwave a frozen pizza or cook the evening meal over wood scavenged and carried for miles. Consider these facts of global energy production and consumption:[46]

- From 1850 to 1970, while Earth's population tripled, energy use rose twelvefold.
- Transportation accounts for about 30 percent of world energy use and 95 percent of oil consumption.
- Globally, about one-third of all energy use is in buildings: heating, cooling, cooking, lighting, and running appliances.

Just as early humans were characterized as the only "fire makers" among Earth's species, modern **economies** and **cultures** are often characterized by their energy production and consumption. As developing countries build their **infrastructures** for transportation and industry, they typically shift from renewable sources of energy, such as wood, to nonrenewable **fossil fuel** (oil, coal, and natural gas) sources for cooking, heating, and transportation.

Fossil Fuel Supplies

Fossil fuels are **nonrenewable resources**: they cannot be replaced as they are used up; thus, there is a finite amount of these resources on Earth. At some point in time, therefore, we will run out of these resources. Most economists and geologists agree that oil supplies are declining and believe that we will run out of this energy source sometime between 2010 and 2035.[47]

Although we may in fact be witnessing the gradual disappearance of plentiful oil, so far there is no immediate global shortage. The oil supply question hinges more on access to oil deposits. Geologists estimate that there may be more than 25 billion barrels of untapped oil in the Gulf of Mexico—but these reserves are 4 miles beneath the Earth's surface and therefore not easily accessible. Tar sand (sand infused with oil) in Alberta, Canada, may hold as much as 1.6 trillion barrels of oil, but no technology has been developed yet to efficiently extract the oil from this substantial source.[48]

Fossil Fuel Use Worldwide

At the beginning of the twenty-first century, most of the world's people remain reliant on **fossil fuels**. These nonrenewable energy sources provide the majority of the world's energy.

This is especially significant in the case of rapidly developing countries, where energy use is increasing at a high rate. If the average Chinese citizen, for example, used as much oil as the average U.S. citizen, China would require 90 million barrels of oil a day—11 million more than the entire world's daily production in 2002.[49]

For the future of the Earth, what does it mean if millions more people become dependent on fossil fuels?

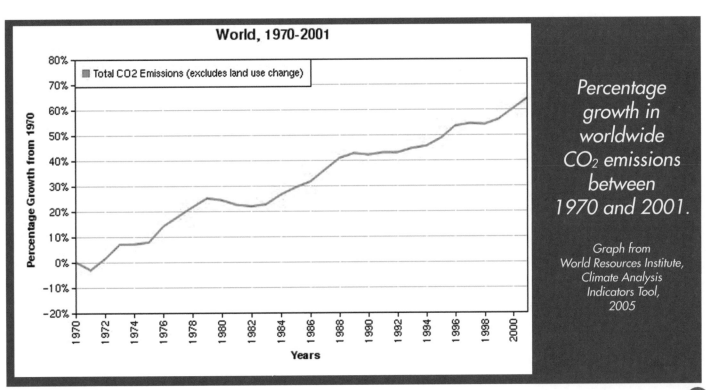

World, 1970-2001

Total CO2 Emissions (excludes land use change)

Percentage growth in worldwide CO₂ emissions between 1970 and 2001.

Graph from World Resources Institute, Climate Analysis Indicators Tool, 2005

Impacts of Fossil Fuel Use

The impacts of worldwide fossil fuel use are many. Most scientists now acknowledge that the phenomenon of global warming is caused by fossil fuel **greenhouse gas** emissions. Global temperatures have been above the norm every year since 1977, and the sixteen warmest years on record have occurred since 1980.[50] Global warming already threatens low-lying areas with flooding as ocean water levels rise. Arid regions of the world, such as the Sahel region of Africa and parts of northern China, are threatened by increased desertification caused by global warming.[51] **Acid rain**, a direct result of the combustion of sulfur-containing coal to generate heat and electricity, can damage plant life and render large bodies of water unable to sustain aquatic plants and animals.

Arid regions of the world are threatened by increased desertification caused in part by global warming.

Photo by Pittet, P.A, UNESCO

Transportation uses, including the automobile, account for the greatest portion of energy consumption in the United States.

Photo by Djordje Zlatanovic

Another impact of fossil fuel use occurs with the exploration, extraction, and development of oil resources. These processes can have direct consequences that affect human and environmental health. The construction of pipelines, which stretch over long distances from oil fields to ports, as in Africa and Alaska, have significant effects when natural habitats and animal **migration** patterns are disrupted.[52] Such disruptions can also adversely affect **indigenous peoples**, who depend on these habitats and animals for their survival. Oil spills, resulting from transportation in supertankers and the pipelines themselves, affect local plants and animals in a variety of ways, especially when spills occur in sensitive marine habitats.[53]

What impacts of fossil fuel use can you identify in your community?

Fossil Fuel Use in the United States

Before the 1900s, the United States relied almost entirely on renewable energy resources. These included wood for heating homes and fueling industry, vegetation for feeding work animals, water mills for grinding grain, and wind for pumping water. By the 1920s, coal and oil had largely replaced renewable energy sources. By 2001, approximately 86 percent of the energy consumed in the United States came from fossil fuels (oil, coal, and natural gas). Renewable energy sources (hydroelectric, biomass, geothermal, wind, and solar) supplied about 6 percent, and nuclear power plants supplied 8 percent of U.S. energy.[54]

Many economists and historians agree that from the perspective of economic development, oil has been a good friend to the United States, especially in the twentieth century.[55] The United States' successful development of its own oil reserves and its access to major reserves around the world fuel its automobiles, factories, agriculture, and military. It is hard to imagine that the current standard of living and per capita income in the United States could have been achieved without a century of ready access to relatively inexpensive oil. Oil has undoubtedly been a quality energy source for the United States in terms of the tremendous boost it has provided for industry, jobs, homes, and recreation.

One reason why the United States continues to rely heavily on oil as a primary energy source for transportation is that the price of gasoline in the United States is relatively low. In 2004, for example, the inflation-adjusted price of gasoline in the United States was half of what it was in 1920 and much lower than its price elsewhere in the world (in 2004, the average price per gallon of gas in Germany was about $5.10 as compared to $1.60 in the U.S.)[56] Some experts argue that the at-the-pump price of gasoline does not reflect the total cost of oil. These "hidden" costs include oil spills, economic disruptions and unemployment due to oil shortages, global warming from **carbon dioxide** emissions, effects of local pollution on respiratory health, and the value of time and fuel wasted in congested traffic.[57] They argue that if these total costs were accounted for, the price of gasoline would likely more than double.

How might people's transportation choices be affected if these hidden costs were included in the price of gasoline?

The reliance on fossil fuels is the reason that the United States has a significantly larger energy footprint than any other nation in the world. Although U.S. citizens comprise less than 5 percent of the Earth's total population:

- U.S. citizens consume 26 percent of all oil and 25 percent of all coal.[58]
- U.S. citizens own about one-quarter of the world's automobiles—one car for every three people, including children.[59]
- U.S. subsidies to oil and gas industries amount to about $5 billion annually. This creates artificially low prices and encourages consumers and businesses to use more of these fossil fuels, contributing to air pollution and global warming.[60]

Oil and U.S. Foreign Policy

Some international development experts question whether or not the U.S. reliance on oil causes it to enter into undesirable alliances or conflicts abroad.[61] The vast majority of the world's oil reserves are in the Middle East. Africa is also now producing an important share of world oil supplies. Both of these regions continue to suffer from conflict and war. Many people question how the United States can be a force for peace and **sustainable development** in these regions when its own oil needs are so immense—and growing.[62] They wonder how the United States can position itself fairly in the Arab-Israeli conflict and other regional wars when secure sources of oil have been named as a vital national interest of the United States.

Chapter 5. Sustainable Solutions: Energy Enough for People and the Planet

Our universe is a sea of energy—free, clean energy. It is all out there waiting for us to set sail upon it.

—Robert Adams (twentieth-century pioneering scientist in clean energy)

Both structural and personal solutions can contribute to sustainable energy uses. Structural solutions require changes in national policies and an international focus on renewable energy. Individuals can contribute to energy solutions by reducing use of energy resources and supporting renewable energy products.

Structural Energy Solutions
Strategies to Reduce Demand and Increase Supply

Energy and environmental experts have identified numerous strategies that could simultaneously reduce energy demand and increase the supply of renewable sources of energy.[63] Many of these strategies mean that governments, businesses, and energy organizations have to work together to develop sustainable energy policies.

1) Develop wind energy. Wind power is clean, abundant, inexhaustible, and inexpensive. China could double its electricity production from wind sources alone. The United States has enough wind in just three states (North Dakota, Kansas, and Texas) to potentially meet the entire nation's energy needs.

Wind power is a promising renewable source of energy.

Photo © 2001, Spirit Lake Community School District, Iowa, USA

2) Promote alternative transportation. Shifting from a car-centered urban transportation system to a system combining light rails, buses, bicycles, and pedestrians would not only save gas and energy from transportation and manufacturing, but also reduce air pollution.

3) Shift from internal combustion engine automobiles to hybrid vehicles. Hybrid vehicles use both gas and electric power sources, recharging their batteries when using gas power, when traveling downhill, and when braking. Current tax credits and high gas prices have put demand for hybrids far ahead of supply.

4) Expand use of biodiesel and biomass fuel. Biodiesel, a biodegradable transportation fuel used in diesel engines, is produced from organically derived oils or fats. It can be used either as a replacement for or as an additive to diesel fuel and can shift reliance away from fossil fuels.[65] Biomass fuels are renewable fuels derived from living organisms or their byproducts, such as wood, dung, methane gas, and grain alcohol.

Biodiesel, a biodegradable transportation fuel used in diesel engines, can help shift reliance away from fossil fuels.
Photo courtesy of Bio-beetle

5) Expand production of hydrogen fuel cells. A **fuel cell** is an electrochemical engine (having no moving parts) that converts the chemical energy of a fuel, such as hydrogen, and an oxidant, such as oxygen, directly to electricity.[66] Fuel-cell engines emit water vapor as exhaust rather than carbon compounds. In the short term, natural gas can provide the main source of hydrogen, but hydrogen generation for fuel cells could be greatly facilitated by the development of wind energy.

6) Expand use of solar energy. No country uses as much energy as is contained in the sunlight that strikes its buildings every day. Solar (or photovoltaic) cells, first developed in 1952 by scientists at Bell Laboratories, have grown in popularity, especially for use in remote locations such as in rural villages or scientific outposts. Residential use of solar energy has grown in countries where governments have offered users financial incentives, such as tax credits.

7) Increase use of geothermal (heat) energy. Geothermal energy from the Earth's core typically escapes unused. It has already proven useful for electricity generation through steam power; other current uses include industrial heat pumps for manufacturing and space heating for greenhouses, residences, and aquaculture. For decades, Iceland's capital, Reykjavik, has heated its houses with hot-water radiators and provided all its hot-water needs with geothermally heated water. You may smell the sulfur of geothermal water while you shower, but you'll never run out of hot water, no mater how long your shower!

8) Price energy to reflect its hidden costs. True cost pricing would include production, environmental, and health impacts. Energy prices could be "internalized," to reflect true relative usefulness and costs, rather than "externalized," where hidden costs get passed on to consumers.

Government Leadership and Renewable Energy

Governments are an important player in establishing programs and policies that promote renewable energy. Following the lead of a number of successful state-run programs, in 1987 the U.S. federal government established national standards for energy efficiency, tripling the efficiency of new refrigerators between 1972 and 1999 and, in the process, saving consumers money.[67] Similar mandated efficiency measures have been effective for other energy uses as well, such as automobile fuel efficiency (better gas mileage), building heat-loss reductions through insulation, and recycling of paper, glass, and metals.

The U.S. Department of Energy is aware of the huge potential of renewable energy resources, claiming that renewable energy could annually provide 250 times the total U.S. energy consumption in "clean" rather than nonrenewable energy.[68] Currently in the United States, electricity from renewable energy sources is being promoted and certified as **Green Power**. Green Power is presently generated mostly from wind and from gases (such as methane) emitted as a byproduct from landfills. Such electricity is usually sold at a higher price than electricity produced from fossil fuels because it costs more to produce; however, today there are more than 300 electric utilities in thirty-two states that offer Green Power to their customers. Government could encourage the development and distribution of Green Power by shifting subsidies from nonrenewable energy to these growing programs for sustainable energy.[69]

Several U.S. states are also furthering the use of renewable energy through renewable portfolio standards (RPS). An RPS is a legal requirement that a specific amount or percentage of power generation come from renewable energy sources. These standards have been established in several states, and a national RPS has also been proposed.[70]

Developing Nations Solution: Leapfrogging to Sustainable Energy

Internationally, wealthier developed nations have a unique opportunity to export their existing technologies and knowledge of renewable energy to developing countries that are in dire need of clean, cheap, and sustainable energy sources to improve their quality of life. This type of transferred, sustainable technology is known as **leapfrog technology**: it provides the possibility for developing nations to raise their standards of living while "jumping over" the unsustainable models used by developed countries. Instead of spending more than a century dependent on fossil fuel (like the United States has), developing countries can, with the right assistance, leapfrog from wood fuel directly to renewable energy. This would serve the planet well, reducing the rate of fossil fuel use by the large and growing populations in China and India and in many African nations.[71]

Leapfrog technology is a way for developing countries to jump over unsustainable technologies to sustainable ones.

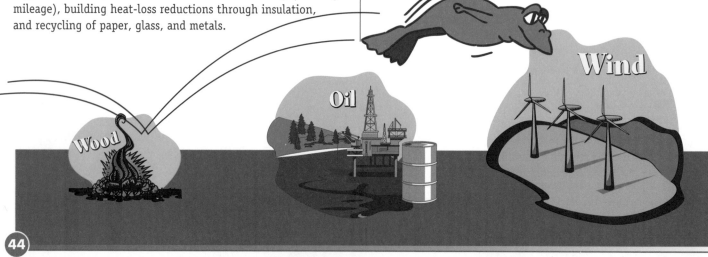

Personal Energy Solutions

In addition to the structural solutions outlined above, individuals play an important part in energy solutions.

Reducing Demand and Conserving Energy

Responsibility for energy sustainability rests partly with individuals, especially with people in wealthier nations, where energy use is significantly higher than in developing countries. Individuals can start by asking, "How much energy is contained in the products I use?" and "What are the impacts of my energy use?"

Consumers in the developed world can support renewable energy technologies (such as those described below) by letting elected officials and energy companies know that they support these. Individuals can directly reduce their demand for energy through energy conservation measures such as installing energy-saving lightbulbs, purchasing energy-efficient appliances, driving hybrid cars or those that run on alternative fuels, and using public transportation.

Civic and Consumer Action

Organizations and governments are primarily responsible for developing policies to establish structural solutions that address energy needs, but individuals have an essential role in this process. Through lobbying and voting, energy consumers can demand that governments enact energy-efficiency mandates in the form of legislation, such as fuel efficiency standards for cars. Citizens can voice their support for redirecting government subsides toward renewable energy sources such as wind and solar power. Individuals can also educate themselves, express their opinions, and exercise their political will by participating in organizations that promote energy conservation and the development of renewable energy.

A future of sustainable energy is within our reach. Meeting the food, water, and energy needs of humanity amid continuing population growth and high consumption rates requires solutions that are sustainable and realistic. Implementing these solutions entails questioning one's own worldview—the beliefs, assumptions, and ideas that underlie our actions regarding energy use.

Bringing the Future to the Present
—Wind Power in Spirit Lake, Iowa[72]

Cities, counties, agencies, and other organizations can take advantage of local, state, and federal funding for wind projects to install their own wind turbines. On-site wind power can be used to power anything from school buildings to wastewater treatment plants—and they can be a highly visible and educational way to increase energy independence, reduce environmental impact, and even gain additional sources of revenue.

The Spirit Lake Community School District in northwestern Iowa has taken advantage of the wind resources blowing across the grounds of its schoolyards by becoming the first school district in the United States to use wind power as a primary energy source. Up until this point, the region had been 94 percent dependent on nonrenewable sources of energy, including coal, petroleum, and natural gas.

The school district received a grant from the U.S. Department of Energy and a low-interest loan from the Iowa Department of Natural Resources (IDNR) to fund the purchase and installation of a 250 kilowatt turbine in 1992. A few years later, a second turbine came on-line that fed directly into the electricity grid, generating enough power for all the remaining buildings in the school district.

Iowa state laws allow the school district to bank the electricity it generates until it is needed. The district can purchase electricity from the local utility in times of peak demand or low wind and, conversely, it can sell electricity back to the utility when the wind power is in excess of the school's demand. Excess turbine electricity has already turned a profit for the school. A wind education program at the elementary school has engaged the students in the project with hands-on understanding of the benefits of renewable energy.

Wind turbines and playground at Spirit Lake Community School.

Photo © 2001, Spirit Lake Community School District, Iowa, USA

The Spirit Lake wind energy project is a powerful blend of cutting-edge technology, public will, political support, progressive economic incentives, and innovative education. There are ever-growing opportunities for renewable and decentralized energy projects. Organizations that serve as clearing-houses for such projects include the International Institute for Sustainable Development (http://www.iisd.org) and the Climate Knowledge Change Network (http://www.cckn.net).[73]

Birds and Wind Energy

One concern about wind energy is the bird fatalities that result from birds flying into the turbines. Although the U.S. government estimates that in 2001 roughly 15,000 wind turbines in the United States killed around 33,000 birds (2.2 birds per turbine annually), this is only a fraction of the number of birds that are killed by flying into cars, trucks, and buildings.[74] The Audubon Society, an environmental organization devoted to conservation of birds and bird habitat, generally favors wind energy for its vast superiority over fossil fuels in terms of overall environmental impacts that harm birds. But Audubon also urges these efforts to minimize potential negative impacts of wind power: properly assessing sites prior to construction of wind turbines, avoiding placement of wind energy developments in high-risk areas, and thoroughly evaluating bird mortality at existing and new wind turbine facilities.[75] The intersection of wind energy and bird health is an interesting example of how sustainable solutions must balance the economy, society as a whole, and the environment.

TECHNOLOGY CONNECTION:

THE DASHBOARD OF SUSTAINABILITY— AN ON-LINE ASSESSMENT

Compare different nations' levels of sustainability by downloading the International Institute for Sustainable Development's "Dashboard of Sustainability." The institute coordinated development of a unique on-line tool that uses the metaphor of a vehicle's instrument panel to display country-specific assessments of economic, environmental, social, and institutional performance toward (or away from) sustainability. Designed using international experiments and measurements and using United Nations indicators for sustainable development, the Dashboard of Sustainability is a tool for experts, the **media**, policy-makers, and the general public. The "Policy Performance Barometer" gives viewers a quick assessment of weak and strong points, areas of conflict, and areas of potential solutions. Visit and download the dashboard at:

http://www.iisd.org/cgsdi/intro_dashboard.htm.

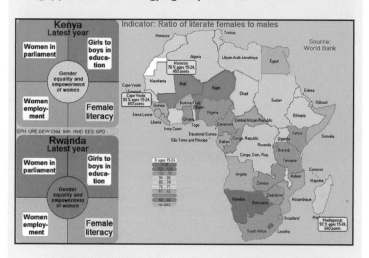

UNIT 3

FACING THE FUTURE ACTIVITIES

- **Shop Till You Drop?**
  (Explore different people's access to food, water, energy, and other human needs)

- **Toil for Oil**
  (Model the extraction of a nonrenewable resource)

To download activities visit **http://www.facingthefuture.org**

UNIT 3

FURTHER INFORMATION

For studies on global warming and the effects of climate change: United Nations International Panel on Climate Change (IPCC) Annual Assessment on Climate Change (four comprehensive on-line reports), The Scientific Basis; Impacts, Adaptation, and Vulnerability; Mitigation; and Synthesis Report. http://www.ipcc.ch/.

United Nations Food and Agriculture Organization, State of Food Insecurity in the World 2003, http://www.fao.org.

For an exposé of the fast-food industry and its associated agricultural, labor, and health impacts: Eric Schlosser, Fast Food Nation. New York: Perennial, 2002.

For a video exploring the impact of globalization on our food systems: Old Dog Documentaries, "The Global Banquet: The Politics of Food" (video), http://www.olddogdocumentaries.com/ vid_gb.html. By taking examples from all over the world, this video makes "difficult" issues understandable to the nonspecialist.

For a detailed analysis of the links between food, water, and climate change, as well as a full range of solutions: Lester R. Brown, Plan B: Rescuing a Planet Under Stress and a Civilization in Trouble, New York: W. W. Norton & Company, with Earth Policy Institute, 2003.

For an overview of renewable energy sources and current programs: U.S. Department of Energy, Energy and Renewable Energy, Contribution of Renewable Energy to the U.S. Energy Supply. http://www.eere.energy.gov/consumerinfo/ factsheets/da8.html.

UNIT 4
ENVIRONMENT: KEEPING OUR HOUSE IN ORDER

We have a special responsibility to the ecosystem of this planet. In making sure that other species survive, we will be ensuring the survival of our own.

—Wangari Maathai
(2004 Nobel Peace Prize Laureate and founder of the Kenyan Green Belt Movement)

Essential Questions

- **What is the condition of Earth's plants, animals, forests, air, and oceans?**

- **What are sustainable ways to conserve and protect the Earth's ecosystems?**

- **Why is environmental justice a critical component of sustainable solutions for the environment?**

Chapter 1. Introduction

Earth produces everything that human beings need to survive—food, water, shelter, and energy—as well as the beauty and diversity of nature. It is important to understand not only how people use Earth's resources, but also the ability of the environment to supply resources over the long term. Consider these basic facts:

- During modern times, half of the planet's tropical rain forests have been destroyed or degraded.[1]

- Human activities are linked to warmer temperatures around the world, which threatens **ecosystems.**[2]

- On average, every hour three unique plant and animal species become extinct.[3]

Elephants occur in a wide variety of habitats on the African continent—from deserts to tropical forests.

Photo © Charles Steinberg

Biodiversity

The health of the planet depends on the health of its many ecosystems. An ecosystem is a community of organisms (plants, animals, and other living organisms) that together with their environment function as a unit.[4] It is impossible to think of ecosystems, whether **terrestrial**, fresh water, or marine, without thinking of the biological diversity of plants and animals that help define and shape them.

Biodiversity falls into three main categories: species, community, and genetic. **Species biodiversity** refers to the variety of living creatures found within a region or **habitat** (the environment in which an organism or population lives or grows). Earth hosts an estimated 10 to 20 million species, but only about 1.75 million species have been officially named and classified by scientists. **Community** or **ecological biodiversity** refers to the variety of habitats and ecosystems that exist on the planet. **Genetic biodiversity** refers to the range of genetic variation within a single species—such as in size, coloration, and behavior—that have evolved to allow the species to survive in its own particular ecosystem.[5]

Unfortunately, all three types of biodiversity are disappearing at an alarming rate.[6] Each year as many as 27,000 species of animals, plants, insects, and microorganisms vanish forever.[7] Mountain gorillas, giant pandas, and snow leopards are just a few of the more well-known animal species on the brink of extinction. Many scientists believe that between 20 percent and 50 percent of all species on Earth could disappear in the next 30 years.[8]

Public awareness about the key role that people can play in protecting nature is growing. By choosing sustainable strategies for keeping our house (Earth) in order, we can help the planet continue to meet basic human needs.

This unit explores the relationship between forest habitats and biodiversity in plants and animals, and then it turns to the state of oceans and the air. Solutions for healthy ecosystems are presented in each chapter. The unit concludes by looking into **environmental justice**, an important ingredient in **sustainability**.

Stories from the World:
Global Warming in the Solomon Islands[9]

Have you ever wondered how your actions can affect someone across the world? A day in the life of Selna, a young woman living in the South Pacific Solomon Islands, serves as an example of the reach and impact of **global warming**, a critical environmental problem.

Selna paddled her dugout canoe up to the dock on Kolombangara Island—one of the 992 islands and atolls that make up the Solomon Islands. As she stepped from her canoe, Selna reflected on the information she had gathered from elders in the community as part of

Home on Solomon Islands.   *Photo © Kim Rakow Bernier*

a science class assignment about global warming. Selna's homework was to interview members of her community to find out if they had noticed any differences in the shoreline water levels over the course of their lifetime.

Most of the 4,000 residents of the 426-square-mile island live along the southwestern shore, with no village farther than a third of a mile from the sea. In doing her interviews, Selna already knew from her studies that global warming can contribute to rising sea levels. But she was still surprised to learn that people in her village were making preparations to move the local market and the leaf-and-stick homes inland. If the temperature of the planet continues to increase, predicted rises in sea level will have an enormous impact in South Pacific countries like the Solomon Islands as shorelines rise and some atolls disappear altogether.

As Selna unloaded the coconuts, fish, cabbage, and papayas from her canoe to sell at the local market, she looked forward to returning to school the next day to share her research with rest of the class. As one of the few girls in her community still in school at age sixteen, Selna hopes to play a role in the **sustainable development** of the Solomon Islands. She also hopes that more people who have the opportunity to reduce **greenhouse gas** emissions will know about the Solomon Islands and the potential impact of global warming on her life.

Youth in Action!
Do You Have Global Eyes?[10]

In 1997 Global Eyes was established in Japan by Kwansei Gakuin University students who were interested in studying and taking action on environmental problems. The Global Eyes mission is to "think globally," linking people to people and organizations to organizations, and to "act locally," making environmental problems known to the Japanese people and coordinating a campus group network.

Global Eyes was initially founded as a research and action group for climate change. In December 1997, Global Eyes members participated as observers at the United Nations Framework Convention on Climate Change, held in Kyoto, Japan. Global Eyes sponsored symposiums for the purpose of getting citizens interested in global warming and other environmental problems.

Global Eyes describes three current projects that reflect their mission:

1. Education Project. Through education and outreach, help Japanese people overcome their traditional reluctance to be concerned with environmental issues.

2. Recycling Project. In order to reduce resource **consumption**, sponsor a "paper recycling fair" and use campus "recycling markets" to encourage students and graduates to donate their used furniture, electric appliances, and books to be reused by incoming freshmen.

3. Research Project. Conduct research on campus environmental impacts, calculating the consumption of electricity, gas, water, and amount of waste, and then present research and recommendations for waste reduction.

Global Eyes is a positive model for youth environmental activism because the organization pursues personal and local issues as well as more structural issues, such as educating Japanese people about their impacts and their power as citizens of a wealthy, developed nation.

Chapter 2. Biodiversity and Forest Habitats

Prayer of the Woods
(ancient Portuguese prayer)

*I am the heart of your hearth
on a cold winter's night
I am the beam that holds your house
The board of your table
The bed on which you lie and
the timber that builds your boat
I am the handle of your hoe
The door of your homestead
The wood of your cradle
The shell of your coffin
Ye who pass by
Listen to my prayer
Harm me not*

Photo courtesy of the U.S. Fish and Wildlife Service

Although oceans contain the majority of species on Earth, forests are home to nearly two-thirds of known terrestrial (land-based) species.[11] This chapter discusses the benefits of forests and the impacts that result from forest degradation. The chapter concludes with an example of how sustainable practices can conserve and protect forests for habitat value and human resource use.

The International Union for Conservation of Nature and Natural Resources identifies habitat loss as a main threat to 85 percent of all species officially classified as "threatened" or "endangered."[12] Almost 40 percent of the Earth's surface has been converted to cropland or pasture.[13] Overuse of pastureland has led to rapid **desertification**; this problem is exacerbated in the parts of the world where limited rainfall already makes domestic animals' grazing an uncertain endeavor.[14]

The interdependence among organisms and their environments creates and sustains the conditions needed for survival. When any species is taken out of an ecosystem, the integrity of the complex system that evolved over millennia is weakened.[15] This is similar to the way in which, when one item is removed from a mobile, the entire structure tips, often imperceptibly but sometimes wildly, depending on the weight of that particular object.

Bald Eagles Soar to Recovery
The Endangered Species Act protected the bald eagle in 1967 when scientists counted fewer than 450 nesting pairs of eagles in the continental United States. The government also acted to ban DDT, a farming pesticide that often ran into streams and contaminated fish eaten by bald eagles. The chemical interfered with the bald eagle's ability to develop strong shells for its eggs. As a result, bald eagles—and many other bird species—began laying eggs with shells so thin they often broke during incubation or otherwise failed to hatch. Happily, there are now more than 5,000 nesting pairs of bald eagles, and in 1999 the U.S. Fish and Wildlife Service recommended taking bald eagles off the list of endangered species.[16]

Photo © Paul Bannick

Forest Benefits

Forests are an important environmental and human resource. They contain much of the world's biodiversity, they provide resources for human use, they produce oxygen and absorb carbon dioxide, and they help keep our water clean, control erosion, and slow desertification.

One incentive for humans to preserve species diversity is that we may not yet know what essential benefit a particular species may offer ecosystems or humans. One estimate poses that less than 1 percent of the plants that are likely to help us find additional medicines have been tested.[17] If such species become extinct, we may limit our ability to treat disease and illnesses now and in the future. Species loss may also limit our ability to invent new technology that borrows chemical components or design elements from nature.

Tanzanian women cut wood for fuel and building materials.
Photo © Sarah Bones, courtesy of CARE

Biodiversity

Forests provide habitats for a variety of creatures, ranging from large mammals such as elk and bears to small birds including the marbled murrelet to even smaller organisms such as spiders. When forests are permanently converted to other uses or become fragmented, animal and plant species are pushed out and sometimes driven to extinction. Organisms that depend on the forest for their nourishment and survival not only take from the forest, but they also give back to it. They are dependent on the trees, and the trees are dependent on them.

Human Uses

For humans, a number of important benefits are derived from forests. Because wood is a **renewable resource**, if forests are managed carefully they can provide for human needs today and into the future. Forests provide us with products such as building materials for homes, paper products, and fuel from firewood. Forests also provide wilderness for recreation and other human pursuits.

Oxygen Creation and Carbon Dioxide Absorption

Forests release oxygen and they take in carbon dioxide, which helps regulate the atmosphere and reduce the risks of global warming. Scientists call forests *carbon sinks* because they capture carbon dioxide and keep it out of the atmosphere. Forests in the United States remove approximately 25 percent of total carbon dioxide emissions yearly.[18] When forests are removed and replaced with deforested areas such as homes, roads, and grazing pasture, we lose these essential benefits.

Erosion Control

Prevention of soil erosion is another important function of forests. When too many trees are cut from a mountainside or riverbank, there is a higher chance of erosion, which can cause mudslides and flooding. Soil fertility is reduced as topsoil and organic materials needed to restore soil are washed away in flood runoff. Deforestation has been linked to disastrous flooding in India, China, Honduras, and the Caribbean.[19]

State of the Forests

Between 1990 and 2000, forestland in the United States increased by about 2 percent.[20] Worldwide, however, the amount of forestland has declined, primarily from human impact. About half of the forests that once blanketed the Earth—almost 3 billion hectares—have disappeared. Every year at least 16 million additional hectares are destroyed by humans.[21]

Humans impact forests in two main ways. One is through the permanent removal of forests for conversion of land to other uses such as housing, agriculture, and roads. The other is through the logging of wood for fuel and wood products, which disturbs or destroys forest habitats but can potentially lead to forest regrowth.

Growth in population and resource consumption are the main reasons why forests are cut down. Clearing forests to make way for farmland to increase food production is a major cause of deforestation in **developing countries**. Harvesting wood for fuel in those countries is another cause. Worldwide, fuel wood accounts for about half of all wood harvested.[22] In southern Africa, for example, 80 percent of the people use wood to cook their food and heat their homes.[23] Land conversion for agriculture and harvesting for fuel wood are good examples of how poverty limits peoples' ability to conserve their natural resources.

Rwanda, in Central Africa, provides an example of how population growth and consumption of wood for fuel can contribute to ecological—and humanitarian—disasters. Population there grew from 1.9 million in 1950 to nearly 8 million in 1994. By 1991, demand for firewood was double what the forest could yield. In addition, there was a loss in soil productivity as the desperate population harvested and burned straw and other crop refuse that, if left in place, would normally replenish the soil's organic content. Soil fertility declined, food production plummeted, and the country was ripe for conflict. Though not the sole cause, competition for scarce fuel and food resources contributed to the catastrophic ethnic genocide in 1994, which resulted in more than 800,000 deaths.[24]

Girls in Burkina Faso, Africa selling fuel wood for cooking and heating.
Photo © Saskia Everts/TOOL Consult, courtesy of Photoshare

Another reason that forests are cut down is for wood used in construction and paper manufacturing. People from Europe, the United States, and Japan, who make up less than 20 percent of the world's population, use more than 50 percent of the world's timber and more than 66 percent of its paper.[25] Home construction is a major culprit. For example, since 1970 the average home size in the United States has grown from 1,400 square feet to 2,200 square feet.[26]

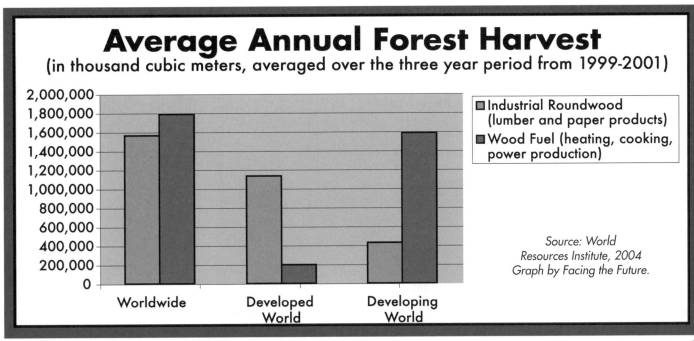

Average Annual Forest Harvest
(in thousand cubic meters, averaged over the three year period from 1999-2001)

Legend:
- Industrial Roundwood (lumber and paper products)
- Wood Fuel (heating, cooking, power production)

Categories: Worldwide, Developed World, Developing World

Source: World Resources Institute, 2004 Graph by Facing the Future.

Strategies for Sustaining Forests

Logging for timber, fuel wood, and other wood products can be sustainable. A range of structural and personal strategies can help conserve forest resources for today and into the future. In North America, many laws and regulations focus on sustainable forest management; many other parts of the world do not have such well-developed environmental management systems.

Personal Solutions

Individuals can further the structural strategies outlined below by following these steps:

- Reduce use of wood products such as paper, packaging, and lumber. This could include building smaller homes and using scrap or reclaimed lumber where possible, using different materials (such as bamboo, clay, or plastic that looks like wood) for construction, and using recycled paper products.
- Avoid use of wood products from endangered trees or forests.
- Get to know your local forest areas and enjoy them for recreation.
- Support sustainable forest harvesting by consuming "green" certified lumber.
- Advocate for the conservation of endangered species and forest habitat.

Structural Solutions

Structural solutions for sustaining forest resources include using specific harvesting techniques, fuel-efficient stoves, and community forestry. These solutions are explained below.

Selective Harvesting

One example of sustainable forestry is **selective harvesting**, in which only a portion of the forest is cut each year. This leaves many trees standing so that the forest remains intact and can provide habitat and recreation space and can continue to convert carbon dioxide into oxygen. Sustainable tree harvesting may appear costly in the short term because the volume of trees harvested in a single cut is lower than in conventional **clear-cut logging** (in which all the trees in an area are cut indiscriminately). Studies have shown, however, that selective harvesting does less damage to the forested area and leads to higher retention of soil nutrients, promoting better growth of the remaining trees. Experts believe that the cost of selective harvesting will drop in the future and that, in the long run, it creates a more sustainable timber supply. Sustainable logging ensures a future for logging, recreation, and forest biodiversity.[27]

Efficient stoves such as this one burn less fuel, leading to an overall reduction in logging.
Photo courtesy of FAO

minum stovepipe. The stove burns very efficiently by channeling heat toward the cooking pot rather than letting most of the heat escape to the sides, as occurs with an open fire. The smokeless Chula requires two-thirds less wood to cook the same meal, reducing the amount of wood needed for cooking. It also channels smoke out of the cooking space, reducing illness in those who inhale the vapors. The total cost of installing a smokeless Chula in India is around $9 U.S.[28]

Community Forestry

One way to help rural communities in the developing world become responsible for management of their local forests is through *community forestry*. In community forestry, management of the forests is given to a group of local people able to demonstrate their commitment to managing and conserving forest resources, while still providing forest products to the people who rely on them. In Nepal, for example, community forestry has led to the conservation and regeneration of forest resources, particularly in areas that were previously degraded. Community forestry can also have unexpected and unintended benefits. In Nepal, when efforts focused on involving women in the development of management skills, training included **literacy** classes and led to the development of leadership roles for women.[29]

Sustainable solutions do exist to help conserve forest habitats and biodiversity, and there are numerous benefits to sustainable logging practices. People can protect forests as the sites of much of the planet's biodiversity, upon which the survival of the human species may ultimately depend.

A clear-cut hillside in the United States.
Photo courtesy of the U.S. Fish and Wildlife Service

Fuel-Efficient Stoves

Providing and encouraging the use of fuel-efficient stoves to replace wood-burning stoves in the developing world is another strategy to help preserve forests. One example is a simple technology called the "smokeless Chula," a small stove built from clay, with an alu-

Community forestry has restored natural habitats while also providing an income from wood products such as those produced from this mahogany forest in the Philippines.

Photo © 2000 Liz Gilbert/David and Lucile Packard Foundation, courtesy of Photoshare

Flooding in the Caribbean and Preserving Trees in China

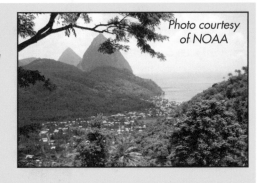

Photo courtesy of NOAA

Haiti is the poorest country in the Western Hemisphere. During recent years, pressures from population growth and poverty led rural people in the area to harvest hillside trees to make charcoal, considered to be one of the only valuable Haitian **cash crops** (crops grown for sale rather than for feeding local populations). In late May 2004, torrential flooding in Haiti and the Dominican Republic caused the loss of more than 1,000 lives, one of the worst natural disasters in Caribbean history. Two weeks of unusually heavy rainfall, totaling as much as 5 feet during one 36-hour period, led to severe flooding. Deforested hillsides quickly eroded under the torrent, causing houses and even entire villages to wash away and greatly increasing mortality rates. Now a painful irony in Haiti (as in other areas around the world that suffer from the cycle of poverty, deforestation, and flooding) is that Haitians may have no choice but to resettle in river valleys, where they will be even more vulnerable to lowland flooding.[30]

Governments can take decisive action through implementing conservation mandates and restructuring **subsidies** to favor forest health—which ultimately favors human health. In 1998, after weeks of flooding in China's Yangtze River Basin caused $30 billion in damages, the Chinese government banned tree cutting completely. The government calculated that due to its critical role in flood control, a standing tree was worth at least three times what a cut tree was worth as a timber product. Determined government intervention like this can help limit the devastating effect of floods, which result in about 50 percent of all deaths caused by natural disasters.[31]

Beans for Biodiversity and Economic Development —Taking the "Natural Step"

Photo © Paul Bannick

The western tanager depends on the shade of the forest canopy for its survival.

In the developing world, cultivation of single cash crops such as coffee or cocoa is often promoted over small-scale agriculture that includes food crops. In the 1980s, to meet rising worldwide demand for coffee, forests in Latin America and other developing countries were extensively cut and replaced with high-yield coffee trees. This resulted in hillside erosion and habitat loss for many species, especially for birds including the western tanager that depend on the shade of the forest canopy, rather than sunny coffee fields, for survival. Additionally, the extensive application of pesticides to maximize coffee-tree yields often pollutes nearby rivers and the lungs of coffee workers.[32] Agriculture workers in the coffee industry often toil for long hours in difficult conditions, and many small coffee farmers earn prices for their coffee that are less than the costs of production. This perpetuates a cycle of poverty and debt, as farmers borrow money to get from one coffee season to the next.

The United States consumes about one-fifth of the world's coffee, more than any other single country. After oil, coffee is the second largest U.S. import. Fortunately, people in the United States can now purchase "shade-grown," "organically certified," and "fair-trade" coffee. The shade-grown and organic options benefit forest health and biodiversity, while the organic and fair-trade options benefit agricultural workers. Fair-trade certification assures consumers that the coffee was purchased under fair conditions. To become fair trade–certified, an importer must meet stringent international criteria, paying a minimum price per pound, which provides much-needed credit to farmers, and providing farmers with technical assistance such as help making the transition to organic farming.[33] Although there are 25 million coffee farmers in the world, it is estimated that sustainable coffee production has already improved the living conditions of almost a million farming households in the Southern Hemisphere alone.[34]

The dominant player in the world coffee market is Starbucks, holding about 25 percent of the world market share. Since 1998, Starbucks has developed programs to lessen its **ecological footprint** by encouraging practices that promote biodiversity and economic well-being during coffee production, transportation, and store operations. These practices include ecologically sound growing and harvesting, reduction of emissions during roasting, use of recycled materials for the storage and transport of beans, and use of recycled paper coffee cups.[35] A portion of Starbucks coffees are shade-grown varieties and purchased at fair-trade prices.[36]

Starbucks collaborated with an international advisory and research organization, The Natural Step, to develop tools and standards with which to measure progress and improve its social and environmental responsibility. Using a systems-thinking approach, The Natural Step designs models and tools for businesses by assessing the business's practices against the test for sustainability. They ask, is the practice good for business, is it good for society, and is it good for the environment?[37]

The Natural Step helps businesses become sustainable by (1) avoiding concentrations of pollutants from synthetic substances and from substances mined or pumped from the Earth's crust; (2) avoiding overharvesting and displacing natural systems; and (3) being efficient in satisfying human needs by maximizing the benefit from the resources used.[38] The Natural Step also works with other corporate giants such as Bank of America, McDonalds, Home Depot, IKEA, and Nike to collaborate on sustainable models of business. To learn more about The Natural Step, visit their website at: **http://www.naturalstep.org**.

Collins Companies and Home Depot
—Private-Sector Pioneers for Sustainable Forestry

Sustainably-managed forestland in Lakeview, Oregon.

Photo courtesy of Collins Companies

style in Oregon, California, and Pennsylvania. Collins Companies, which in 2003 had $220 million in sales, was the first company in the United States to hire a third party to certify its forest as sustainably managed. Certification requirements include demonstrated sustainable-harvest techniques, a commitment to ecosystem health, and provision of social and economic benefits to local communities.

In adherence with the standards set by the certification system, Collins foresters strive to achieve sustainable management above and beyond what government regulations mandate. The forests managed by the Collins Companies are not clear-cut. Instead, they maintain 200-year-old trees, public trails, and campgrounds. To help maintain vital ecosystems, they leave more debris after logging, thus returning more nutrients to the soil. Snags (dead but standing trees) are also left for animals that need them for habitats. Collins is a pioneer of green certification in logging and a business leader for social, environmental, and economic sustainability.

Home Depot sells more than $5 billion worth of wood products annually in 1,450 stores around the world. In the mid-1990s, forest activists organized boycotts, advertising campaigns, and shareholder activism to pressure Home Depot to phase out the sales of all old-growth wood (virgin timber) and stop buying Lauan, a rare Indonesian wood. Home Depot responded, and within a year the company put forth new policies for "green-certified" lumber labeling and wood purchases. Soon many other wood retailers and two of the nation's largest home builders had adopted similar practices in support of sustainable forestry.[39]

One company supplying green-certified lumber to Home Depot is Collins Companies. For 143 years, this family-owned company has nurtured a sustainable selective-harvest management

Although the demand for green-certified wood products has been slow to grow, millions of customers at Home Depot and other retailers of green lumber can ensure that companies practicing environmentally sustainable forestry will be economically viable.

Chapter 3. A Breath of Fresh Air

The thickness of the air, compared to the size of the Earth, is something like the thickness of a coat of shellac on a schoolroom globe. Many astronauts have reported seeing that delicate, thin, blue aura at the horizon of daylit hemisphere and immediately, unbidden, thinking about its fragility and vulnerability.

—Carl Sagan
(twentieth-century American author and scientist)

Few people will have the opportunity that astronauts get to "see" the atmosphere, the relatively thin layer of air that blankets the Earth and that fuels and protects life here. From our earthly perspective, when the air appears clear, our actions often reflect

the saying "Out of sight, out of mind." In other words, when we cannot *see* the air, it often doesn't concern us. Increasingly, both in urban areas suffering from industrial- and transportation-related air pollution and in rural areas affected by acid raid and dust storms, we *can* see the air—and we are impacted by it.

Air-Quality Impacts

Numerous human activities pollute the Earth's atmosphere, contributing to global warming and causing **smog**, **acid rain**, and damage to the **ozone layer**.

Smog

Smog (generated from the words "smoke" and "fog") is heavy air pollution that can persist for an extended period of time, especially in warmer climates. It is found in geologic basins surrounded by hills or mountains, such as Los Angeles or Athens, and over densely populated cities, such as Tokyo and Bangkok. Emissions from cars and industrial factories are the major causes of smog. Worldwide, more than 600 million cars and trucks are in use each day, and nearly 50 million new vehicles are added each year.[40]

Air pollution has severe local impacts on the health of plants and animals, and it is a major contributor to respiratory illness in humans. Pollution has economic consequences when it causes sickness and keeps people home from work. In Mexico City, smog is so thick on some days that schools and factories close and cars have to drive with their lights on. Researchers there estimate that reducing two of the most serious air pollutants by 10 percent would save an average of $760 million a year.[41]

Dry deposition refers to acidic gases and particles. About half the acidity in the atmosphere falls back to the Earth through dry deposition. The wind blows these acidic particles and gases onto buildings, cars, homes, and trees. Dry-deposited gases and particles can also be washed from trees and other surfaces by rainstorms. When that happens, the runoff water adds those acids to the acid rain, making the combination more acidic than the falling rain alone.

Disease-conscious street vendors in Halong, Vietnam wear face masks to block air pollution.

Photo © 2003 Harvey Nelson,
courtesy of Photoshare

Health experts also believe that pollution contributes to asthma, which continues to increase by 50 percent worldwide every decade.[42] In the United States, 17.3 million people have asthma—more than double the number just fifteen years ago. Every day, an average of fifteen U.S. citizens die from asthma.[43]

Acid Rain

Acid rain is another airborne threat.[44] The pollutants that cause acid rain—sulfur dioxide and nitrogen oxides—interact in the atmosphere to form fine sulfate and nitrate particles that can be transported long distances. Acid rain is a broad term used to describe several ways that acids fall out of the atmosphere, and it includes both wet and dry deposits. Wet acid rain deposits refer to acidic rain, fog, and snow. As this acidic water flows over and through the ground, it affects a variety of plants and animals.

Acid rain is caused by sulfur-dioxide and nitrogen-oxide emissions from primarily electric power generation that relies on burning fossil fuels such as coal. Industrial acid rain is a substantial problem in China, Eastern Europe, Russia, the eastern United States, and areas downwind from them.

Acid rain can have serious impacts on people and the planet. It can harm both land-based and water-based plants and animals, especially trees, phytoplankton (microscopic plants that live in the ocean), and fish. Dry-deposited gases and particles can be transported long distances by winds and inhaled deep into people's lungs. Fine particles can also penetrate indoors. Many scientific studies have identified a relationship between elevated levels of fine particles and increased illness and premature death from heart and lung disorders, such as asthma and bronchitis.

Thinning of the Ozone Layer

A specific long-term problem in the upper layer of the atmosphere, or *stratosphere*, is the thinning of the ozone layer. Both the ozone layer and clouds block out the sun's harmful ultraviolet rays, but in different ways. Clouds reflect ultraviolet sunlight back out to space, whereas the ozone layer absorbs it. Ozone in the stratosphere acts as our planet's natural sun block.[45]

Ozone destruction is caused when chlorofluorocarbons (CFCs), chemicals formerly used in refrigerators and air conditioners, and emissions from paints, solvents, pesticides, gasoline, and other petroleum-based chemicals escape into the atmosphere and diffuse up to the stratosphere. When the ozone layer thins or develops holes, too much ultraviolet light can get through and cause harm ranging from skin cancer and eye cataracts to crop damage.

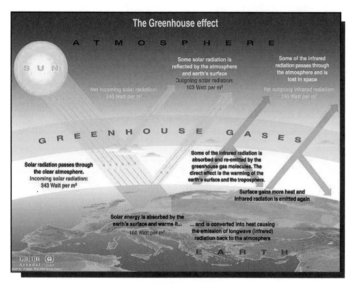

The Earth has a natural temperature control system. Certain atmospheric gases are critical to this system and are known as greenhouse gases. On average, about one third of the solar radiation that hits the Earth is reflected back to space. Of the remainder, some is absorbed by the atmosphere but most is absorbed by the land and oceans. The Earth's surface becomes warm and as a result emits heat. The greenhouse gases trap the reflected heat, thus warming the atmosphere. Naturally occurring greenhouse gases include water vapor, carbon dioxide, ozone, methane and nitrous oxide, and together create a natural greenhouse effect. However, human activities are causing greenhouse gas levels in the atmosphere to increase.

Graphic and text by UNEP and GRID Arendal.

Global Warming

Perhaps the topic of greatest concern related to the atmosphere is that of global warming. Global warming occurs when greenhouse gases such as carbon dioxide build up in the atmosphere and trap heat from the sun, raising the temperature of the Earth's climate. Burning fossil fuels such as coal, oil, and natural gas is the main way that these harmful greenhouse gases are created. As a result, most of the world's temperatures are rising. The ten warmest years on record have occurred since 1980, with the five hottest years occurring since 1997.[46] The United Nations Intergovernmental Panel on Climate Change projects a 3°F to 10°F rise in temperatures during the twenty-first century. The planet is facing the fastest rate of climate warming in the past 10,000 years.[47] Although scientists have shown that the Earth's temperatures have varied over hundreds of thousands of years, most scientists agree that human activity is the major cause of the current extremely rapid warming trend.[48]

We are used to seeing outdoor temperatures vary by season, from more than 100°F in the summer to below 0°F in the winter. Why, then, should people be concerned about global warming heating up the Earth a few degrees? To answer this, think about your body; when healthy, the human body runs at a very steady temperature of 98.6 degrees. A few degrees colder, and you will experience hypothermia; a few degrees warmer, and you have a fever, indicating you are sick. If your body temperature were to change by 5°F–10°F in either direction, you would soon die.

Cartoon © Andy Singer

The Earth is similar in that a permanent change of just a few degrees can drastically change its natural systems, including sea levels, seed germination, and animal and bird **migration** patterns. For example, during the last ice age, when Canada was covered with ice sheets as Antarctica is now, the global average temperature was only 10°F lower than it is today. Heat waves, hurricanes, droughts, and floods are all thought to be related to increasing temperatures.[49]

Air Quality Solutions

Some air quality solutions focus on those countries producing the most pollution. Currently, people living in **developed countries** create 60 percent of all carbon dioxide emissions.[50] However, since most future population growth will occur in developing countries, energy demand and possibly pollution are likely to increase in these areas. As people in developing countries improve their standards of living, they will create more carbon dioxide emissions if they are dependent on fossil-fuel technologies such as the gasoline-powered engine.

Many governments have air pollution standards that limit industrial pollution in order to protect the health of citizens. For example, fifty years ago Los Angeles County formed the nation's first comprehensive smog-fighting agency. In 1972 the state of California passed tighter automobile emission standards than the nationwide standards of that time. Reformulated gasoline, a cleaner-burning gasoline that reduces smog and other air pollution, has reduced pollutants by 3.2 million pounds daily, the equivalent of taking 3.5 million cars off the road across the state. Clearly, governments can play a critical role in improving air quality.

Air-quality problems are often **transboundary** and international in scope, especially in the case of acid rain, ozone depletion, and global warming. These phenomena can affect broad regions of the globe, regardless of which countries may be primarily responsible for creating the problems. A hopeful sign is that many governments have taken action on global warming with international agreements such as the **Kyoto Protocol**, which requires countries to reduce their production of greenhouse gases. Not all countries, including the United States, have signed on to the agreement, however. Because of international treaties, the production of chemicals that destroy the ozone layer has fallen sharply. If these trends continue, scientists predict that the Antarctic **ozone hole** will begin shrinking in the next decade and be fully recovered by 2050.[51]

Other sustainable measures of improving air quality have to do with new technologies that create less pollution. For example, **biodiesel**, **fuel cell**, and **hybrid vehicles** create less carbon dioxide than do gasoline-powered cars. Hydrogen-powered vehicles, which also have the potential to significantly reduce air-quality impacts, are being tested in some countries. Solar panels and wind turbines create electrical power with very little pollution. Geothermal energy is increasingly used for the central heating of houses; in Iceland they are using almost exclusively geothermal energy.

The opportunity to use more of these sustainable technologies —especially in places where many people don't yet have cars or electricity—can help developing countries **leapfrog** over the polluting technologies of developed countries. This allows people to raise their standard of living while using renewable and less-polluting sources of energy.

Clean air is a vital resource.
Photo courtesy of NOAA

The Climate Change Knowledge Network
—It's About Communication[52]

Human-caused climate change is a relatively new variable that could have a profound influence on other global issues. How can those who research climate change work together with governments and policy makers to be sure that the most current and accurate scientific information informs public policy? As people try to understand and respond to climate change, communication will surely be one of the keys to success.

The Climate Change Knowledge Network (CCKN) exists to bring together scientific expertise, experience, and perspectives from research institutes in both developing and developed countries. CCKN offers a forum for research on the issues within the international climate change community and a means for furthering dialogue between countries as they undertake efforts to address climate change.

Visit CCKN for an excellent example of how the Internet helps diverse and geographically dispersed people communicate about a global issue of common concern: **http://www.cckn.net**.

Chapter 4. The Ocean Planet

The oceans affect and sustain all life on Earth. They drive and moderate weather and climate; provide us with food, transportation corridors, recreational opportunities, pharmaceuticals, and other natural products; and serve as a national security buffer.

—U.S. Commission on Ocean Policy,
"An Ocean Blueprint for the
Twenty-First Century," 2004

Oceans cover 70 percent of the Earth's surface, but great ocean depths remain substantially unexplored. An ocean scientist on a team exploring California's 2-mile-deep Monterey Canyon explains, "The deep sea is the largest habitat on our planet, and yet it's still the most unexplored. ...It's a world so unlike our own that we really shouldn't be surprised to find animals that defy our imagination."[53] On a near-daily basis, this team of scientists finds previously unknown organisms. Scientists are still in the early stages of learning what these organisms are and how they may be tied to the health of marine, and possibly terrestrial, ecosystems.

Nearly every day a new species is discovered in the ocean depths.
Photo courtesy of NOAA

The Ocean—A Workhorse for Life on Earth

How inappropriate to call this planet Earth when clearly it is Ocean.

—Arthur C. Clarke
(twentieth-century British author)

Oceans perform a number of essential tasks that enable life on this blue planet called Earth. Covering almost three-quarters of Earth's surface area, the five interconnected oceans account for 95 percent of all the space available for life on the planet. Oceans produce 70 percent of our oxygen and function as a vital carbon sink, absorbing about one-third of human-generated carbon dioxide that would otherwise add to the greenhouse effect.[54]

Oceans dominate world weather systems. They function somewhat like the human circulatory system, absorbing and redistributing heat around the globe and watering the planet's terrestrial surfaces. The engine driving this circula-

tion is **thermohaline circulation**, in which warm, salty water flows north and loses heat, then sinks deep into the ocean. As surface water moves to replace it, a powerful circulating flow is created.

The oceans and seas host much greater biodiversity than the land does. Estimates of numbers of ocean species vary from the thousands to tens of millions. Yet more people have traveled into space than have ventured into the ocean's depths.[55] Although approximately 90 percent of trade between countries is carried by ships over long-established trade routes, humans have explored less than 10 percent of the oceans.

Humans have a long history of dependence on the ocean, despite most of it remaining largely unknown. It provides not only most of our oxygen, but also the habitat for fish that supply the principal source of protein for more than 1 billion people. By 2010 an additional 15.5 million tons of fish will be required just to maintain the current rates of fish consumption around the world. Although the United States manages all major **fisheries** (organized fishing efforts) to a distance of 200 miles from its coast and enforces many environmental regulations in its own waters, vast ocean areas off foreign coasts are unprotected.

If the oceans are so important to humans, why are the seas so little understood and largely unprotected?

Oceans cover over 70 percent of the planet and provide 95 percent of the space available for life.
Photo courtesy of NOAA

Human Impacts on Ocean Health

The oceans are so big that it might seem that humans couldn't significantly impact ocean health. Unfortunately, the facts tell another story. Marine scientists have grouped human impacts on the ocean into seven major categories of damage caused to ocean ecosystems: [56]

1. Chemical Pollution and Marine Debris

More than 60 percent of the world's coral reefs could be destroyed within fifty years due to stresses placed on these fragile ecosystems.[57] Sources of marine pollution include commercial, military, and recreational shipping and boating; soil and chemical runoff from agricultural fields; oil-drilling installations; and land-based industry and sewage treatment plants. **Nonpoint source pollution**—pollution whose source is not specific, such as grease and oil from paved areas that runs off with rainwater—occurs as runoff picks up pollutants and washes them into bodies of water such as the oceans.

2. Fishing

Humans draw deeply from ocean fisheries. The global fishing fleet is 2.5 times larger than what the oceans can sustainably produce, and 75 percent of the world's fisheries are classified as fully exploited or overexploited.[58] An average of 27 million tons of fish caught annually are *by-catch*: fish that are caught along with the target species and remain unused.[59] Some commercial fisheries employ bottom-dragging fishing gear, which damages or destroys sea-life communities and can significantly alter food chains.

3. Nutrient Pollution

This is the discharge of nutrients and other substances—including human sewage, fertilizers and animal waste from farm runoff, and emissions from coal and oil-burning electric utilities, factories, and gas vehicles—into the marine environment. Effects include oxygen depletion of waters near shores, promotion of harmful algae blooms, and dramatic reductions in the richness of sea-life communities.

4. Coastal Development

Coastal development includes **urbanization;** road construction; port and marina activities such as boating, dredging, and dumping; mining; and coastal agriculture, forestry, and **aquaculture** (the farming of marine species in controlled pens or ponds). These activities reduce, fragment, or degrade coastal habitats and cause reductions in plant and wildlife populations, even causing or threatening species extinction. Coastal development is a primary cause of nonpoint source pollution.

The distinct blue in this image is caused by copper contamination from a nearby inactive mine in Idaho; nothing can live in this environment. Photo courtesy of NOAA

5. Exotic (Foreign) Species Introduction

This is largely due to the transport and discharge of species from ships' ballast water into environments where these species did not previously live. (Ballasts are large tanks of water that stabilize ships and determine their buoyancy.) Aquaculture may also be to blame for introducing exotic species into local waters. The introduction of nonnative species and their **pathogens** (disease-causing organisms) can cause the disruption of natural systems on a global scale.

6. Damming Rivers

The growing human demands for power generation, flood control, domestic water, and irrigation are primarily responsible for the construction of river dams. This results in significant reductions or changes in the timing of fresh water flow to the sea, reduced sediment flow into deltas and wetlands, and loss of fish spawning habitats. Impacts include fishery reductions, loss of biodiversity, increased concentrations of pollutants, salinization (accumulation of salt) of surrounding coastal lowlands, and the alteration of estuaries.

7. Global Warming

By raising ocean temperatures, global warming can damage fish eggs, larvae, and tiny planktonic animals and plants that live in the surface waters of the ocean. Higher temperatures may cause sea levels to rise and lead to changes in precipitation patterns—all of which can impact coastal and ocean environments. Some experts believe that oceans will ultimately determine the rate of global warming, because changes in ocean temperatures could disrupt thermohaline circulation enough to slow or possibly halt this engine that creates weather. This would result in even more drastic climate changes in time periods as brief as a decade. Temperatures are already rising in all ocean basins and at much greater depths than scientists had previously expected.[60]

An Ounce of Prevention

The cumulative interaction of ocean temperatures, wind, currents, tides, marine species, and chemical relationships between marine organisms can be surprising. There is sometimes a time lag between a damaging human action and its final impact on the ocean. Also, the immense spatial scale of the ocean may allow people to remain unaware of the relationship between final impacts on the environment occurring at great distance from an initial environmental disturbance.[61]

In its book *Research to Protect, Restore and Manage the Environment*, the United States National Research Council (NRC) addresses the challenges of time lag and spatial scale that are associated with ocean issues. It concludes, "Faced with a combination of potentially very serious consequences but great uncertainty about when or where the troubles will arise, an ounce of prevention is likely to be worth a pound of cure."[62] For this reason, many fisheries managers now advocate a precautionary approach in the management of fish stocks. This approach assumes that a declining fish stock should enjoy the benefit of the doubt and that a lack of information should not prevent managers from taking action. If they wait until they have absolute proof that something is wrong with a threatened fish stock, it may already have collapsed.[63]

Personal Action for Healthy Seas

Despite humans' incomplete understanding of the ocean, substantial knowledge and technology already exist that can protect the oceans and make them healthier. These are specific personal actions that would help sustain the oceans:

- **Support ocean research and conservation organizations.** This will serve to protect ocean ecosystems and further our understanding of and relationship with the oceans.
- **Buy sustainable seafood.** This is seafood obtained from fisheries where sustainable practices are already in place or taking hold. Helpful organizations on the topic of sustainable fisheries include Seafood Choices Alliances and the Monterey Bay Aquarium's Seafood Watch Program.
- **Become informed about and involved in marine policy issues.** An informed public is more likely to support sustainable fisheries and the creation of marine conservation areas.
- **Conserve resources through daily actions.** Individuals can reduce their ecological impacts by lowering their consumption of resources and services that degrade ocean environments, such as aspects of a lifestyle that contribute to global warming, ozone depletion, or acid rain.

Individuals can help sustain oceans and protect fish worldwide.
Photo courtesy of NOAA

Structural Solutions for the Seas

Given the vital importance of the oceans and growing knowledge about the damaging impacts humans have had on the oceans, structural solutions that address the underlying causes of species depletion and marine habitat destruction are essential. The U.S. Commission on the Oceans urges that reform needs to start now.[64] The commission recommends ecosystem-based ocean management, a new national ocean policy framework, and more support for ocean science and marine education efforts.

Marine Conservation

Marine conservation requires international management of shared and interconnected ocean resources and agreements that span boundaries and differences between nations. Just as land management systems around the world act to conserve habitats and biodiversity of wildlife and plants, intergovernmental agreements that require expansion of national conservation and management programs to larger ocean areas will help maintain natural and healthy marine habitats and biodiversity.

Progress is already underway to create more ocean preserves. An alliance of Latin American nations, conservation groups, and United Nations agencies recently succeeded in creating what will be the largest marine reserve in the Western Hemisphere.[65] Linking the region's five existing protected areas, the Eastern Tropical Pacific Seascape will span 521 million acres of ocean, from Costa Rica's Cocos Island to Ecuador's Galápagos Islands. This coastal reserve will extend environmental protection and resource management regulations and offer greater protection to a wide range of ocean species, including sperm whales, dolphins, tuna, sharks, and turtles.

Fisheries Management

For traditional ocean fisheries, the case of the sustainable Alaska ground-fish fisheries (including pollock and cod fisheries) is important because it shows that sustainability is within our means and reach. Rather than waiting for an irreversible decline in ground-fish stocks, in the 1970s the federal government took measures before it was too late by setting firm, scientifically based annual catch quotas. That quota has never been exceeded, and recently pollock was allocated on a boat-by-boat quota basis that resulted in less by-catch, extended employment, and higher product yields.[71] Although we cannot always predict with certainty when resource depletion becomes irreversible, we can predict with some certainty that "an ounce of prevention" will go further toward a cure than will a race to consume the dwindling bounty of the seas.

Aquaculture

Although the number of fish in the ocean is declining, demand for fish as an important source of protein is increasing as world population grows. To meet this need and reduce demands on traditional open-ocean fisheries, the aquaculture industry has developed efficient ways to grow fish on farms. However, experts believe that some fish farms can cause environmental damage through pollution from their waste or that farmed fish, when they escape, can threaten the gene pool of existing stocks of wild fish. Still, because fish are highly efficient at converting calories from

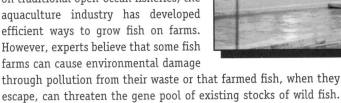

Aquaculture (fish farm) facility in Asia.
Photo courtesy of NOAA

plants into protein (especially when compared to beef), fish farms can be an important step to producing protein needed to feed the planet's growing population.[66]

China has made great progress with both inland and coastal fish farms, accounting for two-thirds of global aquaculture production. **Fish polyculture** is also successful in China, which practices simultaneous farming of four different types of carp that feed at different levels of the food chain, from bottom feeders to phytoplankton-, zooplankton-, and vegetation-eaters. This provides greatly increased yields over single-species fish farming.[67]

The Tragedy of the Commons and Fishing for the Future[68]

Sustainable Alaskan fishery.
*Photo courtesy of
Marine Conservation Alliance*

To understand the relationship of personal and structural solutions to the oceans' troubles, it makes sense to study humans' personal connections to the ocean through the seafood we consume. The over-harvesting of seafood resources held "in common" by fishers can lead to tragic reduction of marine biodiversity. On the other hand, existing sustainable fisheries can serve as models for struggling fisheries.

Biologist Garrett Hardin explained human relationships to common resources through his concept of the **tragedy of the commons.**[69] **Commons** are those resources that all members of a community may use, without payment. Examples include rivers and lakes, the air we breathe, and the vast oceans that no one person can own. Commons can be destroyed by uncontrolled use, when consumers or resource harvesters race to extract diminishing supplies. The less of a desired resource there is, the fiercer the competition and the speedier the resource is depleted. There are a number of examples of the tragedy of the commons: congestion on urban highways, pollution of the air and atmosphere, and overfishing of many fish stocks in global waters.

Fish is a key food source in the world today. One billion people rely on fish as their primary source of animal protein, and 60 percent of all people live within 200 kilometers of a seacoast. Around the world, 200 million people depend on fishing for their livelihood. Unfortunately, today 70 percent of all fish and seafood that people

depend on are being fished to capacity or overfished, meaning that the remaining fish cannot continue to reproduce at levels high enough for future harvests. [70] In the United States, 50 percent of the domestic fishery production occurs sustainably in Alaska, but in many places, including the East Coast of the United States, some stocks of fish are so low that the fishing industry that depends on those stocks is threatened.

Within a fishery, when there is no catch limit to restrain him, a fisherman's best short-term interest is to fish aggressively before other vessels outfish him and take home a larger share of the total catch. As the catch dwindles, fishermen compete even more intensively to maintain a profitable existence and pay for their salaries, boats, and fuel. Technology also plays a role, as faster boats and improved fishing technology speeds this race to a point where the fish stocks in the commons fall below commercial viability. At this point, fishermen often shift to harvesting other species. This tragedy of the commons can repeat itself until many stocks are diminished or overfished.

How can we avoid the tragedy of the commons with wild fisheries? Just as sustainable forests can preserve habitats and meet human needs for wood, sustainable fisheries can preserve fish species and provide humans with valuable protein. One model of a more sustainable wild fishery is the Alaskan ground-fish fishery. This is the largest U.S. fishery by volume and value, and it yields half of all U.S. fish production. Between 1980 and 1990, the Alaska ground-fish harvest experienced nearly **exponential growth,** but since 1990 it has been maintained at a stable level.[71]

Alaskan ground-fish management and regulation evolved through four stages: from minimal restrictions on foreign fleets in the 1970s, to aggregate quotas in the 1980s, to numerical limits on vessels in the 1990s, and finally to boat-by-boat quotas. Although some people within the fishing industry call these regulations unfair or biased (as not all fishermen can obtain a permit or catch as much as they would like), many agree that the regulations have resulted in more efficiency and lower operating costs to fishermen, higher market value for fish, safer fisheries for fishermen, and greater industry interest in resource protection.[72] The ground-fish fishery in Alaska has succeeded admirably, whereas most other fisheries worldwide are in rapid decline and a state of significant depletion.

LITERATURE CONNECTION:
The River God Meets the Ocean God

People have been inspired by oceans and rivers for centuries. The following story from Chuang Tzu, a fourth-century Taoist philosopher, is one such example.

Autumn Floods: The River God and the Ocean God
By Chuang Tzu

The autumn floods had come. Thousands of wild torrents poured furiously into the Yellow River. It surged and flooded its banks, until, looking across, you could not tell an ox from a horse on the other side. Then the River God laughed, delighted to think that all the beauty in the world had fallen into his keeping. So downstream he swung, until he came to the ocean. There he looked out over the waves, toward the empty horizon in the east, and his face fell. He came to his senses and murmured to the Ocean God:

"Well, the proverb is right. He who has got himself a hundred ideas thinks he knows more than anybody else. Such a one am I. Only now do I see what they mean by expanse!"

The Ocean God replied:

"Can you talk about the sea to a frog in a well? Can you talk about ice to dragonflies? Can you talk about the way of life to a doctor of philosophy? Of all the waters in the world, the ocean is greatest. All the rivers pour into it day and night; it is never filled. It gives back its waters day and night. But am I proud of it? What am I under heaven? Compared with the sky, I am a little rock, a scrub oak on the mountainside."

(Excerpt from *The Way of Chuang Tzu*, by Thomas Merton, copyright © 1965 by the Abbey of Gethsemana, reprinted by permission of New Directions Publishing Corp.)

Chapter 5. Sustainable Solutions: Environmental Justice

If you are neutral in situations of injustice,
you have chosen the side of the oppressor.
If an elephant has its foot on the tail of
a mouse and you say that you are neutral,
the mouse will not appreciate your neutrality.

—Bishop Desmond Tutu
(South African leader for independence
and post-independence reconciliation)

Social Sustainability and the Standard of Equity

The interconnection of the **economy** and environment is fairly clear when we consider biodiversity and habitat conservation. For example, when a marine ecosystem is depleted or damaged, it can no longer serve the economic needs of current or future generations of fishers. When a fishery collapses, the fishing industry as a whole suffers, as does the fishery's role in a national economy.

A true measure of sustainability, in addition to economic and environmental considerations, should also include *society*. When determining whether an issue or solution is socially sustainable, one might ask:

- What are the social impacts associated with the use of a resource?
- What groups of people have access to which resources?
- Who suffers under what kinds of environmental conditions?

These questions address the issue of environmental justice—whether or not people's **human rights** and resource needs are being met equitably and without discrimination in matters relating to the environment and pollution. Sometimes people do not get enough of the resources they need (such as food and water), or they are not involved in the decision-making process that determines resource distribution. Other times, people get too much of things that detract from their **quality of life,** such as environmentally based pollution, illness, and disease. Regarding environmental justice, the Environmental Protection Agency (EPA) says:

No group of people, including a racial, ethnic, or socioeconomic group, should bear a disproportionate share of the negative environmental consequences resulting from industrial, municipal, and commercial operations or the execution of federal, state, local, and tribal programs and policies. ... Environmental justice is achieved when everyone, regardless of race, culture, or income, enjoys the same degree of protection from environmental and health hazards and equal access to the decision-making process to have a healthy environment in which to live, learn, and work."[73]

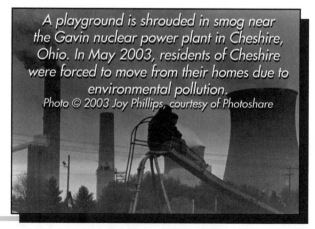

A playground is shrouded in smog near the Gavin nuclear power plant in Cheshire, Ohio. In May 2003, residents of Cheshire were forced to move from their homes due to environmental pollution.
Photo © 2003 Joy Phillips, courtesy of Photoshare

Environmental Justice in the United States

In the United States, minority populations and low-income populations bear a disproportionate burden of poor health due to environmental factors. This is a sampling of some of the environmental injustices occurring in the United States:[74]

- **Hazardous-waste landfills.** Virtually all hazardous waste in the southern states of the United States is disposed of in African-American communities, yet African-Americans comprise just 20 percent of the region's population. Three out of every five African-Americans in the South live in communities with abandoned toxic-waste sites. The community around the nation's largest hazardous-waste landfill, in Emelle, Alabama, is 95 percent African-American. The landfill accepts hazardous wastes from the Lower 48 and several foreign countries.
- **Lead-based paint.** According to the Centers for Disease Control and Prevention (CDC), the number-one environmental health threat to children is lead paint in older housing. Although 40 percent of American homes still have lead-based paint in them, low-income children are eight times more likely to live in areas with lead paint, and African-American children are five times more likely than white children to suffer from lead poisoning.
- **Asthma and air pollution.** There is a particularly strong correlation between asthma hospitalization caused by air pollution and the percentage of African-Americans and Latinos in a community. A positive correlation also exists between asthma and poverty and between asthma and the percentage of children in a population.[75]

In 1994 growing awareness about environmental injustice in the United States led President Clinton to issue Executive Order 12898 addressing environmental justice in minority and low-income populations. The EPA responded by developing the *Environmental Justice Strategy*. Unfortunately, the EPA's own 2004 self-study revealed that it had "not fully implemented the 1994 Executive Order 12898 on environmental justice or even developed the necessary criteria for doing so."[76] It remains important for grassroots organizations, as well as ordinary citizens, to continue to be aware of and vocal about the cause of environmental justice in the United States.[77]

Environmental Justice Around the World

Environmental justice is also a global issue. Certain populations around the world suffer from many of the same environmental inequities and injustices that exist in the United States, sometimes with drastic consequences involving food security, environmental pollution, toxic wastes and pesticides, and human rights abuses, especially in workplaces.

Many developing countries have extraction-based economies (such as drilling for oil, logging, and mining) that supply the raw materials for distant industrialized nations. Taxes may be waived for foreign companies, and environmental regulations are sometimes relaxed or disregarded, with negative economic and health results for local people. In developing countries where large oil refineries

are located, the health of those living in the area can be directly affected. One example was the 2003 oil pipeline explosion in Nigeria that killed 250 people living in the vicinity of the pipeline.[78]

Global environmental injustices may also take the forms of economic imbalance and gross social inequity. For example, whereas the chief executive of British Petroleum anticipates an annual retirement pension of $1.97 million, most people in Nigeria (one of the world's largest oil-producing nations) earn less than $1 per day, and the percentage of people living beneath the poverty level there has increased from 27 percent in 1980 to 66 percent in 1996. This means that these people will suffer from **structural scarcity,** because they will be unable to afford sufficient resources to meet their basic needs.[79]

Youth working for environmental justice.
Photo courtesy of Greenaction

Pursuing Environmental Justice

Social sustainability maintains that an equitable distribution of resources and reasonable protection from environmental hazards are essential to the current and future well-being of people and the planet. When local people are involved in decision making and the distribution of resources, local populations are healthier and better able to pursue a livelihood that allows for a better quality of life. This results in both less conflict over and competition for scarce natural resources and also conservation of biodiversity and natural ecosystems. Environmental justice can be pursued on both the personal and structural levels.

Personal Solutions

Citizen advocates for environmental justice are important, both locally and globally, because they can voice their compassion for those who lack the voice or power to change their own situations. Being an advocate for environmental justice can include supporting businesses that have a good track record on environmental pollution in minority and low-income neighborhoods.

Citizen groups have been especially important in seeking improved quality of environmental health for different groups and communities. Organizations concerned with domestic environmental justice pursue a wide variety of issues, including nuclear energy and waste disposal; air and water pollution; industrial toxins; pesticides; and the concentration of serious health concerns such as asthma and cancer in certain ethnic and economic communities.

Structural Solutions

Both intergovernmental organizations (such as the United Nations Development Programme) and **nongovernmental organizations (NGOs)** are dedicated to environmental justice. These organizations try to find ways to protect the natural environment, and the people and wildlife that depend on it, by linking environmental security, human rights, and social needs.

One way to pursue environmental justice on the international stage is to explore new forms of **economic development** that do not depend on resource extraction. Another is to develop international policies based on measures of progress that consider social and environmental impacts rather than just monetary exchanges. A third way is to include antipollution and resource protection clauses in private and public contracts, with substantial penalties for violators.

A number of agreements and protocols have been adopted by the United Nations with the purpose of setting environmental standards for industries, ranging from the Convention on the International Trade in Endangered Species to the Montreal Protocol on Substances that Deplete the Ozone Layer. Almost every practice that is harmful to the environment is covered, including the dumping of hazardous materials, destruction of wetlands, and overfishing of endangered marine species. The most recent addition is the Kyoto Protocol on climate change, which sets clear standards for carbon emissions.[80] Although these agreements may not claim environmental justice as their immediate goal, their targeted results include improved environmental health and economic opportunity for everyone.

Seeking a Safe and Sustainable Livelihood: The Hazards of Shrimp Farming[81]

Local community involvement is a critical part of achieving environmental justice. Organizations such as the Environmental Justice Foundation (EJF) play an important role in helping implement international environmental justice solutions that include local people. One example of their work is in the shrimp industry.

Photo courtesy of NOAA

In their campaign to study and reform the impacts of shrimp production around the world, the EJF determined that in tropical seas such as the Philippine waters, shrimp trawlers catch and discard up to 20 kilograms of by-catch for just 1 kilogram of shrimp. Shrimp trawling has also decimated many local fish stocks, leaving many fishermen unemployed. When farmed, shrimp consume more than twice their weight in fish food before they are sold, making them inefficient protein producers. Because of the large amount of waste they produce, shrimp farming can destroy coastal forests and threaten coral reefs and marine wildlife. They have ruined agricultural lands, polluted fresh water sources, reduced food security, and even brought conflict to coastal communities. One Filipino fisherman said, "The shrimp live better than we do. They have electricity, but we don't. The shrimp have clean water, but we don't. The shrimp have lots of food, but we are hungry."[82]

In local communities in the developing world, EJF trains people to investigate, expose, and combat environmental degradation and inequity in shrimp aquaculture. EJF supports local populations in their struggle to regain a sustainable livelihood. Globally, EJF lobbies for political solutions and mobilizes consumers to boycott products that contribute to environmental injustice, such as shrimp grown through unsustainable aquaculture in the Philippines.

EJF involves people in the developed world by encouraging them to be advocates for environmental justice. This citizen advocacy includes signing petitions and lobbying shrimp retailers to purchase shrimp only from suppliers who can certify that the shrimp were produced without harming natural environments or local communities.

LITERATURE CONNECTION:
Gandhi Is Fasting

The famous African-American writer Langston Hughes wrote the following poem in 1943, when Mahatma Gandhi was imprisoned by the British in India for leading mass protests, strikes, and boycotts of British products.

Under British rule, India was forced to increase exports of food grains and other cash crops while in the midst of a growing famine. In this case, agriculture was an "extractive" industry that removed raw materials from the people and provided minimal economic development. Indo-British trade practices in the form of tariffs favoring England literally forced British products on India. As a result, millions of artisans and craftspeople, spinners, weavers, potters, smelters, and smiths were rendered jobless and were compelled to become landless agricultural workers.

In his poem, Hughes highlights the power of one man's fasting against an oppressive colonizer whose racism fueled economic and environmental injustice. Hughes draws a parallel with the Jim Crow system of laws and practices that legalized segregation in the United States, beginning during the Reconstruction period following the Civil War and continuing through the 1950s, finally ending with the 1960s civil rights movement, when Dr. Martin Luther King Jr. also used fasting as a protest tool.

Gandhi Is Fasting By Langston Hughes

Mighty Britain, tremble!
Let your empire's standard sway
Let it break entirely—
My Gandhi fasts today.

You may think it foolish—
That there's no truth in what I say—
That all of Asia's watching
As Gandhi fasts today.

All of Asia's watching.
And I am watching, too,
For I am also jim crowed—
As India is jim crowed by you.

You know quite well, Great Britain,
That it is not right
To starve and beat and oppress
Those who are not white.

Of course, we do it too.
Here in the U.S.A.
May Gandhi's prayers help us, as well,
As he fasts today.

(From The Collected Poems of Langston Hughes, by Langston Hughes, copyright © 1994 by the Estate of Langston Hughes. Used by permission of Alfred A. Knopf, a division of Random House, Inc.)

UNIT 4
FACING THE FUTURE ACTIVITIES

- **Fishing for the Future**
  (models concepts of tragedy of the commons and sustainability)

- **Take a Step for Equity**
  (explores equity and environmental justice issues around the world)

To download activities visit http://www.facingthefuture.org

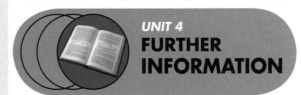

UNIT 4
FURTHER INFORMATION

For a detailed assessment of environment and sustainability around the world: State of the World—2004, World Watch Institute, New York: W. W. Norton & Company, 2004.

For a wide range of information on forests, oceans, sustainability, and climate change that is aimed at a general audience: David Suzuki Foundation, http://www.davidsuzuki.org/.

For an intergovernmental approach to global environmental issues: the United Nations Environmental Programme, http://www.unep.org/.

For a wide range of information on environmental issues and regulations in the United States: Environmental Protection Agency, http://www.epa.gov.

For information on wildlife and the oceans: World Wildlife International, http://www.panda.org.

For studies on global warming and the effects of climate change: The United Nations, The International Panel on Climate Change (IPCC), Third Annual Assessment on Climate Change, which offers four comprehensive online reports: The Scientific Basis; Impacts, Adaptation, and Vulnerability; Mitigation; and Synthesis Report, http://www.ipcc.ch.

For information on environmental justice in the United States: Greenaction for Health and Environmental Justice, http://greenaction.org/; The Environmental Justice Resource Center, http://www.ejrc.cau.edu/; and Environmental Protection Agency: http://www.epa.gov.

For information on international environmental justice: The Environmental Justice Foundation, http://www.ejfoundation.org.

UNIT 5
QUALITY OF LIFE: CULTURE, HEALTH, EDUCATION, AND HUMAN RIGHTS

The quality of a life is determined by its activities. —Aristotle (Greek philosopher, 384–322 BCE)

Essential Questions

- **What determines quality of life and happiness?**
- **What roles do culture, government, and business have in determining quality of life?**
- **How are consumption and the media connected to quality of life?**
- **How are health, education, and human rights tied to quality of life?**

Chapter 1. Introduction

The "American dream" of prosperity idealizes accumulation of material possessions, from large homes and cars to stereos and the latest season's fashions. The underlying assumption of this dream is that wealth and happiness are linked.

Photo © CARE 2002/Jason Sangster

What is the connection between wealth and well-being? The word *wealth* derives from "weal," which means prosperity and well-being.[1] In modern times, wealth has come to imply material goods and financial success, especially for individuals rather than communities or groups.[2] Recently in the developed world, where many (but not all) people have more than sufficient financial resources to meet all their basic needs, the qualities of physical health, leisure time, the bonds of family and community, and a happy state of mind are increasingly being sought over material goods as the defining traits of well-being.

Many people in **developing countries** struggle to meet the most basic human needs of food, water, shelter, and personal safety. For them, working less in exchange for the luxury of more leisure time could spell disaster in the form of insufficient food or water for the survival of their families. If they are able to save money beyond the amount required for **subsistence**, this meager surplus might be directed toward **primary health care** or possibly education for someone in the family.

This unit explores various definitions and components of well-being. It examines the relationships between **quality of life** and **culture**, health, education, and **human rights**.

Stories from the World: *Oglala Lakota Tribe*

—Putting a Value on Cultural Knowledge[3] (excerpted from *YES!* magazine, www.yesmagazine.org)

Photo © Marcel Salvaro,
courtesy of UNESCO

Can countries look to **indigenous people** (people whose ancestors are native to a region) for sustainable solutions for health care, **governance**, and **ecosystem** management? With serious problems on U.S. reservations in the areas of education, health, and poverty, many Native Americans are focused on the preservation and rediscovery of traditional values of interconnection, **sustainability,** and reciprocity. These values can guide them in developing new **economies** that fit within their traditional culture.

Indigenous peoples of North America live according to a variety of economic systems, some more *egalitarian* (equal) and other more *hierarchical* (ranked by levels of importance). Sherry Salway Black is a member of the Oglala Lakota Tribe and vice president of the First Nations Development Institute in Fredericksburg, Virginia. When teaching about indigenous economics, she focuses on Native American economies that emphasize **equity.** She explains that many Native American cultures emphasize *relationship* in a way that values connectedness and community over individual achievement. The commonly held Native American idea that "all of my human relatives and all other living things are related to me, to each other, and I to them" leads many tribes to consider how present decisions and actions will impact future generations. For example, the Menominee Tribe harvested their forest only two and a half times in the past century, providing a model of sustainability that results in a positive distribution of wealth and the long-term well-being of the tribe as a whole.

Salway explains that, traditionally, resources in Native American communities were distributed through kinship systems that put leaders on the same economic level as other community members, because the principle of *reciprocity* ensured a return of favors and material goods in the future. Tribes evolved complex systems of laws, activities, and institutions through the value placed on sharing wealth.

For the better part of two decades, the First Nations Development Institute has been working with native peoples to use these cultural values to develop productive yet sustainable business practices. Other nations may do well to look to them for guidance on sustainable economic practices.

Youth in Action! Hip-Hop Artist Redefines Cool[4] (excerpted from *YES!* magazine, www.yesmagazine.org)

Ricardo "Kool Aid" Chavez is a hip-hop and rap artist and son of Cesar Chavez, cofounder of the United Farm Workers Union. Ricardo grew up poor but politically aware, and he believes that artistic expression in music should not be controlled by record companies. When he began producing his music, record companies' message to him was, "If you want to get played, you should rap about sex, drugs, and violence. You should be more mainstream." Ricardo refused to play by their rules.

Ricardo believes that the mainstream rap promoted by record companies is just one part of the artistic spectrum. His group, *La Paz* ("The Peace"), is at the other end, using their independence from a major recording contract to write lyrics that make people feel respected and challenged. Performing for benefits, community

events, and fundraisers, *La Paz* celebrates women—sisters, mothers, and grandmothers—as the "backbone" of society. The group takes their inner-city message across the country to diverse communities, many of which previously associated rap only with "gangsta" lyrics celebrating violence and drugs.

Ricardo finds solace in music, but he also warns of its power: "Music is like a force of nature. It's as basic to the human condition as anything else in the natural world. But, like nature, it can be productive or destructive. Fire can keep you warm, but it can also burn down the house." In an era of increasing corporate ownership of **media** outlets, Ricardo Chavez reminds us, "You don't have to play to anybody else's tune. You can march to your own drum."

Chapter 2. Well-Being and Happiness— In Search of the Good Life

The gross national product does not allow for the health of our children, the quality of their education, or the joy of their play. It does not include the beauty of our poetry or the strength of our marriages, the intelligence of our public debate or the integrity of our public officials. It measures neither our wit nor our courage, neither our wisdom nor our learning, neither our compassion nor our devotion to our country. It measures everything, in short, except that which makes life worthwhile. And it can tell us everything about America except why we are proud that we are Americans.

—Robert F. Kennedy (U.S. senator, 1925–1968)

What is the good life? How can we measure quality of life? Although the **gross domestic product (GDP)** measures a nation's annual income, other **quality-of-life indicators** such as the Human Development Index (HDI), **Genuine Progress Indicator (GPI)**, Well-being Index (WI), and Fordham Social Indicator (FSI) attempt to measure quality of life more broadly. These alternative indicators consider not only income and the basics of survival (food, water, and shelter) but also factors such as work satisfaction, personal health, social relations, **ecology,** personal safety and security, freedom, and human rights. This chapter contrasts quality of life in the United States, a developed, wealthy nation, with quality of life in developing countries.

The United States—Got Happiness?

The United Nations Development Programme ranked the United States seventeenth among industrialized nations for quality-of-life indicators such as longevity (life expectancy), poverty, and **literacy** (the ability to read and write).[5] No one in the developed world works more hours than U.S. citizens. The average American worked 199 hours more in 2000 than in 1973, an increase of almost five weeks annually.[6] The average U.S. citizen has ten days of paid vacation each year, while European workers get at least twenty-eight days.[7] However, recent trends indicate that European countries may be moving toward the forty-hour work week.[8]

In the United States, incomes grew and buying power doubled between 1957 and 2002. However, psychologists who study happiness and well-being found that the percentage of people reporting themselves to be "very happy" over that period did not change significantly.[9] Another study collected thirty years' worth of data between 1970 and 2000 on indicators such as teen suicide, income inequity, and limited health insurance. The study concluded that the social health of Americans had declined.[10]

Photo © Chris Calwell

Social psychologist David Myers studies quality of life in the United States. Reflecting on the last few decades, he says that Americans were "finding ourselves with big houses and broken homes, high incomes and low morale, secured rights and diminished civility. We were excelling at making a living but too often failing at making a life."[11] Women's entry into the workplace after WWII presented both opportunities and challenges. Two-income families drove up the price of housing, and women were faced with employment stress on top of the traditional responsibilities of parenting and housework.[12] Studies show that today U.S. citizens live in a "culture of envy," in which they judge themselves and establish their happiness not by what they have or need but by comparing what they have to what their neighbors have.[13]

The average U.S. citizen worked 199 hours more in 2000 than in 1973.

Photo courtesy of the U.S. Census Bureau

In the world's most powerful **democracy**, one might expect active citizenship to be a fundamental contributor to the quality of life: one might expect that people are informed about political issues and vote at every opportunity. However, researchers cite relatively low voter turnouts as evidence of weak **civic engagement** in America.[14] This has been attributed to many factors, including time limitations, residential sprawl, and excessive television viewing. U.S. citizens work long hours to support their consumption of fast food, cars, and the latest technology, and they spend a great deal of time commuting and watching television. In the industrialized world, television viewing averages three hours daily. It is no longer considered a luxury to own a television, but a necessity.[15] Television advertising, in turn, promotes a consumer lifestyle in an escalating cycle of overwork and overconsumption.[16]

LITERATURE CONNECTION:
A Different View of Work

In the following poem, Peter Spiro critiques some commonly held views about work and time. What is Spiro's view of work? How do you think it compares with most people's view of work? Do you agree or disagree with him?

Work by Peter Spiro

They say,
What would you like to do
or where would you like to work.
I think, Earth. I'd like to work
on Earth, third in from the sun.
Does the bear say,
I work in this section of the forest.
Does the eagle say,
I work in this part of space.
Does the shark say,
I swim only here.
Does the air work or the wind.
And what kind of work do I want to do?
I say,
I want to eat and sleep and explore
like the bear and the eagle and the shark.
I want to speak like the wind and breathe air
period.
I want to hang a sign on my door:
Do not disturb while I'm at work
dreaming.
They say,
this is lazy.
They say,
you are worthless.
They say,
you have no ambition.
And I tell them,
I am an unambitious worthless problem
Like the air and the wind.
I will sleep and dream like the air and
move in passion like the wind
When it pleases me and for
no one.

(Work, by Peter Spiro,
from The United States of Poetry,
copyright © 1995
by Harry N. Abrams, Inc.
Reprinted by permission
of Peter Spiro.)

Photo © Paul Bannick

Meeting Basic Needs in the Developing World—How Much Is Enough?

As per capita earning rises slowly in some developing countries, where limited income is devoted first to meeting basic survival needs, the opportunity arises to address these questions: How much is enough? How does increased income affect happiness for people in the developing world? A study found that in sixty-five developing countries tracked between 1990 and 2000, increasing annual income to just $13,000 led to increased happiness and only modest gains in happiness resulted as income topped $13,000.[17] The resulting implication is that income growth increases well-being as survival needs are met, but that past this point, happiness is not substantially increased by more money.

Unfortunately, most people in poorer countries do not make anywhere near the $13,000 annually that seems to grant basic needs and a peak in happiness gains. According to the Well-being Index rating of 180 countries, two-thirds of the world's people received a "bad" or "poor" rating for human well-being, and half of Earth's land area received poor ratings for environmental health.[18] This means that poverty and a damaged environment combine to keep quality of life low for many people in the world.

While people in wealthier nations contemplate how to reduce their stress and reclaim some of their time, people in poorer areas face a daily struggle to meet their needs of food, water, and shelter. Naturally, people in poor countries spend a greater percentage of their income on basic needs than do people in wealthier countries. For example, in Tanzania, with per-person living expenses of $375 for 1998, 67 percent of that went to pay for food; in contrast, Japanese per capita living expenses were $13,568, with only 12 percent spent on food.[19]

The irony of quality of life in the world today is that many people in **developed countries** are trapped in a cycle of over-work and overconsumption, while the majority of the planet's residents are too concerned with daily survival to worry about how to reduce stress and increase free time.

Field workers in Sierra Leone.
Photo © 2002 Valenda Campbell,
courtesy of CARE

Building the Happy Life in Bogota, Colombia[20]

Photo © Institute for Transportation and Development Policy

Beginning in the late 1990s, Bogota Mayor Enrique Peñalosa initiated a bold campaign to improve the quality of life in his city by orienting urban life around people and communities. In doing so, he effectively countered the stereotype of Colombia as being rife with **intrastate** or **civil war**, the cocaine trade, and violence.

Immediately upon taking office, Peñalosa scrapped a plan to build a $600 million elevated highway intended to reduce growing traffic congestion. Instead, the mayor expanded the city's less-expensive bus system to carry more than 780,000 passengers daily (more than ride the subway system in Washington, D.C.). Building his inspired vision of people and communities, Peñalosa created or revived more than 1,000 parks that are now used by 1.5 million visitors annually, invested in hundreds of kilometers of bike- and pedestrian-only paths and rights-of-way, and constructed new public buildings with direct benefits to citizens, such as libraries and schools.

Sometimes, as in the case of Bogota, developing countries can **leapfrog** the pitfalls of overconsumption and poor planning by not following the examples of excess set by developed nations. Peñalosa judges his own success with a commonsense measurement:

"A city is successful not when it's rich, but when its people are happy."

The Good News about the Good Life

If increased income beyond a modest level does not guarantee improved quality of life, what does?

Researchers have identified a number of key ingredients to happiness and well-being. At least a dozen long-term studies in Japan, the United States, and Scandinavia report that the chance of dying in a given year (of any cause) is two to five times greater for people who live in relative isolation than it is for more social folks.[21] The connection, meaning, and hope found in spiritual and faith communities have also been cited as positive quality-of-life factors. Researchers note another happiness factor called "flow," which occurs when, in work or leisure, we are "unself-consciously absorbed in a mindful challenge."[22]

Bangladesh mother and child.
Photo © 2000 Billy Howard, courtesy of CARE

The goal for improving quality of life on Earth is relatively simple: to improve well-being in a sustainable way. This goal entails addressing economic needs, a healthy environment, and social equity for present and future generations. Research shows that many people in wealthy nations want to live simply and find ways to downsize their **ecological footprint.** One study found that 75 percent of U.S. workers would like to have a simpler society with less emphasis on material wealth.[23] By lowering their level of consumption, wealthier people can actually enhance well-being by reclaiming their time and reconnecting themselves with family and community.

Progress toward a simpler life in the developed world can enhance opportunities for access to resources in the developing world. The longer the world's wealthy avoid addressing quality of life and environmental problems, the costlier the effects become.[24] Ignoring the needs of the world's poorest people will eventually threaten the well-being of the more prosperous around the world. For example, dust storms from the rapid **desertification** of northern China have affected air quality as far away as Korea and Japan.

When citizens of developed countries shrink their ecological footprint, they shrink their disproportionate consumption of food, water, and energy, which can have a positive effect on other global issues.

Can You Make the Time to Take Back Your Time?

Millions of Americans are overworked, overscheduled, overwhelmed, and just plain stressed out. The promise of leisure remains elusive for the rich and poor alike. Gains in productivity have resulted in economic growth and more material goods, but not in more time to enjoy life. In fact, American workdays and workweeks are longer than ever before—and longer than those in any other industrialized nation. Technology may make us more efficient, but it has not delivered on the promise of easing workloads. Rather, technology makes Americans more available (with cell phones, faxes, E-mail, etc.) and more accountable for their work. For many people, the end result of technology is more work, not less work.

As an antidote to overwork and stress, the Simplicity Forum launched "Take Back Your Time Day," the first of which was held on October 24, 2003. Now an annual international event, this date is nine weeks before the end of the year, symbolizing the nine additional weeks worked by Americans each year in comparison to Europeans. Modeled after Earth Day, which ushered in a new era of environmental awareness and ecological legislation, Take Back Your Time Day events are held in at least 200 communities in the United States and Canada. The campaign earns endorsement and praise from labor unions, religious and family organizations, and some local and state **government** entities.[25]

It appears that reclaiming time is of international concern. Starting in 1986, Italy combined its traditional fine cuisine with a desire to live more simply and slowly, resulting in the Slow Food Movement. With at least 60,000 members on five continents, the Slow Food folks are killing two birds with one stone in the time-food continuum by taking plenty of time to shop for ingredients and prepare fine, healthy food and then share a leisurely meal with family and friends. This serves human health in a world dominated by fast food. Beginning in 2000, an offshoot movement, called the League of Slow Cities, was formed. Cities in this movement seek to reclaim community spirit and time by featuring outdoor cafés, town squares, pedestrian walkways, and parks.[26]

Do you have the time to take back your time?

Chapter 3. Improving Quality of Life— Government, Business, and Individuals

Gross national happiness is more important than gross national product.
—Jigme Singye Wangchuk (King of Bhutan, 1972–)

Governments and businesses can help improve people's quality of life in many ways. One is by promoting **sustainable development**, which results in healthier environments and more efficient use of Earth's resources. This chapter explores some examples of governments and businesses improving people's quality of life through promoting sustainable development in both the developed and developing world. The chapter then turns to personal actions that individuals can take to enhance their own and others' well-being and happiness.

Government's Role in Quality of Life

Governments in developed countries can play a major role in advancing sustainability and quality of life by using their considerable might and resources to both push and pull for reduced resource consumption and smaller ecological footprints. Governments can exert pull through incentives, usually in the form of tax-based **subsidies**, for sustainable goods and services. Government pull also occurs when subsidies for unsustainable practices in agriculture, **fisheries**, forestry, development of energy sources, and road transportation are reduced or eliminated. Instead, governments can restructure taxes and subsidy programs to favor renewable energy, efficient technology, clean production and manufacturing, and mass public transit.[27]

Subsidies can work for or against sustainable living. In the United States, taxpayer money subsidizes the automobile industry and auto use in the amount of $257 billion annually (about $2,000 per taxpayer). This means that taxpayers who cannot afford a car are, in effect, supporting those who can.[28] In the European Union, on the other hand, ecological tax reform is taking hold. This ensures that a product's market price includes its full environmental costs. Between 1980 and 2001, some European Union nations increased taxes fourfold for gas, diesel, and auto sales.

Additionally, government agencies and large public institutions around the world have begun to experiment with *green procurement*, in which they purchase only goods that are considered environmentally sustainable. Private businesses and public agencies can require that their suppliers offer products with attributes including recycled components, efficiency, low toxicity, biodegradability, and reduced packaging waste. Green procurement has the potential to direct trillions of dollars in the world's industrialized countries toward environmentally sustainable suppliers of goods and services.[29]

In addition to the pull of restructuring taxes and subsidies, governments can build quality of life into laws, with mandates that emphasize humans and environmental health. For example, regulatory standards can be used to reduce industrial pollution and automobile emissions. Regional and national standards are also useful tools in saving energy and water. Between 1980 and 2000, the number of countries implementing household appliance efficiency programs grew sevenfold, to forty-three. This approach provides a push, or consequence, if manufacturers do not meet minimum standards, as well as a pull, or incentive, for consumers to make responsible choices.[30]

The net result of governments pushing and pulling for sustainability is improved quality of life, healthier environments, and less competition for increasingly scarce resources.

Businesses with a New Bottom Line

Businesses can also play an important role in sustainable development. A number of business-based solutions for increasing consumer choices in sustainable products are beginning to take root.[31] Businesses can label products in a variety of ways to maximize information. They can build their market share and increase profits by meeting "green" certification requirements and labeling their products as such. For example, many food products in recent decades have been successfully marketed as "natural" and "organic." Home Depot has employed this green strategy by purchasing, labeling, and marketing green-certified lumber products. In 2004 Germany's Blue Angel, a label for numerous green products in Europe, celebrated its twenty-fifth anniversary of providing sustainable products.[32]

It makes economic sense, as well as environmental sense, for businesses to shift to green products, green labeling, and efficient design principles. All these measures can be reflected in labeling and advertising to maximize product exposure and profitability. In the United States, about 63 million adults, representing 30 percent of all households, do some form of environmentally conscious purchasing, from buying organic produce to choosing energy-efficient appliances.[33] Although skeptics warn that the labeling strategy must require the oversight of an official agency that determines "green" standards, industry and advertisers have already begun to track and cater to the growing number of green buyers.[34]

Personal Actions for Quality of Life

There are a number of actions that you as an individual can take to improve quality of life for yourself and for others:

- Ask yourself, what contributes to happiness and the "good life"? Consider both material and nonmaterial indicators of well-being.
- Become aware of your consumption patterns. What do you want? What do you need? What do you buy? Consider food, clothing, and recreation.
- Take inventory of how you use your time. Ask yourself, do I spend enough time on things that matter to me, things that help me live a good life?

Lifecycle Design: Manufacturing and Public Planning with a Vision of Sustainability

Cradle-to-grave design is a **lifecycle design** approach that tries to anticipate environmental consequences throughout the entire life of a given product—from the extraction of raw materials to the disposal of the product, from energy used in production and operation of the product to its transportation to market. The underlying assumption of this approach is that everything in the chain of a product's development,

The Mirra office chair is made using a cradle-to-cradle design approach.
Photo courtesy of BuildingGreen.com

use, and disposal—"from cradle to grave"—is part of its ecological footprint. The product's ecological footprint becomes part of our own ecological footprint when we purchase and use it.

Even while many industries are just beginning to embrace and develop cradle-to-grave design as a vast improvement over more traditional production, others propose that the time has come for **cradle-to-cradle design**.[35] The cradle-to-grave lifecycle does account for ecological footprints, but it still assumes disposal—the product's "grave." Instead, the emerging cradle-to-cradle alternative suggests that disposal is not inevitable; it merely reflects a design flaw. With cradle-to-cradle design, products provide benefits for industry and nature even after their normal useful lifecycle is complete.

Cradle-to-cradle design imitates the regenerative cycles of nature, using renewable energy and resources that can be perpetually recycled. The model uses a system in which biological **nutrients** can return to the environment to nourish other living things (as with biodegradable packaging). Resources are recycled in a closed loop of production, recovery, and remanufacture.

A variety of innovative companies are successfully using the cradle-to-cradle principle in their design and manufacturing. Shaw Industries, the world's largest carpet manufacturer, is developing sustainable carpet products that can be continually broken down and reused, returning old carpet to new carpet through a closed-loop, cradle-to-cradle design. Studio 7.5 Berlin manufactures the green, award-winning Mirra chair, in which 96 percent of its content is specifically designed for recycling. Each part of the chair is labeled for future disassembly and refurbishing or recycling.[36]

Lifecycle design principles have also found a place in the public planning and management of large construction projects, such as freeways and hospitals.[37] The approach is also gaining widespread use for hazardous waste management and urban planning in the United States and around the world.[38] China announced in 2002 that it will work with the China-U.S. Center for Sustainable Design to apply cradle-to-cradle design to industries, products, and villages.

As cradle-to-cradle design moves from theory to practice in the design of manufacturing, construction, and public projects, it can be a powerful force for improving quality of life and sustainability.

Chapter 4. Tradition, Technology, and Media— Preserving Culture

Culture is a matrix of infinite possibilities and choices. From within the same culture matrix, we can extract arguments and strategies for the degradation or ennoblement of our species, for its enslavement or liberation, for the suppression of its productive potential or its enhancement.

—Wole Soyinka
(twentieth-century Nigerian Nobel Laureate)

This chapter focuses on how culture and **worldview** are affected by the **globalization** of technology and media.

Worldview and Culture

When people travel to other countries, to different regions in their own countries, and even to unknown neighborhoods in their own cities, they often are surprised by subtle differences in language, behaviors, and the material artifacts of culture. Visitors may sense an entirely different perspective on life that underlies this range of differences, whether the differences are obvious or subtle. This perspective is sometimes called a culture's worldview. Our worldview gives identity and purpose to the structures, patterns, and events that we experience in life.

Worldview also encompasses all the things that make up quality of life, including values (such as a work ethic), activities (how time is spent in work or leisure), and material things (needed for survival and enjoyment).

One way of studying worldviews is to examine different cultures. One can think of worldview as both a cause and an expression of culture. From the Latin root *colere* ("to inhabit, to cultivate, or to honor"), culture refers broadly to all forms of human activity and expression, including beliefs, behavioral norms, and artifacts.[39] Culture thus includes material things such as the products of art and technology, as well as the ideas and behaviors that combine to create those artifacts. In turn, material things themselves can express and influence ideas and behavior.

People all over the world are familiar with and influenced by western popular culture. In wealthier nations, the culture of consumption exerts great influence over peoples' ideas and behavior. American culture in the form of mass consumption is also a profoundly influential export to the rest of the world.

A Thai man weaves hats from native grasses.
Photo © 2001 Pairat Saensawat, courtesy of CARE

Globalization and Culture

Our [indigenous people's] sustainable lifestyles and cultures, traditional knowledge, cosmologies, spirituality, and values of collectivity, reciprocity, and respect and reverence for Mother Earth are crucial in the search for a transformed society in which justice, equity, and sustainability will prevail.[40]

—Declaration by the Indigenous Peoples Organization of the United Nations Development Programme, 1999

Where traditional cultures hold valuable knowledge and clues to sustainability, how can they benefit the world without being destroyed, co-opted, or commercialized by the impacts of globalization? Often, the answer involves protecting the natural ecosystems in which indigenous people live. Their wealth of knowledge and sustainable practices are often closely tied to the land, plants, and animals of their ancestral homelands. When we preserve native lands, we often preserve the **biodiversity** that is the foundation for culture.

One tension between globalization and culture has to do with whether or not cultural knowledge can or should be owned by corporations. For example, some corporations seek legal rights over plant species that can be used for medical or agricultural uses. Many farming communities and indigenous peoples, however, want local control over their plants and crops to ensure sustainable and productive use for local communities' needs. In Latin America, a variety of organizations are seeking to establish goals and strategies for indigenous groups to conserve biodiversity and protect against *bioprospecting* on indigenous lands, a practice in which outside governments or corporations seek patent rights over plants for medical or agricultural purposes.[41]

A Senegalese West African woman wearing traditional wedding jewelry.
Photo by Elizabeth Benedict Huttman

Globalization raises the question of whether or not indigenous peoples' knowledge about native varieties of plants will become a **commodity** (an article of trade or commerce) for profit. How might the interests of people in the developed world be affected if the indigenous ideas, practices, and technologies supporting sustainable agriculture are compromised?

As an assortment of people in developed countries are searching for ways to reclaim happiness by downsizing and trying to live simply, indigenous people often hold essential clues and strategies for sustainable living and alternatives to the culture of consumption. While people in the developing world often lack the most basic ingredients for a good quality of life (sufficient food, water, and shelter), an important resource that they do *not* lack is culture. Long histories of traditional ideas, behaviors, and technologies can provide invaluable models for sustainable living. In fact, the cultural knowledge of indigenous people is itself an asset that is perhaps more important to the long-term health of the planet than are raw materials.

Anthropologist Rodolfo Stabenhagen has said, "Cultural diversity is to the human species what biological diversity is to the genetic wealth of the world."[42] Cultural knowledge is itself a valuable resource—and not necessarily a **renewable resource.** Like plant and animal species, once a culture is gone, it may be irreplaceable. For the future of the planet, it may prove wise to protect culture with a passion equal to that felt for protection of biodiversity and **habitat.**

Telecommunications—For What and for Whom?

*Whoever controls the media,
the images, controls the culture.*

—Allen Ginsberg
(twentieth-century
American poet)

Media and communications technology increasingly influence traditional cultures. Media is anything—from books to telephones and computers—that can be used to store or deliver information. **Mass media** is the body of media that can reach wide public audiences, and it includes radio, television, movies, magazines, newspapers, and the Internet. *Telecommunications* refers specifically to the more recent electronic tools of media, starting with telephones and radios and including the latest Internet, computer network, and satellite technologies for communication.

Technology proponents include author and engineer Samuel Florman. He does not find evidence that frequent contact with nature is essential to human well-being. Instead, Florman contends that technologies such as medicine, manufacturing, agriculture, and communications have saved us from the hardships of life prior to modern technologies.[43] Along the same lines, author O. B. Hardison promotes a faith in silicon devices and computer technology that is similar to some religious beliefs.[44] Florman, Hardison, and others are confident that technology will help people through the global age, just as twentieth-century **Green Revolution** agricultural technology fed swelling populations during the late twentieth century.

Others argue that the issue is not whether technology itself is good or bad. They take the position that it is the technology gap between rich and poor nations that presents a serious obstacle to reducing poverty and increasing quality of life. Developed countries have nearly unlimited access to the latest telecommunications and computer-age technology. Computers are taken for granted in the businesses of the developed world, where they provide essential tools for gathering data, processing documents, and conducting research, planning, analysis, and communication. Only a few developing countries, such as Brazil, have made significant progress in providing Internet access to the poor. Some claim that this technology gap serves to further economic and trade inequities on both regional and international stages.[45]

Girls in Bangladesh learn to use computers.
Photo courtesy of the
U.S. State Department

By itself, access to computer technology does not close the technology gap. Unless literacy rates improve substantially in developing countries, people will not be able to utilize the vast amounts of information available on the Internet. Also, unless people become literate in languages that dominate the Internet, such as English, content will need to be made available in hundreds of local languages for developing-world citizens to be able to benefit.[46]

Still others counter that although the technology gap is indeed significant, what developing countries really need is not modern telecommunications but more basic technology to meet survival needs, such as water treatment and distribution systems, basic medical technology, electricity generators, and better agricultural technology, including farming equipment, water pumps, and irrigation systems.[47]

Cell Phones for All?[48]

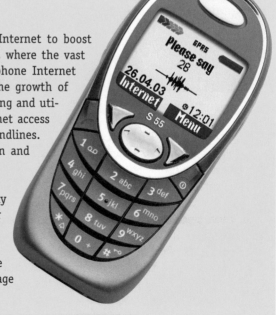

Ibrahima N'Diaye, the mayor of Mali's capital, Bamako, is counting on the Internet to boost democracy in Africa via specially outfitted cell phones. For developing countries, where the vast majority of people do not have Internet access, N'Diaye claims that new cell phone Internet technology will help to spread information, a tremendous asset in promoting the growth of democracy. Although limited electricity and illiteracy pose problems for establishing and utilizing computer networks, the technology that outfits mobile phones with Internet access is readily available and is not dependent on computer hardware or electrical landlines. Because of their Internet capability, such cell phones can be used for education and citizenship, including remote voting!

A cell phone with Internet access will not substitute for the basic and readily available technology that can result in increased food production, fresh water for agricultural and domestic use, or improved health care services. However, it can serve personal and business needs efficiently, even substituting for some of the advantages that more expensive and unlikely Internet access might afford. For example, the business earnings from the average Nigerian cell phone is twice that of the average American's because of the amount and type of business conducted over the phone.[49]

Media, Democracy, and Culture
Don't hate the media, become the media.
—Jello Biafra (twenty-first-century
rock musician and free speech activist)

In this era of globalization, the mass media has become a sort of **commons,** much like public lands, air, and the oceans. Just as fishers cast their nets wider to catch dwindling numbers of fish, large media corporations have accelerated their expansion to all corners of the globe in order to capture larger audiences. There are fewer and fewer places where traditional cultures have not been influenced or overtaken by mass media. Radio and television first became widely available during the twentieth century, but the instant global connection provided by the Internet and the increasing deregulation and consolidation of print, radio, television, and music industries present new and challenging questions.

One concern over the role of the media is the topic of democratic debate. When a few large corporations control major portions of the media, consumers may lose the diversity of ideas and debate that are essential to healthy democracies.[50] In the 1940s, after watching totalitarian regimes such as Nazi Germany foster **genocide** during World War II by dominating the media, the U.S. Federal Communication Commission (charged with regulating media and communications systems) restricted how many news media outlets one company could own, within a city or nationally. Since the 1980s, however, there has been a steady relaxing of media ownership rules; noting this, some people worry that the public's interest in diverse and independent media has been eroded by increasingly large corporations that span not only different types of media but also worldwide networks. The concern is whether healthy democratic debate can take place within such a concentrated, corporate media environment.

Another concern about the role of media has to do with the preservation of indigenous cultures in the face of popular culture carried abroad by mass media. As the entire world increasingly participates in one global market system, commercial media has followed the trend toward globalization.

Western brand advertisements are visible even in the poorest of countries. Here, a Coca-Cola sign is displayed in a Zambian marketplace.
Photo © CCP, courtesy of Photoshare

The global media system is dominated by ten huge *conglomerates,* large companies that own many other companies. These conglomerates or **transnational** corporations include some well-known companies such as Time Warner, Turner Broadcasting, American On-Line, and Twentieth Century Fox.[51] Media corporations can have a positive impact on culture when they enter countries controlled by corrupt media systems (as in much of Latin America) or countries that have significant state censorship over media (as in parts of Asia). In these cases, however, media giants may find no economic benefit in promoting democratic debate or fostering indigenous culture.[52]

Sustaining Cultures in a Globalized World
There are both structural and **personal solutions** for sustaining culture in our increasingly globalized world.

Structural Solutions
Nonprofit organizations such as Cultural Survival have been formed to resist the increasing expansion and influence of mass media conglomerates by promoting the voices, rights, and visions of indigenous people.[53] The goal of this organization is for local people to control their own independent media. Cultural Survival cites both specific and general examples of how the media has threatened indigenous peoples and cultures. For example, when the federal government of the remote Asian country of Brunei introduced color television sets and generators, children there gave up their traditional games to imitate the television detective hero Kojak. In a recent worldwide phenomenon, advertising-created crazes for MacDonald's hamburgers have changed dietary habits everywhere, leading to increased rates of obesity and diabetes.[54]

Cultural Survival works to ensure the preservation of indigenous cultures. They pose the questions, "will media be a vehicle for the preservation or destruction of traditional culture?" and "will globalized media accelerate consumerism in developing and developed countries?"

Personal Solutions
The following are actions that individuals can take to help understand and address media impacts and support native cultures:
- Track how much time you spend daily or weekly consuming different types of media: television, Internet, books, magazines, newspapers. Ask yourself, which ones contribute to quality of life for you and for others?
- Get your news and cultural information from a variety of sources, especially independent media groups and international media.
- Be a critical consumer of media and advertising. Learn to identify origins, perspectives, and biases of media and advertising messages.
- Celebrate, participate in, and preserve your own culture—its art, music, language, and values.
- Be aware of your own cultural biases. Learn to identify stereotypes. Speak out against discrimination.
- Support indigenous cultures—their arts, products, and businesses.

Taking Back the Media

Many people believe that democracy cannot exist without freedom of information and an informed public. Citizenship, it is held, goes hand in hand with media. Despite increasing deregulation and concentration of mass media, there are promising countercurrents of people taking back the media and giving it a new voice. For example, radio media presents both public (noncommercial) and private (for-profit) alternatives that specifically seek to promote democracy through programming that includes a variety of ideas and opposing viewpoints.[55]

Neoradio, a new style of private commercial FM radio based on eclectic music and informed commentary, points in the direction of media decentralization and independence.[56] Since the United States' deregulation of radio in 1996, media critics have expressed concern over the proliferation of advertising that has taken the place of the music content, which used to be the hallmark of FM radio. For years, narrow play lists, "shock" talk radio, and constant commercial inserts were promoted by media corporations and station managers as the formula for financial success.

Today, neoradio can be viewed as a backlash against the radio industry's consolidation and commercialization. It allows for long periods of music listening, interspersed with commentary by independent-minded disk jockeys. Many stations that have tried the neoradio format have actually gained in listenership and netted impressive advertising revenue. Although neoradio reduces the amount of ad time per hour, advertisers have been willing to pay more for it, confident that listeners will be more likely to listen through the fewer commercials, rather than switching from station to station as they hunt for music.

Chapter 5. World Health

> *The first wealth is health.*
> —Ralph Waldo Emerson
> (nineteenth-century American philosopher)

Quality of life is determined first and foremost by health. Without good health, other desirable aspects of a good quality of life—vibrant culture, sufficient income, a good education, and adequate technology—are worth little. This chapter reviews the general state of human health worldwide and explores factors contributing to declining world health, including the **AIDS** epidemic.

Health in the Developing World

What is the state of health in the developing world? The last two centuries have witnessed remarkable growth in medicine and health science. It is unfortunate that in this era of accelerating medical advances, so many of the planet's people remain unhealthy. Advances in medicine over the past fifty years have meant that more people around the world are surviving past childhood and the average life span is increasing, but for millions worldwide, longer lives have not necessarily been healthier lives. Despite progress that has been made toward the material well-being of many and the reduction of infant mortality and some diseases, life expectancy is significantly lower in the world's poorer countries than it is in the wealthier countries, and many people, especially women and children, suffer from poor health.

- Every year, 11 million children die—most before the age of five and more than 6 million from preventable causes such as malaria, diarrhea, and pneumonia.[57]
- Each year, approximately 300 million to 500 million people are infected with malaria; approximately 3 million people die as a result.[58]
- Tuberculosis (TB), a treatable disease, claims 2 million lives each year. In some parts of Africa, 75 percent of people with **HIV** also have TB.[59]
- About 530,000 women of reproductive age die every year. A woman living in sub-Saharan Africa has a 1 in 16 chance of dying during pregnancy or childbirth. This compares with a 1 in 3,700 risk for women in North America.[60]
- Tobacco-related illnesses are responsible for about 5 million deaths worldwide each year.[61]

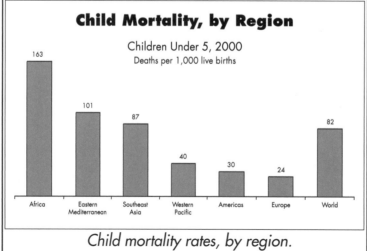

Child Mortality, by Region

Children Under 5, 2000
Deaths per 1,000 live births

Region	Deaths
Africa	163
Eastern Mediterranean	101
Southeast Asia	87
Western Pacific	40
Americas	30
Europe	24
World	82

Child mortality rates, by region.
Source: World Health Organization

Factors Contributing to Worldwide Disease and Illness

Insufficient food and lack of **potable water** are the main problems contributing to illness and disease. Food and water are essential human needs, without which people become more susceptible to disease and less able to recover from illness. Both ends of the economic spectrum are affected by diet. Affluent countries suffer from cardiovascular disease and other diseases associated with obesity and unhealthy diet, while many of those whose lives depend on basic food crops are simply malnourished.

A Haitian child lies in a hospital bed in Port-au-Prince, where medical supplies are scarce.

Photo courtesy of the U.S. State Department

Larger human populations and poverty can also make diseases harder to treat and cure. Sick people need doctors, clinics, and medical supplies, but in many developing countries, adequate health services may not be available or affordable to the poor. [62]

New and reemerging diseases put a strain on the ability of scientists and health-care providers to deliver medical treatment. Also, humans are currently encountering new diseases that are truly international in scope. Since 1970, at least thirty-five previously unknown diseases with serious potential for causing international epidemics have been identified, including Acquired Immunodeficiency Syndrome (AIDS), Sudden Acute Respiratory Syndrome (SARS), and the West Nile virus. [63] Additionally, twenty well-known diseases that had largely disappeared, including tuberculosis, malaria, and cholera, have reemerged or spread to new areas. [64]

Lack of water weakens healthy people and can be fatal to those suffering from illnesses such as diarrhea, in which dehydration is a mortal threat. Also, contaminated water can spread disease. During crises or disasters, there is often a downward spiral of people drinking tainted water and then further contaminating water supplies with their illness.

A number of human activities hasten the spread and reemergence of disease. Increasing population densities and globalized trade have virtually erased geographic and national boundaries, which previously might have slowed the spread of **pathogens.** Transportation systems have made it easier for people to travel around the world—bringing their diseases with them. As people cultivate new land and engage in intensive farming practices, they often unknowingly create and spread disease from animals to humans. Increasing global temperatures allow pests and diseases to survive in places where they never could in the past.

The Equity Link to Health in Developed Countries

Some research indicates that in developed countries, there is a negative link between economic inequality, sometimes called the rich-poor gap, and a population's health. [65] Economic inequality is greater in the United States than in any other industrialized nation. Despite the greatest health expenditures on the planet, the United States' record has continued to fall on various health and quality-of-life indicators in comparison to other industrialized nations. Other developed nations spend on average only 44 percent of what the United States spends on overall health care, but their citizens typically enjoy better health. [66] According to this research, better health is tied to higher levels of economic **equality.** [67] Although this is not widely agreed on, it raises some interesting questions.

The Global Challenge of AIDS

Most health experts agree that the HIV/AIDS **pandemic** (a worldwide epidemic) is the greatest threat to world health in terms of its proven potential for spreading. Human Immunodeficiency Virus (HIV) is the virus that causes AIDS, a group of symptoms that includes infections and/or cancers, as well as a decrease in the number of certain cells in a person's immune system.

With improvements in antibiotics, vaccines, food supply, and public health services, average life expectancy had been on the rise worldwide since the 1950s. However, by the turn of the millennium the AIDS epidemic had dropped the average life span in sub-Saharan Africa from sixty-two to forty-seven years.[68]

The United Nations 2004 Report on the Global AIDS Epidemic presents these statistics:[69]

- Since the first case was identified in 1981, more than 20 million people have died of AIDS.
- Worldwide, about 42 million people are living with HIV/AIDS.
- In Africa, women are 3.4 times more likely than men to be infected with AIDS.
- Nine out of ten people needing AIDS medications do not receive them.

AIDS is an example of how health problems have the potential to reduce economic output to the point that entire regions are destabilized. The HIV/AIDS pandemic has had this effect on Africa, where, in some countries such as Uganda, Botswana, and Malawi, nearly an entire generation of farmers has died, crippling the ability of these countries to support themselves.[70]

Because AIDS is spread primarily through sexual contact and intravenous drug use, many nations and cultures continue to see it as a point of shame, rather than as a preventable and treatable health hazard. Reluctance to deal directly and quickly with AIDS sometimes allows it to spread at epidemic proportions, not only in developing countries in Africa but also in China, Russia, and in Eastern Europe, which currently has the fastest-growing rate of HIV infection in the world.[71] Eastern Europe and Asia, which hold 60 percent of the world's population, are the new frontlines for halting the spread of AIDS. Successes in the struggle with AIDS have been identified in Brazil, Uganda, and Thailand. A key factor in these successes is behavioral change—specifically, widespread condom use among sex workers in Thailand and restriction of multiple sexual partners in Uganda. Other factors contributing to progress against AIDS in these countries include lower costs and improved availability of treatment, increased international aid, preventive education, and stronger political will and leadership.

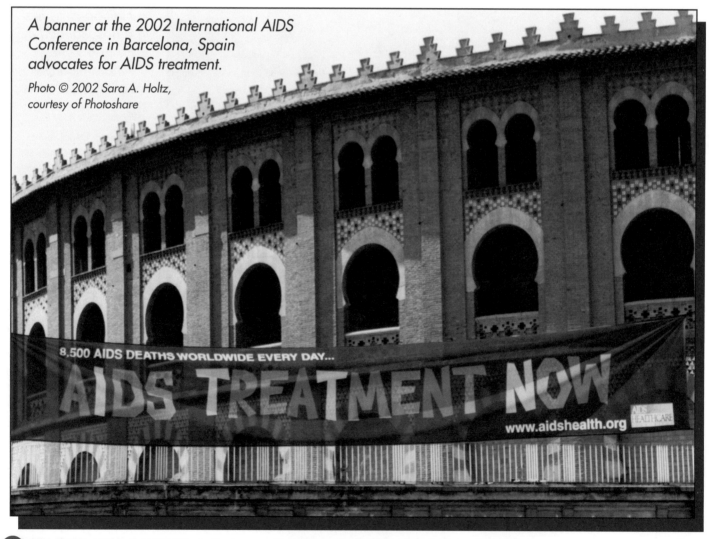

A banner at the 2002 International AIDS Conference in Barcelona, Spain advocates for AIDS treatment.

Photo © 2002 Sara A. Holtz, courtesy of Photoshare

8,500 AIDS DEATHS WORLDWIDE EVERY DAY...
AIDS TREATMENT NOW
www.aidshealth.org

SCIENCE CONNECTION:

Understanding AIDS

What Is HIV/AIDS?[72]

The Acquired Immunodeficiency Syndrome (AIDS), first recognized in 1981, has since become a major worldwide pandemic. AIDS is caused by the Human Immunodeficiency Virus (HIV), which infects *helper T cells*, critical cells in the immune system, and causes their functional impairment. HIV progressively destroys the body's ability to fight infections and certain cancers.

An HIV-infected person is diagnosed with AIDS when his or her immune system is seriously impaired and manifestations of HIV infection are severe. The U.S. Centers for Disease Control and Prevention (CDC) defines AIDS in an adult or adolescent age thirteen years or older as the presence of one of twenty-six conditions indicative of severe immunosuppression associated with HIV infection, such as *Pneumocystis carinii pneumonia* (PCP), a condition extraordinarily rare in people not infected with HIV. Most other AIDS-defining conditions are also "opportunistic infections" that rarely cause harm in healthy individuals.

How Do People Get HIV/AIDS?

HIV may be passed from one person to another when infected blood, semen, or vaginal secretions come in contact with broken skin or mucous membranes. HIV can be passed through sexual contact or needles carrying the virus, and infected pregnant women can pass HIV to their babies during pregnancy or delivery, as well as through breast-feeding. A person cannot get AIDS from being bitten by mosquitos, coughing or sneezing, sharing household items, or swimming in the same pool as someone with HIV.

AIDS Prevention

Sexual abstinence (refraining from sexual activity) is the only sure way to prevent HIV transmission through sexual contact. The use of latex or polyurethane condoms is highly effective in preventing transmission, but only if condoms are used correctly and consistently. Many organizations and nations have had success with "needle swapping" programs, in which sterile needles are made available to drug users free of charge, so that users will not infect others through the sharing of a used needle.

Education is an essential element in the prevention of HIV infection.[73] Basic AIDS prevention education includes avoiding HIV infection by means of sexual abstinence, loyalty to an uninfected sex partner or spouse, careful use of condoms, and safe use of intravenous drugs. Whether through schooling or informal means such as public outreach by mass media or community organizations, prevention education works, when properly and broadly implemented. HIV/AIDS prevention education means offering learning opportunities for all people to develop the knowledge, skills, competencies, values, and attitudes that will limit the transmission and impact of the disease.

Where the epidemic has been slowed, education has been the foundation. Education provides protection against individual vulnerability and gives the tools for understanding and avoiding risk. It creates a context in which the epidemic can be discussed and understood and in which those infected and affected are cared for and included in society. Education is necessary for galvanizing the political momentum and community mobilization that are central to success against HIV and AIDS.

Aids Treatment

Although some people may die shortly after developing AIDS, others may live for many months or even many years. Treatments are increasingly effective, but scientists and health-care providers still do not have a full understanding of HIV or AIDS.

Although there is no cure for AIDS, it can be treated with anti-retroviral (ARV) drug therapy. ARV drugs do not kill HIV, but they do slow its spread. When spread of the virus is slowed, so is the progression of AIDS. ARV therapy for AIDS faces significant obstacles because it can be expensive and often involves the administration of multiple medications in specific sequences.

There is, however, reason for hope. By the end of 2004, 700,000 people living with AIDS in developing countries were receiving ARV treatment. This is an increase by approximately 75 percent in the total number of patients receiving treatment from the previous year.[74]

This progress has been made because of efforts to increase the availability of ARV therapy in poor countries by the World Health Organization (WHO), the Joint United Nations Programme on HIV/AIDS (UNAIDS), the United States government, and the Global Fund to Fight AIDS, Tuberculosis, and Malaria. While this is certainly good news, these organizations warn that continued major efforts are still needed to reach the goal of access to treatment for all who need it.

WHO and UNAIDS estimate that, overall, 72 percent of the unmet need for treatment is in sub-Saharan Africa and 22 percent is in Asia. India, Nigeria, and South Africa alone account for 41 percent of the overall need for treatment. In the region with the heaviest burden—sub-Saharan Africa—the number of people on treatment more than doubled, from 150,000 to 310,000, from June 2004 to January 2005; in Asia, the figure doubled from 50,000 to 100,000. Building on years of AIDS awareness and prevention programs, Uganda and Thailand expected to be treating 50 percent or more of people needing ARV therapy during the first half of 2005.

A vaccine that prevents AIDS by building up the body's defenses prior to HIV exposure has not yet been developed. However, therapeutic vaccines are sometimes used to help the body resist HIV in infected persons by boosting their immune system. Vaccine development is a major priority for many biotechnology and pharmaceutical companies, with new developments and discoveries being made every year.

Adolescents work on an AIDS mural at the University of Durban in Westville, South Africa.

Photo © 1999 Gary Lewis/CCP, courtesy of Photoshare

AIDS— Hope on the Horizon

AIDS Prevention in Thailand— A Model for the World?

Along with drug users, prostitutes and their customers are most at risk for HIV infection. Prostitutes' rights organizations, such as the Empower Foundation, and public health advocates including Thai movie star–legislator Mechai ("Mr. Condom") Viravaidya have been instrumental in launching one of the world's most effective AIDS prevention efforts: a condom promotion campaign targeting the Thai sex industry.[75] By combating the stigma associated with HIV/AIDS that victimizes the poorest Thais and by promoting the use of condoms in the sex industry, between 1991 and 2003 Thailand reduced its rate of new HIV cases by 80 percent.

The Thai model for combating AIDS serves as one example of a successful prevention program. It has been estimated that protecting the developing world and Eastern Europe from the danger of HIV would require about 8 billion condoms per year, while currently only 1 billion are being distributed. The cost (at three cents apiece) of distributing this 7 billion shortfall in these regions would be about $1.9 billion, just a fraction of the potential medical costs for those populations if AIDS continues to spread at its current rate.[76]

Women and AIDS Prevention

Uganda is one of the few African countries to have actually lowered its HIV infection rate, which it did through a campaign of prevention education and associated behavior changes. Women's organizations in Uganda have been especially important in building a culture of support for AIDS victims there. In addition to the social stigma associated with AIDS, another challenge has been that its victims often already suffer from discrimination, as is the case for women. The impact of the disease on mothers has even greater implications, because women are primarily responsible for their children's future. Uganda has been an inspiration, with its remarkable array of women's rights and advocacy organizations, such as the National Community of Women Living with HIV/AIDS. This organization publishes newsletters in five languages, organizes income-generating activities, conducts children's seminars, and trains mothers in communication skills.[77]

Zambia, too, has reduced HIV infection rates in young people through a church-based national prevention campaign, while Senegal successfully checked the spread of AIDS in its early days, reducing it to its current rate of only 1 percent.[78] Education, behavioral changes, and women's support networks were at the heart of these countries' success.

Heroes Against AIDS

Some AIDS victims suffer discrimination and inferior medical treatment due to their situation in life, as in the case of prison inmates. Dr. Stephen Tabet almost single-handedly reformed prison health care in the states of Alabama and Washington by improving AIDS treatment and documenting unequal and inferior medical treatment received by inmates. In addition to his dedication to prison populations, Dr. Tabet used his bilingual skills to help typically underserved Hispanic patients and communities. His work has fueled successful class-action lawsuits and raised the quality of AIDS care for U.S. prisoners.[79]

A group of women sing and dance to raise awareness about HIV/AIDS in Kampala, Uganda.
Photo © 2001 Sara A. Holtz, courtesy of Photoshare

Chapter 6. Sustainable Solutions: Human Health

He who has health has hope,
and he who has hope has everything.
—Arabian proverb

This chapter discusses a range of **structural solutions** for improving world health and concludes with actions that individuals can take to lead healthy lives.

Structural Solutions for Health

The Millennium Development Goals (MDGs) adopted by the United Nations in 2000 set out an ambitious and far-reaching road map for international efforts to improve quality of life during the first part of the twenty-first century. Three of the six goals target improvements in health as a way of reducing poverty.[80]

Specifically, the MDGs to be met by 2015 include reducing infant **mortality rates** by 60 percent, improving maternal health by 75 percent, and halting the spread of AIDS, malaria, and other major diseases.[81] Although hopeful that these goals are attainable, the United Nations and World Health Organization (WHO) are concerned that progress toward these goals has thus far been insufficient.

From Knowledge to Action—Practical Steps Toward Better Health

Many experts are confident that the solutions and resources to substantially improve the health of the world's people are already available. In a major study, WHO reported that most of the world's health challenges come from HIV/AIDS, tuberculosis (TB), malaria, childhood diseases, unsafe pregnancy, infant illness at the time of delivery, and tobacco-related illnesses. Almost one-third of deaths in low- and middle-income countries are due to communicable diseases, maternal conditions, and nutritional deficiencies. WHO points out that all of these diseases are preventable and, with the exception of tobacco-related illnesses, all are treatable.[82]

Immunization and oral rehydration are two of the most important and relatively inexpensive interventions for the prevention and control of many of the most common illnesses and diseases. Immunization programs dramatically reduce infant mortality, as does oral rehydration therapy (ORT) for children who risk fatal dehydration from diarrhea.[83]

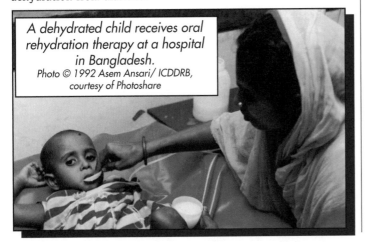

A dehydrated child receives oral rehydration therapy at a hospital in Bangladesh.
Photo © 1992 Asem Ansari/ ICDDRB, courtesy of Photoshare

Worldwide access to reproductive health care would be a significant step toward the increased health and well-being of women and their families. Access to **reproductive health care** is a practical step toward relieving the pressure that population growth places on worldwide capacity to meet its needs. Population stabilization lowers the ratio of people to health services, making it more likely that those who need care will get it. The ability to make choices about family size permits parents to safeguard their children's health by focusing on the improved hygiene and diet of fewer children, rather than on the survival of more.

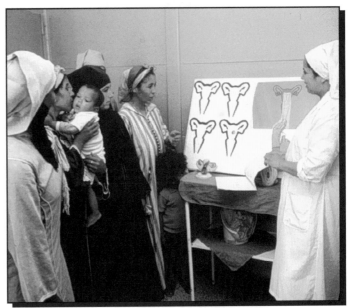

Reproductive health education in a Moroccan clinic.
Photo courtesy of FAO

Funding and Decentralizing Health Care in Developing Countries

WHO suggests that about half the total increase needed in health-care spending should come in the form of international development assistance from wealthier, industrialized nations.[84] Developing countries would need to provide the other half by reprioritizing their budgets and increasing the portion of funds devoted to public health care.[85] This could be greatly facilitated through reduction of the overwhelming national debts of the poorest nations of the world—money owed due to loans from international development organizations such as the World Bank and International Monetary Fund. These loan debts could either be adjusted downward or excused completely. Although more money does not necessarily translate into bigger health budgets, relief from this debt could be an essential factor in helping poorer countries fund better health care.

Some health experts recommend close-to-client (CTC) systems, in which local health providers in developing countries are given a high budgetary priority. The effectiveness of CTC systems hinges on efficiency and accountability at the local level. Access to health care for all citizens is prioritized by maximizing spending on local clinics and practitioners, where direct health services are actually delivered, rather than on government health bureaucracies or larger and more distant hospitals.[86]

The Big Payback—Health and Economic Productivity

In the long run, increased investments in health for the world's poor would not only save millions of lives but also produce enormous economic gains through enhanced productivity. Experts estimate that by 2015–2020, increased health investments of $66 billion per year above current spending would generate annual returns of at least $360 billion.[87] About half of this gain would result from direct economic benefits: if the world's poorest people live longer, they will have many more days of good health and will be able to work longer and earn more. The other half of the gain would result from the indirect economic benefits of greater individual productivity. For example, healthy citizens would not require as much state support for medical treatment and economic welfare. Good health makes good economic, as well as humanitarian, sense.

Personal Solutions for Health

In addition to the work that organizations are doing to address world health issues, there are actions that individuals can take for a healthy life:

- Determine what factors contribute to your physical and mental health. Consider diet, exercise, recreation, and rest. Set goals to live a healthy life.
- Be safe and smart about health issues such as sexual activity and drug use.
- Become knowledgeable about public health issues such as communicable diseases. Volunteer your time with public health organizations.
- Support organizations that are working toward improved world health.

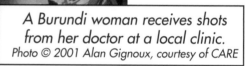

A Burundi woman receives shots from her doctor at a local clinic.
Photo © 2001 Alan Gignoux, courtesy of CARE

What else can you think of to improve your health and the health of the world's people?

Sharing the Wealth for World Health
—A New Global Health Giant

The Bill and Melinda Gates Foundation Global Health Program has made a substantial commitment of resources to the cause of world health. It focuses on reducing global health inequities by speeding up the development, delivery, and sustainability of health solutions that will save lives and reduce the disease burden in developing countries. The program targets "global health equity," citing the large disparity between the average life expectancy in the United States (more than seventy-five years) compared to that of the poorest African nations (thirty-seven years).

Through mid-2004, grants from the Global Health Program totaled more than $3.8 billion, supporting these key goals:

1. Preventing and treating infectious diseases such as hepatitis B, malaria, measles, and polio through funding of research, immunization, and vaccination.
2. Supporting strong political leadership and a dramatic increase in resources to treat HIV/AIDS as a global responsibility.
3. Empowering women and saving the lives of millions of mothers and children through interventions, adequate nutrition, and quality care during pregnancy, during delivery, and following childbirth.

The Bill and Melinda Gates Foundation provides a good example of how individual people can turn wealth into health.

Chapter 7. Education—Issues and Solutions

Only the educated are free.
—Epicletus (Greek philosopher, CE 55–135)

Education is fundamentally linked to health and economic **self-sufficiency**. In poorer countries, illiteracy—especially for women—is a reliable indicator of poverty, hunger, disease, and higher population growth rates. Where there is illiteracy in the developing world, there is usually a significant reduction in the quality of life. Conversely, education and literacy address the underlying, root causes of poverty and illness.[88]

Education and Quality of Life

Basic literacy holds great promise for improving quality of life in the developing world. According to experts at the United Nations Development Program, when children (especially girls) attend school and adults (especially women) can read and write, significant progress occurs in the following areas:[89]

- **Income**—Education is a key to breaking the cycle of poverty that grips developing countries.
- **Health**—Educated parents not only can afford more food for their children but they also make more informed choices about nutrition and health care.
- **Population growth rates**—The more educated a woman is, the fewer children she tends to have.
- **Infant and maternal mortality rates**—Education is directly linked to the health of women and children.
- **Food and agriculture**—Literacy about agricultural methods and technology increases food production.
- **AIDS and other infectious diseases**—Education boosts disease prevention and treatment success.
- **Immunization and vaccination rates**—School-based programs improve immunization and vaccination rates.
- **Environmental responsibility**—Education helps people make better choices about using environmentally sound practices and appropriate technology.
- **Democracy**—Education is a prerequisite for an informed citizenry and functional democracy.

The top three countries with the highest adult literacy rate in the world are Norway, Iceland, and Sweden (the United States holds seventh place).[90] These Scandinavian nations also enjoy a high standard of living. Unfortunately, at the present time at least eighty-eight countries are not able to offer universal primary education.[91] Illiteracy rates are especially high in the more populous countries of Asia, Africa, and Latin America, especially India, China, Pakistan, Bangladesh, Nigeria, Egypt, Indonesia, Brazil, and Mexico.[92] Worldwide, 875 million adults are illiterate and 115 million children do not attend school.

Education for Everyone

In light of the widespread need for literacy—and knowing the tremendous power of education to transform lives from despair to hope and from illness to wellness—the United Nations named universal primary education as a Millennium Development Goal to be met by 2015. The World Bank responded with its Education for All plan, an ambitious effort to support education for all children in developing countries, with the specific objective that no child will be denied an education because his or her parents cannot afford books or school fees.[93]

According to experts, a variety of strategies already exist for building universal primary education and adult literacy:[94]

- **Educate teachers**—Build the ranks of teachers (especially in countries where AIDS has claimed the lives of many teachers) by providing teacher education scholarships in return for a commitment to teach for a fixed number of years.
- **Educate the poor**—Focus on educating the poorest of the poor in rural areas, especially girls and women, and launch extensive, local, volunteer-based adult literacy programs.
- **Capitalize on local schools**—Use local schools to implement widespread immunization and vaccination programs, and use school lunch programs to improve health and educational performance.
- **Increase international funding**—Increase international funding for universal primary education and adult literacy.

Bolivian women practice their writing skills. In poorer countries, illiteracy—especially for women—is a reliable indicator of poverty, hunger, disease, and higher population growth rates.
Photo courtesy of FAO

Educating Girls and Women—
A Yardstick for Global Progress

Today, 60 percent of illiterate adults worldwide are women. The United Nations emphasizes that educating girls is especially important in order to maximize positive results from all other social and **economic development** goals. In their words, "Gender equality [in education] is not just a goal in its own right—it is central to achieving all other goals."[95]

The benefits of educating females are numerous and significant. Educated girls and women tend to marry later and have fewer children. They usually seek better medical attention sooner, for themselves and their children. Educated women provide better parenting and nutrition for their children. With time, reduced child mortality leads mothers to choose smaller families, with the result of lowering population growth and **fertility rates.**[96]

An Afghani girl learns to read Arabic in school.
Photo © 2002 Jason Sangster, courtesy of CARE

If the world commits to turning the tide of illiteracy rates for girls and women, what would initial progress look like? Now that universal primary education for girls and adult literacy for women have been targeted as essential goals, it is important to anticipate how progress toward this goal will be recognized.

The United Nations recommends that in order to monitor improved education of girls and women, countries should track some specific measurements. These include the ratio of girls to boys attending school, the ratio of female to male literacy in fifteen- to twenty-four-year-olds, the numbers of women with wage employment outside of agriculture, and the number of women serving in elected posts in national government and other positions of authority.[97] Success with these particular measurements would ensure that education for girls and women is part of the formula for human progress.

The United Nations emphasizes that progress for women must extend into both public (government) and private (family) spheres to overcome the systematic discrimination and oppression that have threatened and shortened their lives.[98] Education can help reform the worldviews that perpetuate gender-based discrimination. If maximum progress toward better quality of life is the general goal, it is also in the best interest of men to support women's rights and education so that the fruits of development can be realized for everyone.

As education and literacy rates improve around the world, many other global issues become solvable. In order to act differently, people must be able to think differently. Education can put the world on that path and accelerate the pace of improvement by focusing on girls and women as the yardstick for measuring progress.

Educating Girls for a Healthy Future in Nepal[99]

World Education is a nonprofit organization dedicated to improving the lives of the poor through education as well as economic and social development. Its programs include promoting literacy; environmental education; community development; maternal and child health; HIV/AIDS education, prevention, and care; and **refugee** training. Projects are designed to contribute to individual growth as well as to community and national development.

In recent years, conditions in rural Nepal demanded attention and intervention. Two-thirds of adolescent girls there were not enrolled in school. They faced lives of low status and limited opportunities. Thousands of Nepali girls have fallen victim to sex traffickers who kidnap them and force them into prostitution in India.

To remedy this, World Education began the Girls' Access to Education (GATE) program in Nepal by developing a literacy curriculum that includes adolescent health and girls' empowerment. Through this program, girls acquire basic skills in reading, writing, and mathematics as they learn about reproductive health; the consequences of early marriage, adolescent pregnancy, unsafe sex, and sexually transmitted diseases; and the dangers of prostitution and other forms of abuse. Since its start in 1998, the GATE program has allowed more than 13,000 adolescent girls to achieve a better education and improve their lives.

Personal Actions for Education

There are also actions that you can take as an individual to help promote education in the developed and developing world.

- Make the most of your own educational opportunities. Work hard in school. Discover the subjects you are passionate about, and nurture your interest. Be a lifelong learner.
- Most libraries have an adult literacy tutoring program, and school systems offer mentoring of younger students as community service opportunity. Share your own literacy.
- Support education reform efforts, especially those aimed at closing the "achievement gap" that hinders the advancement of people of color.
- Support organizations that are working to improve worldwide literacy, especially for girls and women.
- Consider a career in education, such as a teacher, Peace Corps volunteer, or coach.

Photo courtesy of U.S. Census Bureau

Education for Sustainability in the Developed World

Fortunately, most people in the developed world enjoy universal public education and the privilege of education beyond basic literacy. How can those in the developed world better apply themselves to the global challenge of sustainability? The two examples below show how education for those who already have basic literacy is progressing in the effort toward sustainability.

Ecology, Far and Near[100]

Educator David Sobel suggests that in addition to learning about faraway ecosystems such as the Brazilian rain forest and the Gobi Desert, we must also nurture students' connection with the local nature that surrounds them. The way to achieve this, he says, is to get primary and middle school kids out of the classroom and into nature, starting close to home and school. For example, by tracing the path of water from where they find it (the faucet) to its natural setting (a local pond), students will understand and care for the resource better than if they learn about the water cycle from a poster, book, or video.

Sobel also favors neighborhood action projects for older students who are drawn to the larger landscape of social life. Adolescents can manage school recycling programs and get involved with their local government. They are receptive to topics of **environmental justice,** from the dangers posed by toxins to the condition of city parks.

The bottom line, Sobel says, is that before educators look for students to care for global issues, they must allow students time to bond with nature and connect with environmental issues outside of the classroom. "If we want children to flourish, to become truly empowered, then let us allow them to love the Earth before we ask them to save it."

Walking the Talk of Education for Sustainability[101]

Teaching young people to care about the Earth is often an easy and natural fit, but what about older students who are leaving high school and entering college? Even if they have already developed a passion for Earth stewardship, how will young adults know how to work toward a sustainable future?

Photo courtesy of the U.S. Fish and Wildlife Service

Educator and environmentalist David Orr proposes a national campaign to make schools, colleges, and universities models of ecological design that can be seen and experienced by students. It is this hidden, physical curriculum of buildings, operations, and grounds that structures how students eat, think, move, communicate, and learn. Therefore, campus design should inspire and teach sustainability and new ways of solving problems through renewable energy, efficiency, and artfulness. The task, Orr says, is to help students expand their sense of ecological and human possibilities.

One example of teaching through this type of hidden curriculum is the Environmental Studies center at Oberlin College in Ohio, planned and constructed using life-cycle design to internalize all costs and impacts. The center features solar power with photovoltaic and **fuel cells,** real-time displays of energy use, natural lighting, wastewater purification via a "living machine," and construction from recycled products.

The Environmental Studies center teaches sustainability in horticulture, gardening, natural systems agriculture, forestry, and **aquaculture,** as well as techniques to preserve biological diversity. When colleges (and other large public and private institutions) can reduce environmental impacts, improve services, and reduce operational costs, they model sustainability with their actions. They really do "walk the talk."

Chapter 8. Human Rights—Issues and Solutions

Recognition of the inherent dignity and of the equal and inalienable rights of all members of the human family is the foundation of freedom, justice, and peace in the world.

—Preamble to the Universal Declaration of Human Rights, 1948

Access to food, water, energy, and other elements of quality of life such as culture, health, and education depends on two of the most basic human rights: the freedom to pursue a good quality of life and **justice** in the face of conflict, discrimination, and competition for resources. This chapter addresses how human rights affect global issues and explores the opportunities and progress underway in the human rights arena.

Understanding Human Rights— Freedom, Justice, and Equality

In the political sense of the word, *freedom* is the right and ability to express oneself, particularly with respect to speech, religious practice, the press, and false imprisonment. If a person lacks any of these key ingredients in life, he or she lacks full freedom.

Justice is a concept involving the fair and moral treatment of all persons, especially in matters of the law. It assumes that people deserve what is "right," which in most cases is determined by either the majority or the logic of law.

Equality is a condition in which people are afforded the same social status according to a particular situation or standard. For gender equality in employment, for example, the people in question are men and women and the social situation is the search for a job. Equality is often the standard used to measure human rights, and the concept raises some important questions: Do all people in a given country have the basic human rights of freedom and justice? Do all people have equal access to resources? Do they enjoy equal living conditions and quality of life?

These bedrock principles of human rights—freedom, justice, and equality—are imbedded in the constitutions and laws of democratic governments. A democracy is a form of government in which ordinary citizens take part in governing, in contrast to a monarchy (rule by kings) or oligarchy (rule by the wealthy or powerful). The word *democracy* originates from Greek, meaning "rule by the people."

Political Injustice and Human Rights Abuses

Unfortunately, not all human beings are treated as equals or are able to live in dignity and freedom. Millions of people have unmet basic human needs and limited basic freedoms. The justice that is taken for granted by the citizens of successful democracies does not exist for these unfortunates.

Political injustice results when individual liberties, such as the right to freedom of speech or religion, are violated. The denial of voting rights or due process and inadequate protection from cruel and unusual punishment are other forms of political injustice. Lacking legal rights and the protections of law and government, many people live under persecution, unjust detention, and fear for their physical safety. The following is an Amnesty International report card for critical worldwide injustices in 2003:[102]

- Extrajudicial (outside of official justice system) executions were carried out in 47 countries.
- People were "disappeared" by state agents in 28 countries.
- Victims of torture and ill-treatment by security forces, police, and other state authorities were reported in 132 countries.
- Prisoners of conscience (those who disagreed with official state policies) were held in 44 countries.
- People were arbitrarily arrested and detained without charge or trial in 58 countries.
- Armed groups committed violent acts and murders in 34 countries.

These statistics point to the scale and significance of human rights abuses and the urgency of pursuing human rights for all people.

Families of jailed dissidents exercise their right to protest in Havana, Cuba.

Photo courtesy of the U.S. State Department

Woman and Human Rights Abuses

Worldwide, women suffer disproportionately from human rights abuses:[103]

- Women account for 85 percent of the victims of domestic violence. Worldwide, at least one out of every three women has been beaten, coerced into sex, or abused in her lifetime by partners, relatives, friends, strangers, employers, colleagues, soldiers, and members of armed groups.
- More than 60 million women are "missing" from the world today as a result of sex-selective abortions and female *infanticide* (the killing of infants).
- Women and children account for nearly 80 percent of the casualties associated with small arms–related acts of violence.

In 1995 the United Nations International Conference on Women was held in Beijing, China, to advance the cause and rights of women. The conference emphasized the important link between women's empowerment and the overall health and well-being of all people. Follow-up work on the conference continues worldwide.

Women wait in line to vote in the 2004 Afghanistan election. Their right to vote was removed under the Taliban regime, from 1996-2001.
Photo courtesy of the U.S. State Department

LITERATURE CONNECTION:

Human Rights for a New Millennium

Eduardo Galeano is one of Latin America's most distinguished poets. He lived in political exile in Spain and Argentina from 1973 until 1985, when he returned to his native Uruguay. The following is excerpted from a poem Galeano wrote at the turn of the millennium. In his poem "Remembering," Galeano imagines a world that dares to claim rights and truths beyond the most obvious human rights.

Remembering by Eduardo Galeano

In 1948 and again in 1976, the United Nations proclaimed long lists of human rights.
But the immense majority of humanity enjoys only the right to see, to hear, and to remain silent.
What about if we begin to practice the never proclaimed right to dream?
What about if we hallucinate for a short while?
Let's set our sights beyond the abominations of today to divine another possible world:

The air will be free of all poisons, except those born of human fears and passions.
On the streets, the cars will be squashed by dogs;
People will not be driven by the automobile,
nor will they be programmed by computers,
nor will they be bought by supermarkets,
nor will they be watched by television sets;
The TV set will cease being the most important member of the family, and will be treated like the washing machine or the iron;

People will work to live instead of live to work;
like the bird sings without knowing it is singing,
and like the child plays without knowing that it plays;
The economists will not call standard of living what really is standard of consumption,
nor will they call quality of life what is quantity of things;
and nobody will take seriously anybody else who cannot make fun of him/herself;
Death and money will lose their magic powers;
Nobody will be considered a hero or dumb for doing what he/she thinks is fair instead of doing what is most convenient;
The world will no longer be at war against the poor, but against poverty,
Food will not be a merchandise, nor communications a business, because food and communication are human rights;
A black woman will become president of Brasil, and another black woman president of the US;
An Indian woman will govern Guatemala and another, Peru;
In Argentina, the Women of the Plaza de Mayo will become examples, because they refused to forget in the times of compulsory amnesia;
We will be contemporary neighbors of all those who search for justice and beauty, no matter where they were born, where they have lived, and regardless of boundaries in the maps or in time;
Perfection will continue to be the bored privilege of gods;
But in this crazy and tough world, every night will be lived like it were the last and every day will be lived like it were the first.

("Remembering" from *Upside Down: a Primer for the Looking-Glass World* by Eduardo Galeano. English-language translation © 2000 by Mark Fried. Reprinted by permission of Henry Holt and Company, LLC)

Organizations for Human Rights and a Lawful World

Throughout the twentieth century, nations around the world entered into an impressive variety of covenants, declarations, conventions, agreements, and laws focused on a wide range of political, economic, social, and cultural rights. These included protections from racial, ethnic, political, gender, or religious discrimination; unfair trial; genocide or **ethnic cleansing;** inhumane treatment or torture of prisoners; child labor; slavery; rape; and workplace abuses.[104] In addition, several governmental and **nongovernmental organizations** are dedicated to the cause of worldwide human rights embodied by the United Nations Declaration of Human Rights. (For more information, see UNDHR feature on page 91.)

The UN High Commissioner for Human Rights encourages the international community to uphold universal human rights, alerts governments when these standards are ignored, and advocates for the victims of human rights violations. The UN also emphasizes that economic development is a human right.[105]

Accepted by the nations of the UN as a lawful, binding document, the Geneva Conventions (signed in 1864, 1949, and 1977) provide international rules for military engagement and treatment of prisoners of war (POWs).[106] The Geneva Conventions are enforced through the United Nations' International Criminal Tribunal (ICT), which can try war criminals and impose sentences. In recent years, the ICT conducted war crimes trials after the 1994 genocide that claimed nearly 1 million people during ethnic killings in Rwanda, Africa. The ICT for Rwanda delivered the first-ever judgment on the crime of genocide. Emphasizing the essential role of international law in regard to Rwanda, Kofi Annan, Secretary General of the United Nations, said, "[T]here can be no healing without peace; there can be no peace without justice; and there can be no justice without respect for human rights and rule of law."[107]

Since the war trials, Rwanda has been on the road to recovery. Though still struggling to boost investment and agricultural production, Rwanda's parliament now leads the world in gender equality, with 49 percent of National Assembly seats held by women.[108] This is an example of how pursuing human rights and justice (in this case, for war crimes) can result in stronger support for underrepresented groups such as minorities and women.

In 1945 the United Nations Charter established the International Court of Justice to judge on a variety of international concerns. The International Court of Justice mediates and passes judgments on international treaties, covenants, and laws for a range of issues, including maritime disputes over shipping routes and fisheries, refugee **asylum,** natural resource and energy rights, airspace, nuclear testing and power, and territory and border disputes.[109]

Nongovernmental organizations such as Amnesty International (AI) and Human Rights Watch (HRW) conduct research and action to prevent and remedy human rights abuses. AI and HRW are concerned with political and wartime persecution, freedom of conscience and expression, and freedom from discrimination. Organizations such as AI and HRW investigate and expose human rights violations and pursue measures to hold abusers accountable. As nongovernmental organizations, they are not aligned with particular governments or political parties, which helps them to remain independent and develop support for the cause of human rights in international communities.[110]

The International Committee of the Red Cross (ICRC) is a nongovernmental organization that concerns itself specifically with the victims of war and internal conflict. The mission of the ICRC is humanitarian, to protect human lives and dignity. It directs and coordinates international relief activities in situations of conflict and natural disasters. The ICRC performs important dual functions in that it not only provides immediate, frontlines food, water, and health-care relief, but it also serves as an observer of human rights conditions during or following conflicts and disasters, when civilians are especially vulnerable to abuses.[111]

Refugee children of the civil war in Darfur, Sudan, 2004.
Photo courtesy of the U.S. State Department

These international and nongovernmental organizations play a vital role as monitors, tribunals, and enforcers of the international rules of law. With their help, the causes of freedom, justice, and equality can contribute greatly to quality of life around the world.

The Universal Declaration of Human Rights— A Future Fit for All

At the heart of international human rights is the Universal Declaration of Human Rights (UDHR), adopted by the General Assembly of the United Nations on December 10, 1948.[112] This document is global in its sweep and humanitarian in its spirit. It provides inspiration and principles for governments, human rights organizations, and citizens everywhere. The Universal Declaration proclaims that respect for human rights "is the foundation of freedom, justice, and peace in the world." To read a complete version of the Declaration, visit the website **http://www.ohchr.org**.

Summary of the Universal Declaration of Human Rights:

1. All humans are born free and equal in dignity and rights.
2. Everyone is entitled to all the rights and freedoms listed in the Declaration, regardless of race, color, sex, or religion.
3. Everyone has the right to life, liberty, and security.
4. No one shall be held in slavery.
5. No one shall be subjected to torture or to cruel, inhuman, or degrading treatment or punishment.
6. Everyone has the right to recognition before the law.
7. Everyone is equal before the law.
8. Everyone has the right to an effective remedy for violation of their legal rights.
9. No one shall be subjected to arbitrary arrest, detention, or exile.
10. Everyone is entitled to a fair hearing.
11. Everyone is innocent until proved guilty.
12. No one shall suffer arbitrary interference.
13. Everyone has the right to freedom of movement.
14. Everyone has the right to seek asylum.
15. Everyone has the right to nationality.
16. Everyone has the right to marry.
17. Everyone has the right to own property.
18. Everyone has the right to freedom of thought.
19. Everyone has the right to freedom of opinion and expression.
20. Everyone has the right to freedom of assembly and association.
21. Everyone has the right to take part in government.
22. Everyone has the right to full security in society.
23. Everyone has the right to work.
24. Everyone has the right to rest and leisure.
25. Everyone has the right to a standard of living adequate for health and well-being.
26. Everyone has the right to education.
27. Everyone has the right to participate freely in the cultural life of the community.
28. Everyone has the right to a social and international order in which these rights and freedoms can be fully realized.
29. Everyone has duties to the community and a duty to respect the rights and freedoms of others.
30. Nothing in the Declaration may be interpreted as giving a right to destroy any of the rights and freedoms set out in it.

Many people will recognize these fundamental rights and freedoms as the birthright of every human and the basis for any healthy democracy. Others believe that the Universal Declaration of Human Rights is unrealistic and goes too far in promoting rights beyond those that would be considered basic. In any case, if the Universal Declaration of Human Rights becomes a reality for more of the world's people, their quality of life will understandably improve and there will be progress regarding other global issues.

None for You, Girl!

When there aren't enough resources to go around, somebody goes without. Whether the resource is food, education, income, or credit, it's most often girls and women who get less.

- Of the 1.2 billion people in extreme poverty, 70 percent are female.[113]
- Two-thirds of illiterate people in the world are female.[114]
- Around the world, women hold only 11 percent of the seats in parliaments or equivalent elected positions.[115]
- It is estimated that up to 2 million people, mostly women and children, are trafficked every year across international borders. (Trafficking is the movement of women and children, usually from one country to another but sometimes within a country, for purposes of prostitution or some other form of slavery.) Trafficking of women is estimated to generate $5 billion to $7 billion every year.[116]

Reversing this trend—supporting equal rights for women and investing in women's education—is essential for sustainable development.

UNIT 5
FACING THE FUTURE ACTIVITIES

- **Who are the Nacirema?**
  (a literary exploration of how people view other cultures)

- **What's Up with the GDP?**
  (a look at traditional and alternative measures of progress)

- **Shop Till You Drop?**
  (a comparison of how basic human needs, including education and health care, are met between different economic groups)

To download activities visit http://www.facingthefuture.org

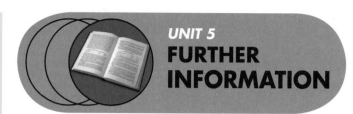

UNIT 5
FURTHER INFORMATION

For a collection of essays incorporating recent research with a focus on consumerism and the environment: Linda Starke, ed., State of the World 2004—Special Focus: the Consumer Society, New York: W. W. Norton & Co. with Worldwatch Institute, 2004.

For lively, humorous, and informative documentary videos about the history and function of consumption in American culture, and a growing movement to live simply and consume less: John de Graaf, Affluenza and Escape from Affluenza, Bullfrog Films, http://www.bullfrogfilms.com/.

For books on consumerism and time: John de Graaf, ed., Take Back Your Time: Fighting Overwork and Time Poverty in America, San Francisco: Berrettt-Keohler Publishers, Inc., 2003; and John de Graaf, David Wann, and Thomas H. Naylor, Affluenza: The All-Consuming Epidemic, San Francisco: Berrettt-Keohler Publishers, Inc., 2001.

For a description of the struggles of living and working as a low-wage earner in the United States: Barbara Ehrenreich, Nickel and Dimed: On (Not) Getting By in America, New York, Owl Books, 2002.

For a "journal of the mental environment" that uses the tools of advertising and graphic arts to explore the relationship of advertising, consumerism, and politics: Adbusters Magazine, http://adbusters.org.

For information on improving health and quality of life for people around the world by advancing technologies, strengthening systems, and encouraging healthy behavior: Program for Appropriate Technologh in Health (PATH), http://www.path.org.

For an intergovernmental approach to human rights: Office of the United Nations High Commissioner for Human Rights, http://www.ohchr.org.

For nongovernmental advocacy for human rights: Human Rights Watch, http://www.hrw.org; and Amnesty International, http://www.amnesty.org.

UNIT 6
BUILDING SUSTAINABILITY: GOVERNANCE, ECONOMIC DEVELOPMENT, AND PEACE

For development to be sustainable, it must integrate environmental stewardship, economic development, and the well-being of all people— not just for today, but for countless generations to come. This is the challenge facing governments, nongovernmental organizations, private enterprises, communities, and individuals.

—International Institute for Sustainable Development, 2004

Essential Questions

- **What are the qualities of effective governance?**

- **How can economic development serve human development?**

- **What are the causes of conflict?**

- **How can conflict be replaced with peace?**

- **What roles do governance, economics, and peace building play in the sustainability puzzle?**

Chapter 1. Introduction

A nation is more than its **government**. The identity and direction of a country is determined by many additional forces, including economics, community and **nongovernmental organizations (NGOs)**, grassroots activism, and the influences of **culture** and the **media**.

It can be argued that neither politics nor governments rule supreme on the international level, either. **Globalization** (integration of the countries of the world) has been fostered not only through government efforts but also largely through the development of communications technology, economic markets, and international trade. This unit examines the ways that government, business, and people exercise power, focusing on successful forms of **governance**, **economic development**, and **peace building**.

Stories from the World:
Government Training in Sierra Leone Helps Improve Community and Family Life[1]

Amadu Suma used to think that there was only one way to solve problems: authoritarianism. For example, he made all the major household decisions by himself. He ordered around his children and didn't listen to what they had to say. He always told his teenage daughter "no" when she asked to go on outings with friends, and his refusals caused constant conflict between the two.

In 2003 Suma attended training in nation-building skills through the U.S. Agency for International Development (USAID). USAID trained 183 community leaders, including men, women, and youth, as part of the larger USAID goal to promote peace, healing, conflict management, reaffirmation of community values, and stability in Sierra Leone. "Now, after the training," says Suma, "I am able to listen to people. The question I ask myself is, 'Suppose somebody else did the same thing to me—how would I feel?'" Participants like Suma have found the training invaluable in learning to demonstrate love and cohesion within one's family and in extending those practices into the community to promote honesty, settle disputes, fight corruption, and rebuild institutions.

Suma and other participants emphasize their desire to see the training extended to recently elected leaders, in order to resolve upper-level disputes and help promote regional stability. "If our rulers are trained to settle problems amicably, they can use these peaceful methods of resolving conflict, even with our neighboring countries."

Youth in Action!
Digital Storytellers[2]
(excerpted from *YES!* magazine, www.yesmagazine.org)

Can young people be involved as effective citizens? Yes! That's what happened when youth from twenty different national organizations were given digital cameras and computers—as well as political and artistic license.

Third World Majority, a collective of women of color who provide training in new media and digital technology, selected young journalists to be digital storytellers. Participants used material from their own lives and communities to compile raw documentary footage, including oral history, music, creative writing, photographs, and news media excerpts. The young journalists explored issues such as **immigrant** rights, failing schools, police accountability, homelessness, and homophobia. In a three-day workshop, they learned how to edit their work into finished documentaries. In 2002 the young video journalists gathered in Oakland, California, to share their documentaries with 300 political activists in a digital storytelling conference.

Third World Majority director Thenmozhi Soundararajan explains that all too often, people of color and **indigenous people** have been adversely affected by technology, with little control over its uses and abuses. Using technology, young people can learn to express their own truths in their own voices. This project is about telling stories and reclaiming histories.

Many of these young journalists are now finding venues to show their work and, in doing so, are discovering the political power of journalism. Thenmozhi reflects, "When people reclaim their stories and reconnect to what is important to them in their communities, that's when the real empowerment begins."

Chapter 2. Governance: Standards of Effectiveness

Good governance is perhaps the single most important factor in eradicating poverty and promoting development.

—Kofi A. Annan,
Secretary General
of the United Nations, 2004

What Is Governance?

Government is defined as an official governing organization that has the power to make and enforce laws for a certain territory; governance, however, is much more. *Governance* is the exercise of economic, political, and administrative authority to manage a country's affairs at all levels. Whereas government is an *entity*, governance refers to a *process* through which people and groups exercise their citizenship. Governance is made up of processes and institutions through which citizens and groups voice their interests, exercise their legal rights, meet their obligations, and mediate their differences.[3]

This chapter first explores **democracy** by focusing on the importance of *citizen involvement* and *government responsiveness* as two standards for effective governance. It then examines the roles of the three interconnected parts of governance: the state, **civic organizations,** and the **private sector.**

Good Governance—
Democracy, Involvement, and Responsiveness

Most people would agree that good governance thrives in the context of democracy. By the beginning of the twenty-first century, the majority of the world's nations hosted some form of democracy in which citizens exercised their will through voting and representation in government.[4] Local and state governments tend to be more effective when they are founded on democratic principles such as the right to vote, free and fair elections, free speech and press, and economic, employment, civil, and family rights.[5] Democratization is certainly an essential part of building good governance, but it requires ongoing education, the development of government structures and institutions, and time. Once established, democracies need to be tended carefully in order to stay healthy and provide good governance for the people.

Ideally, good governance includes the standards of *involvement* and *responsiveness*: involvement from all three parts of governance and responsiveness from each part to the others' needs. In other words, effective governance means that **stakeholders** (those who are affected by governance) feel that they have a voice in matters that affect them.

A women's group in Bangladesh meets to discuss development in their community.

Photo © 2000 Billy Howard, courtesy of CARE

One example of good governance that includes the standards of involvement and responsiveness can be seen in a situation regarding the people of the province of Negros in the Philippines. In 1998, when a U.S. company proposed building a large coal-fired power plant in Negros, local nongovernmental organizations (NGOs), businesses, and the community were outraged. They rallied their government through public demonstrations, press statements, and resolutions. They argued that a coal-fired power plant would set their country back centuries, causing noise, air pollution, and environmental degradation, and would endanger workers' health and well-being. The people of Negros insisted on the implementation of renewable energy technologies to meet their energy expansion needs, reduce their dependence on imported **fossil fuels,** and preserve their natural resources.

In 2002 Philippine government officials responded by withdrawing plans to build the power plant. Negros has taken a lead in promoting and implementing clean power sources in the region, including the construction of wind-powered energy plants throughout the Philippines. Negros's victory is a prime example of good governance—citizen involvement and government responsiveness resulting in a positive outcome.[6]

Three Parts of Governance: The State, Civic Organizations, and the Private Sector

There are three interconnected parts of governance. One is the *state*, which includes political institutions such as a presidency, **legislature,** or parliament and governmental institutions such as a department of defense or a state department of highways. The second part of governance is *civic organizations*, which include community groups and NGOs. The Sierra Club, Amnesty International, and the Boy Scouts are some examples of civic organizations. The third part of governance is the *private sector*, which includes businesses ranging from large companies such as Costco to small neighborhood grocery stores. The media—usually part of the private sector—also plays an essential role in governance by enabling and influencing communication among the three elements of governance.

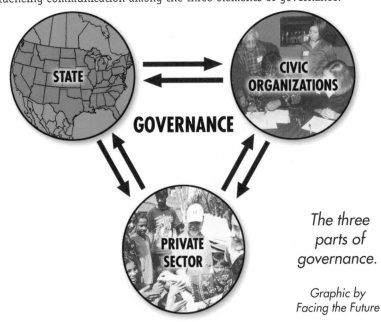

STATE

CIVIC ORGANIZATIONS

GOVERNANCE

PRIVATE SECTOR

The three parts of governance.

Graphic by Facing the Future

Many **developed countries** have reached an impasse in the ability of their own democratic institutions to inspire or support good governance. For example, voter turnout in the United States has declined steadily since the 1960s, even during important presidential elections.[7] Frequently, citizens express cynicism and disenchantment with politics and politicians, claiming that elected officials are out of touch and overly focused on *special interest groups* (large groups organized around a common cause, interest, or issue). This is a problem of responsiveness in governance.

A remedy for such negative attitudes and poor participation involves a combination of strategies. For the three main aspects of governance, key strategies include developing a more **decentralized state,** active civic organizations, and a responsible private sector. These strategies are described below.

The Decentralized State

One important strategy for achieving citizen involvement and government responsiveness is that of decentralization, in which greater responsibility for governance is transferred to local officials, rather than concentrating all decision making in national or regional centers. For the past decade or more, experts have encouraged the capacity building of local governments through decentralization of power. In many **developing countries,** this is the key to narrowing the rich-poor gap and alleviating poverty. These experts believe that if all citizens in a country are actively involved in their governance and have an influential voice in running their country, resource use will be more equitable and the gap between the rich and poor will grow smaller.[8]

Decentralized government can respond faster and more effectively to people's needs, with less corruption and more *accountability* (meaning that politicians say what they do and do what they say) and **transparency** (the full and accurate disclosure of information). More localized delivery of services results in better information flow (which is critical following natural disasters) and more successful and sustainable development projects. It can also improve means for conflict resolution and pro-

vide more opportunities for local political representation and greater political enthusiasm.[9]

In a decentralized system, it is local officials who coordinate development to meet basic human needs such as food, water, energy, health care, and education. This may be difficult to accept for people at higher levels of government who are accustomed to having control over regions or cities and over a government's funds. Nonetheless, decentralization can be a powerful means of achieving good governance because it brings power and decisions closer to the people. This results in governments being more knowledgeable, accessible, and responsive, as has been shown recently in Botswana, Brazil, Colombia, Jordan, South Africa, and parts of India.[10]

Active Civic Organizations

Even an honest, forward-looking country cannot decentralize effectively unless the organizations of civic society provide citizens with opportunities for involvement. Decentralization provides the local governmental structure for citizen involvement, and leadership can guide government toward responsiveness, but it is civic organizations that provide local opportunities for citizens to meet, debate, and work on the particular issues that concern them.

The work of civic organizations is as broad as the interests of the individual citizens who found them and make up their membership. Their work ranges from education, voter registration, and public health to environmental activism, arts development, and the protection of civil liberties. Well-known civic organizations in the United States include the Sierra Club, an environmental organization; the League of Women Voters, an election organization; and the Red Cross, an international health and emergency relief organization. These groups may be public or private, ranging from specialized government programs for citizenship and voting to church groups or private **nonprofit organizations** with a very specific orientation.

Youth volunteers at a Red Cross Service Center serve meals to flood victims.
Photo courtesy of FEMA

Civic groups often raise important questions for government agencies to consider. They can serve as watchdogs and progress indicators on the most pressing issues. Also, civic organizations and political activists can monitor **equity** and provide fresh ideas for the most sustainable solutions to many important issues, ranging from homelessness and health care to the protection of the environment. A broad range of community, regional, and national civic organizations is a sign of a healthy democracy that provides opportunities for citizens to collaboratively work on and solve local and global issues.

A Responsible Private Sector

The private sector includes businesses, industries, and corporations. It is a player of increasing importance and power in the governance equation by exchanging goods and services and providing wages and benefits.

The degree to which the state regulates the private sector varies considerably from country to country. Government intervention in the private sector is usually designed to promote equity, access, and health for its citizens. For example, in addition to **subsidies** and tax incentives designed to favor certain businesses or discourage others, governments can legislate standards for environmental performance (such as maximum levels of pollution), employee wages and conditions of employment, and the role of unions as well as restrictions on business monopolies and mergers.

Environmental, social, and economic **sustainability** can be served when business and industry work with the state and citizens toward the goals of involvement and responsiveness in governance. For example, in response to government regulation and citizen interest, some automobile manufacturers have begun to address **global warming** and oil depletion by developing high-mileage cars and vehicles that run on alternative fuels.

The Web of Democracy:
A Systems Approach to Governance[11]

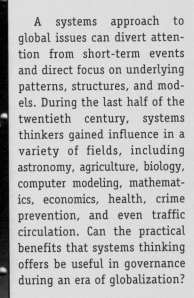

A systems approach to global issues can divert attention from short-term events and direct focus on underlying patterns, structures, and models. During the last half of the twentieth century, systems thinkers gained influence in a variety of fields, including astronomy, agriculture, biology, computer modeling, mathematics, economics, health, crime prevention, and even traffic circulation. Can the practical benefits that systems thinking offers be useful in governance during an era of globalization?

Some experts believe that **systems thinking** is well suited to the challenges of democracy. They say that democracies typically function with a mostly top-down system, a model of governance that often generates low voter turnout and high citizen apathy and cynicism. These experts believe that systems thinking is more suited to the way that most of humanity (and perhaps government and industry) actually functions—through interdependence, relationships, complexity, and networks. Systems thinking may be well suited to building a democratic version of leadership by prioritizing the goals of involvement and responsiveness.

Consider the analogy of a soccer game, with eleven equally talented players on each side. On one team, the players can do *only* what their coach directs them to do and nothing else. The other team gets to interact and build on their shared understanding of the game with intermittent guidance from their coach. The coached-only team would likely lose badly in the face of the more powerful, creative, and *decentralized* (not directed from above) play of the other team. This is because human behavior is naturally self-organizing and complex, and humans are at their best when these traits are emphasized rather than suppressed.

The global challenges of governance and economics are much more complicated than a soccer game, of course. This complexity is why a systems-thinking approach to governance may be appropriate and successful. A systems approach requires that stakeholders be active in a cycle of thinking, acting, and learning—more like the parts of an interconnected mobile than points on a line. This participatory approach may be a good fit for the requirements of good governance, which emphasizes decentralization, the involvement of local and international organizations, and maximum citizen involvement.[12]

Chapter 3. Ineffective Governance: Sources and Impacts

A government is like fire—
a handy servant, but a dangerous master.
—George Washington
(first president of the United States)

Governance, like sustainability, is an ever-evolving process, not a final state of permanent perfection or failure. All the nations of the world have components of both effective and ineffective governance. This chapter discusses some of the root causes of ineffective governance, as well as its impacts.

Sources of Ineffective Governance

Because governance is a complex and dynamic system, several root causes can lead to ineffective governance. Some of the obvious and critical causes—colonialism and lack of funding—are discussed below.

Colonialism

Many ineffective governments have their roots in colonialism. Developing countries that were former colonies have inherited systems of governance in which citizens are not allowed to be actively involved in politics and politicians and civil servants are not responsive to their people. Africa provides perhaps the clearest example of the legacy of colonialism. In the latter portion of the nineteenth century, European powers divided up the continent into their own colonies, or *satellite states*. Lasting effects of these arbitrarily created nations include governments that are ineffective due to longstanding, unresolved tribal conflicts. Today, countries with colonial roots often have difficulty making the transition from colonial rule to more democratic forms of government. They can be subject to government corruption, as well as civil war.

Progress from colonial rule to political independence was a major achievement for most of the world in the twentieth century. As recently as 1945, when the United Nations was established, 750 million people—almost a third of the world's population—were still dependent on colonial powers and seeking self-rule. They lacked the opportunity for democratic self-governance, in which they could exercise their will through voting and representation in government. Today, fewer than 2 million people still depend on colonial powers and live without some form of self-rule.[13]

South African boys watch a game of soccer at an all-white school in Johannesburg. The long period of Apartheid, stemming from British colonial rule, enforced the segregation of blacks and whites.
Photo courtesy of the U.N.

LITERATURE CONNECTION:

The Coming of Colonialism

Things Fall Apart **by Chinua Achebe**

Published in 1958, *Things Fall Apart* is a well-known, widely translated, and influential African novel. The author, Chinua Achebe, develops a complex and sympathetic portrait of a traditional village culture at the point of European **colonization** in what was later to become Nigeria. *Things Fall Apart,* set at the turn of the twentieth century, pits traditional African society against the changes brought by British colonialism. The main character, Okonkwo, struggles to understand what it means to be a man in his Ibo village, unable to adjust to the new ways of the foreigners.

Achebe's book informs the outside world about Ibo cultural traditions, but the story also serves to remind his own people of their past, clearly asserting that tradition contains much of value. During Achebe's youth, many African nations had not yet gained their independence from European colonial powers. All too many Africans were ready to accept the European judgment that Africa had no history or culture worth remembering. Throughout the novel, Achebe describes many African cultures and how they have changed over time. *Things Fall Apart* is a compelling personal story that captures the spirit of African religion and culture at a critical time in history.

Lack of Government Funds

Ineffective governance can also result when weak governments do not have the benefits of a dependable tax base to generate revenue for the operations and services of the state. Without adequate funds to pay its employees and maintain basic services, a country risks collapse. If people stop paying taxes, there is not enough money to run services such as water and sewer treatment, maintain roads and highways, or pay teachers in public schools. Lack of funding can be a major factor in perpetuating ineffective governance.

Impacts of Ineffective Governance

Ineffective governance impacts the **quality of life** of everyone in a country, from the poorest person, whose basic needs go unmet, to the privileged and wealthy, who risk losing property and wealth due to corruption and unstable economic and political conditions. Ineffective governance can result in diminishing food and water security, depletion of natural resources, lack of personal safety, poor health and education services, **human rights** abuses, and conflict.

Lack of Essential Services and Basic Needs

When governance is weak or ineffective, there is often a lack of essential services such as water treatment, **sanitation**, education, and **primary health care** for people living in the lower economic levels of society. In countries with ineffective governance, it is often difficult to ensure that people have enough food to eat and fresh drinking water to meet their basic needs. Furthermore, education may be an option for only the wealthy in these places.

A woman cooks food for her family outdoors in a Bangladesh slum.
Photo © Dan White, courtesy of CARE

Resource Depletion

Ineffective governance can result in resource depletion and environmental degradation. Without accountability to their citizens, corrupt governments may reach economic agreements with businesses or other states that offer short-term profits but have a devastating long-term effect on the environment and economy.

The Maasai, a pastoralist tribe of East Africa, serve as one example of the consequences of ineffective governance and resulting resource depletion. In the early 1900s, British colonization of what is now Kenya and Tanzania reduced ownership of Maasai land by more than 75 percent. The Maasai were forced from their ancestral homes into fringe territories with inadequate resources to maintain their livelihoods and continue their cultural practices. Independence in the 1960s did not bring relief for the Maasai, because even more land was converted into private farms, government property, and wildlife parks. The Kenyan government failed to account for the displaced Maasai tribe and their loss of land, culture, and livelihood.[14]

Limited Government Oversight

Weak or corrupt governance can also mean limited governmental oversight of the activities of businesses. This can result in environmental degradation if a company extracts resources without consideration of the surrounding natural **habitats.** Even if there are laws and rules to protect the environment, when there is limited government oversight those laws may not be enforced. Foreign investors sometimes benefit from such a situation and may take advantage of developing countries experiencing poor governance.

A situation in Ecuador serves as one example of how weak or corrupt governance can result in inadequate oversight of corporations. Between 1964 and 1992, Texaco, a U.S. oil company, managed the oil industry in the northern Amazon region of Ecuador. The Ecuadorian government, both unfamiliar with the oil extraction process and seemingly unconcerned with the environmental impacts of drilling, did not have effective leadership in place to supervise Texaco's activities. After almost thirty years of unsupervised drilling and waste disposal

by the giant oil company, 30,000 Ecuadorian residents brought a lawsuit against Texaco for dumping its highly toxic wastewater, an oil extraction by-product, in rain forests. The lawsuit claimed that the illegal dumping had severely contaminated the environment, destroyed the rain forest, and endangered the health of indigenous people in the region.

In countries with more involved and vigilant governments, Texaco would likely have been required to re-inject the wastewater deep into the ground, far from the immediate environment and daily lives of the local residents.[15] In Ecuador, because the government in this case was weak and ineffective, the oil company was not required to follow such practices.

Human Rights Abuses

Ineffective governance can result in human rights abuses in which people's basic freedoms are repressed. For example, in Myanmar (formerly known as Burma) many human rights violations have been reported following a breakdown of democratic governance.[16] Having gained independence from colonial rule by Britain in the late 1940s, Myanmar suffered many setbacks as it began to build a democratic form of governance. The country underwent a civil war and then many smaller conflicts. In the 1960s, the country fell under military dictatorship. Since then, human rights have been oppressed and many innocent people have been killed by the military government.

Conflict

Perhaps the most devastating consequence of ineffective governance is the likelihood that citizens will suffer from violence and conflict. With weak governance, there are often not enough police to adequately protect people and their property. Weak governance can also result in conflicts between ethnic or religious groups. This was the case in 1994, when the Zapatista National Liberation Army, an indigenous *militia* (local military group) in Chiapas, Mexico, launched a surprise attack and seizure of economic, political, and religious centers. The militia had several grievances against the Mexican government, including electoral fraud, unresolved land disputes, corrupt and racist political officials, and extreme regional poverty. The Mexican government's reluctance to address these issues and integrate indigenous populations into the Mexican political system were central factors in the indigenous militia's decision to revolt. Had Mexico had a stronger and more effective government, this violent conflict might have been avoided.[17]

In 1999, the people of East Timor voted for independence. Following the vote, local militia groups, along with elements of the Indonesian Security Forces, launched a campaign of violence, looting, and arson throughout the territory. Many East Timorese were killed and about 500,000 were displaced from their homes. In this photo, refugees return to East Timor following the conflict.

Photo courtesy of UNHCR

Chapter 4. Governance in the United States

The job of a citizen is to keep his mouth open.
—Günter Grass (1999 German Nobel Laureate author)

Effective Governance in the United States

During the twentieth century, the United States developed certain policies that promoted sustainability and served as examples of government responsiveness.

In the 1930s, the United States passed national laws that restricted child labor. These laws limit the number of hours young people can work and bar them from working on extremely hazardous projects.[18] The United States also has mandatory education laws that require every citizen to complete a high school education. It supplies teachers, schools, and materials in every community in the country and also provides special services for learning-disabled students and for students whose first language is not English.

The civil rights movement of the 1950s and 1960s united powerful civic organizations and impassioned citizens in nonviolent protest and activism against racial injustice. This ultimately resulted in the 1964 Civil Rights Act, which enforced the constitutional right to vote, provided legal relief against discrimination in public places, protected constitutional rights in public facilities and public education, and prevented discrimination in federally assisted programs. The tradition of civil rights legislation continued with the Age Discrimination in Employment Act of 1967, the Americans with Disabilities Act of 1990, and the 1991 Civil Rights Act.

Environmental laws established in the United States have helped to promote sustainability by protecting the environment and ensuring economic vitality.

In 1955 the U.S. government passed the first national law to help fight air pollution. In 1970 the Environmental Protection Agency was founded to further protect the air, water, and land within the United States.[19]

Dating back to the New Deal, which helped put U.S. citizens back to work after the Great Depression of the 1930s, the government has taken action to ensure that the economy is healthy and can provide jobs and opportunities for new businesses. It is a difficult task to balance the needs of the economy, environment, and society, but at key points in history the U.S. government has shown strong leadership in addressing these needs in a sustainable way.

The interior of the Capitol dome, Washington, D.C.

Can the United States Do More to Promote Effective Governance?

Some argue that, as a leader in the world, the United States could do more to improve governance. Some environmentalists assert that the United States has not done enough to curb its large **ecological footprint** or to support sustainable industry. They believe that tax breaks and subsidies to the oil industry continue to accelerate depletion of nonrenewable fossil fuels and emissions of **greenhouse gasses.** Also, with tax cuts for the upper class and the deregulation of banking and other industries through the 1980s and 1990s, there is an increasing concentration of power and money in the hands of fewer corporations and individuals.

Although personal income and the **gross domestic product (GDP)** have grown in the United States for decades, working hours remain the longest in the industrialized world, while personal income, adjusted for inflation, has dropped. Some argue that the government should take action to improve quality of life in the United States by implementing the following strategies:[20]

- Reduce working hours.
- Support flexible work arrangements (telecommuting, work sharing, etc.).
- Redirect government subsidies to sustainable industries and renewable energy development.
- Institute campaign finance reform (limits on campaign funding).
- Restrict advertising to children that promotes harmful habits, such as consumption of junk food.

Government solutions for effective governance can be complicated and controversial. One example is campaign finance reform. Campaign finance reform is a movement to limit the influence that money and big businesses have on elections. Many people believe that this is important because it is growing prohibitively expensive for most citizens to run for political office. More and more, politicians spend an enormous amount of money on television ads and political consultants, often funded by wealthy corporations. For example, the price of the 2004 U.S. congressional and presidential elections was almost $4 billion, up from $3 billion in 1996 and $1.8 billion in 1992.[21]

Critics fear that the growing amount of money spent for political campaigns weakens governance. They believe that the more money that is donated, the more influence that donors—wealthy individuals, companies, labor unions, and interest groups—have over elected officials and public policy. The McCain-Feingold bill passed by Congress in 2002 banned "soft money" (unlimited contributions to the national political parties for "party-building" activities) and placed restrictions on political advertisements.[22] Still, many claim that such measures do not go far enough to limit the influence that money has on elections and policy. A question to consider in this debate is, what is the impact on governance when big donors have more influence in gaining political outcomes than the average citizen?

Personal Solutions for Good Governance

Good governance does not involve just governments, businesses, and organizations. It depends on active and engaged citizens. Below are some ways that you can help create good governance.

- Pursue opportunities to gain hands-on experience in politics. Run for school office. Meet with school administrators to voice your opinions and ideas. Be a student representative to parent and community organizations.
- Attend political meetings and events at the community, city, county, and state levels.
- Follow domestic and international current events through a variety of media: television, radio, Internet, newspapers, and magazines.
- Register to vote—and, most important, vote!

In this photo, young volunteers help distribute food and supplies to hurricane survivors.

Photo courtesy of FEMA

Porto Alegre's Decentralized Budget Process [23]

How would you and your neighbors like to spend $200 million? Local governments around the world may have much to learn from a city in Brazil. Beginning in 1989, 50,000 of the 1.5 million poor and middle-class residents of Porto Alegre, Brazil, undertook a bold move in improving governance through a radical experiment in decentralization that involved all three major components of governance: the state, civic organizations, and the private sector.

Normally, citizens pay taxes and the government decides how money is spent. In this case, the citizens of Porto Alegre got to determine how the city would budget the public money. Because *budgeting* (how money is generated and spent) can be a complicated process, before the citizens could take part, the city provided them with some basic training in how budgets work.

At the heart of the reform effort was a budgeting process in which the local citizens were involved. This process began with dozens of meetings across the city that aimed to include many citizens who experienced discrimination in Brazilian life: middle-class citizens, the poor, those with little education, and black residents. Participants become empowered, knowing that they were gaining the skills to improve their quality of life. Each meeting attracted more than 1,000 residents to address topics such as transportation, health, education, sports, and economic development. Progress throughout the process was posted electronically on the Internet and in print format.

Since the 1989 launch of this experiment in self-government via local control of the budgeting process, benefits have been numerous and impressive. During the project's first twelve years:

- Homes with running and treated fresh water increased from 75 percent to 99 percent.
- Housing assistance rose from 1,700 families served to 29,000.
- The number of public schools increased from twenty-nine to eighty-six, and **literacy** reached 98 percent.
- Government corruption virtually disappeared.

Due to its decentralized approach to budgeting, Porto Alegre has become one of Brazil's most livable cities. Its progressive model of governance has since spread to 100 other cities in South America.

What would you do if you and your neighbors got to decide how to spend millions of dollars for the public's benefit in your city?

Chapter 5. Global Governance and Sustainability

The [United Nations'] Millennium Development Goals commit the international community to an expanded vision of development, one that vigorously promotes human development as the key to sustaining social and economic progress in all countries.

—Millennium Development Goals website, 2004

Many experts argue that, given the interconnected state of the world today, it is time for a global network of democracy. This chapter reviews the history of global governance with a focus on the role of the United Nations.

Roots of International Governance— From Telecommunications to the United Nations

The idea of international cooperation has its modern roots in the nineteenth century, when countries first established international organizations to work together on communication and security issues. The International Telecommunication Union was founded in 1865, and the Universal Postal Union was established in 1874. In 1899 the International Peace Conference was held in The Hague, Netherlands, to develop means for settling crises peacefully, preventing wars, and establishing rules of warfare. The forerunner of the United Nations was the League of Nations, established during World War I in 1919 under the Treaty of Versailles to promote international cooperation and achieve peace and security.[24]

In 1945 representatives of fifty countries met in San Francisco at the United Nations Conference on International Organization to draw up the United Nations Charter.[25] The United Nations (UN) officially came into existence in October 1945, when the UN Charter was ratified by China, France, the Soviet Union, the United Kingdom, the United States, and a majority of other participating countries. In the 1950s and 1960s, the UN played a key role in the transition of many countries from colonial rule to independence. From the 1960s to the 1980s, the UN focused on economic improvement of developing countries, including employment, industrialization, and international assistance. Goals from 1960 through 2000 included improving international literacy, schooling, health, sanitation, and access to fresh water.[26]

Students in Karachi, Pakistan: U.N. development goals include improving international literacy and schooling.
Photo courtesy of the UN

United Nations Today

At the turn of the twenty-first century, the United Nations prioritized the first steps toward attaining a sustainable future by identifying the Millennium Development Goals (MDGs) for humankind. [27] All 191 member states of the UN (including the United States) pledged to meet the following goals by the year 2015:

1. Eradicate extreme hunger and poverty.
2. Achieve universal primary education.
3. Promote gender **equality** and promote women.
4. Reduce child mortality.
5. Improve maternal health.
6. Combat **HIV/AIDS**, malaria, and other diseases.
7. Ensure environmental sustainability.
8. Develop a global partnership for development

(For more information on the Millennium Development Goals, see Unit 7.)

While advances are being made toward many of these goals, the United Nations reports that progress is not satisfactory in all areas and not rapid enough to meet the stated goals by 2015. The UN does note important accomplishments in world health, including the eradication of smallpox and polio, immunization of infants, reduction of infant and childhood mortality, improvement of life expectancy, reduction of hunger, and improvement of access to fresh water. Several important UN goals remain unmet, however, including those related to adult illiteracy, AIDS, and malaria. [28]

Failure to meet a numerical objective is not an entirely fair measure of success for the UN. Merely by setting goals, the UN calls attention to issues facing the international community. Often, organizations and governments respond with programs of their own. Regardless of measurable progress with its specific programs, the UN provides leadership by focusing nations, organizations, and businesses on strategies for sustainability. [29]

Two Kosovar boys with their family's bread rations at a UN refugee camp in Albania.
Photo courtesy of the UN

Life Expectancy at Birth 1995-2000

Years

- World: 64.6
- More Developed Regions: 74.8
- Least Developed Countries: 48.7
- Other Less Developed Countries: 65.4

Note: More developed regions, according to the UN Population Division, include Australia, New Zealand, Europe, North America, and Japan. Less developed regions include Africa, Asia (excluding Japan), and Latin America and the Caribbean; 49 countries within these regions are classified as least developed.

Source: United Nations Population Division, World Population Prospects: The 2002 Revision—Highlights

The media tends to direct attention toward the more dramatic international mediation and conflict resolution work of the UN, but the major focus of the UN's work is on economic and social development. Eighty percent of the work of the UN is devoted to assisting developing countries to build the capacity to help themselves. UN programs aim to promote and protect democracy and human rights; save children from starvation and disease; provide relief assistance to **refugees** and disaster victims; counter global crime, drug trafficking, and **terrorism**; and assist countries devastated by war and the long-term threat of land mines. [30] Beyond peace and security, the UN plays a central role in fostering improved quality of life in developing countries. For example, during the twelve years preceding the 2003 U.S. war in Iraq, the UN helped feed and care for 27 million Iraqi citizens who suffered under international sanctions aimed at removing their leader, Saddam Hussein, from power. [31]

Criticism and Praise for the United Nations

Since its beginnings, the United Nations has been subject to both harsh criticism and strong support. Critics argue that the UN is an oversized, expensive, and ineffective bureaucracy. To support their claims, they cite examples of the UN's failure to resolve conflicts in Somalia, Rwanda, and Bosnia. In 2004 the UN was criticized for mismanaging the "oil for food" program in Iraq and for responding weakly to the crisis in Sudan. Supporters of the UN argue that the budget for the UN's core functions is $1.3 billion per year, nearly $1 billion less than the annual budget for the Tokyo Fire Department.[32]

Supporters of the UN say that although the UN is far from perfect, it does play an important role in a very complicated world. These supporters believe that the UN helps prevent conflicts, mediates disagreements, establishes peacekeeping operations, and assists in the difficult task of postconflict rebuilding. Supporters note that the UN has established itself as the world's only nation-building organization with the resources to address many aspects of development, from health and education to human rights and economic development.[33]

For now, the United Nations exists as the most prominent international body that promotes a global perspective in governance. The work of the UN may never be perfect or complete, but it does have a global vision, and its programs undoubtedly improve the quality of life for millions of people.

UN peacekeepers' gear, Burundi, 2004.
Photo courtesy of the UN

Chapter 6. Economy, Inequality, and Poverty— Past and Present

Poverty is the denial of opportunity.
—Amartya Sen
(1998 Nobel Prize winner in economics)

Experts agree that economic development is essential for progress on other global issues, such as health, education, and effective governance. This chapter defines economy and then reviews the historical roots of economic inequality, the state of the worldwide economy, the structure and impact of poverty, and arguments for and against globalization.

Defining Economy

The word "economy" comes from the Greek *oikonomia*, meaning "management of a household."[34] Economy includes not only the exchange of money and goods but also a range of external social and environmental exchanges and transactions. These external exchanges and transactions include less quantifiable phenomena such as industrial pollution and energy **consumption**, unpaid work of women and children, and destruction of habitat to clear land on which to grow food for one's family. Economy can be as local as the exchange or purchase of food crops between neighbors or as large and global as the workings of a multibillion-dollar corporation.

Photo courtesy of the U.S. Fish and Wildlife Service

Economic Inequality in History

The world's raw resources, from which most wealth is derived, have never been uniformly distributed. Since the days of hunter-gatherers and through early civilizations, raw materials and goods made from them have been redistributed through trade or have been taken by force. Even in the earliest civilizations, distinctions in economic and social class existed, and slave classes were often established as a common fact of life.[35]

The pattern of inequality was widespread over history, intensifying during the colonial era and remaining prevalent throughout recent history. During the era of colonization, economic arrangements such as resource extraction and trade furthered historical inequities. During the end of the fourteenth century, and increasing in scope and intensity during the nineteenth and early twentieth centuries, colonization resulted in economic benefits for the colonizers but not the colonized. The extraction of natural resources by colonial powers slowed opportunities for the colonized countries to develop sustainable economies and build **infrastructure**, such as water and sanitation facilities, schools, hospitals, and roads.[36]

Within nations, particular groups have also struggled to overcome histories of discrimination. In the United States, Native Americans were decimated by the diseases and genocidal wars brought by colonial Europeans. Also, African-Americans suffered from centuries of slavery and discrimination. These **demographic** groups continue to suffer greater poverty and much lower life expectancy than other U.S. citizens.[37]

Economic Inequality in the Modern Era

Like food, water, and energy, money is unevenly distributed around the world. In 2004, two out of every five people on the planet—2.8 billion people—lived on less than $2 a day, and 1.2 billion (one of every five people) lived on less than $1 a day.[38] Since 1960 the gap between rich and poor countries has grown steadily. At the turn of the twenty-first century:

- The richest 1 percent of the global population receives as much income as the poorest 57 percent combined.[39]
- The wealth of the world's 200 richest people equals the combined annual income of the world's poorest 2.5 billion people.[40]
- In 2002, 21 percent of U.S. citizens (34.6 million) lived in poverty and 8.6 percent (14.1 million) lived in severe poverty.[41]

Of all wealthy nations, the United States has the most unequal distribution of income between rich and poor people.[42] In 2002 the richest 10 percent of the U.S. population earned more than 30 percent of national income, while the poorest 10 percent earned only 1.8 percent. Research indicates that this inequality is a fundamental cause of unhappiness.[43] In fact, the degree of economic inequality is identified as a reliable indicator for the degree of unhappiness in all countries. In addition to the United States, forty-eight other countries around the world experienced an increase in economic inequality between 1980 and 2000.[44]

Whatever the causes of poverty and inequality—colonization, discrimination, resource **scarcity**, economic exploitation, or trade restrictions—a person's relative state of poverty or wealth affects his or her ability to have a healthy and fulfilling life.

The Structure of Poverty

Structural poverty occurs when the poor are unable to accumulate the resources required to move out of poverty. In most cases, people are born and raised in desperate conditions of poor health and limited opportunity that tend to perpetuate a state of poverty for their children. The term "structural" emphasizes the interconnected and cyclical nature of poverty and its impacts. These impacts include hunger, diminished health, lack of education, crime, and conflict because of competition for scarce employment and resources. Because the reach of structural poverty is so broad, when poverty is reduced, many other global issues are positively affected.[45]

Because of poverty, housing shortages, and lack of jobs, millions of people around the world live in and around garbage pits. Like these children at a dump in Recife, Brazil, they survive by scavenging food and items to sell. Photo courtesy of FAO

LITERATURE CONNECTION:
Tradition and Economic Change

Nectar in a Sieve **by Kamala Markandaya**

Nectar in a Sieve, Kamala Markandaya's first novel, was published in 1954, just a decade after India gained its independence from its British colonizers. The novel deals with the transition in India's postcolonial history from an agricultural economy to an industrial economy. The story encompasses an economy struggling to gain its feet in both rural and urban India. Poverty is tempered in the story by the main character's resilience in the face of tragedy, devotion to family, resourcefulness, and remarkable spirit for survival.

The story is told through the eyes of Rukmani, a peasant woman from a small village in India. Rukmani's strong and loving arranged marriage and her devotion to her children provide hope and dignity in the midst of deplorable conditions where daily survival is a struggle. The novel portrays the conflicts between a traditional agricultural culture and a growing, postcolonial industrial society. The author addresses important themes, such as the importance of traditional cultural practices, people's reluctance to change, and the impact of economic transformation. *Nectar in a Sieve* has been translated into seventeen languages.

Globalization

Globalization presents new challenges for people and the planet and new potential for solving global issues. It is sometimes a controversial topic, especially with regard to international economics. For example, rapid economic growth and reduced poverty in China, India, and other countries that were poor twenty years ago have been cited as examples of positive aspects of globalization. On the other hand, some of the economic growth resulting from globalization has generated debate over concerns that it has led to increased economic inequalities among people and has contributed to overuse of natural resources and environmental degradation.

The Case Against Globalization— Increasing Inequality

Some experts point to *globalization* (increased levels of international trade and movement of labor and money) as one important cause of global income inequality. They argue that because of globalization, poor countries become increasingly dependent on richer countries, whose interaction with the poorer country can both deplete natural resources and slow its economic development.[46]

Excessive Corporate Power

Large, multinational companies of the twentieth and twenty-first centuries experienced increasing economic power, especially over the agricultural economies of Africa, Asia, and Latin America. Operating under a **free market** system (in which products and services are produced based on people's demand for them), these large companies must ensure that their **shareholders** or **stockholders** (people who own shares of stock in the company) get a return (profit) on their investment. Therefore, these companies focus on what they believe is the best way to make as large a profit as possible. Sometimes this focus on profit results in creating situations of poverty and environmental destruction in the poorer host nations where the companies operate.[47]

Recent research indicates that the economic inequality that can occur along with globalization is due more to the conditions of weak or corrupt governments than it is to globalization itself.[48] In countries with weak governance, a situation of passive globalization may occur, without the benefit of government oversight to keep the best interests of the citizens in mind.

A group of Tanzanian boys in front of a mural of the world.
Photo © Sarah Bones, courtesy of CARE

Race to the Bottom: Sweatshops and Outsourcing

In a competitive market, sales generally go to the business that offers the lowest price. As a result, producers are inclined to lower their prices as much as possible. When this tendency lowers the cost of goods and services through the improved efficiency, the effect may be benign. But when corporations and governments lower costs by reducing environmental protection and employee wages, salaries, and benefits, the result can be negative—a "race to the bottom" for environmental, labor, and social conditions.[49]

One prime example of the consequences of the "race to the bottom" is the use of **sweatshop** labor. Large companies often employ people in the developing world to do low-paying, labor-intensive jobs such as assembling and sewing garments. In some cases, the people working in these jobs are not working under fair or humane conditions. This work is often referred to as *sweatshop labor*. The word "sweatshop" originated in the nineteenth century to describe a subcontracting system in which middlemen earned profits from the margin between the amount they received for a contract and the amount they paid to the workers. The margin was said to be "sweated" from the workers because they received minimal wages for excessive hours worked under unsanitary conditions. Today, a sweatshop is a general term for any workplace where workers are subject to extreme exploitation, including the absence of an acceptable or "living" wage, poor working conditions (such as health and safety hazards), and harsh or even violent discipline.[50]

Sweatshop employment provides little hope of advancement, often causes substantial environmental damage, and generates only a limited infusion of money into the private or public sector of developing nations. Also, even though globalization brings income to people in developing countries, these nations often do not have the infrastructure in place to provide the population with basic services such as health care and education.[51]

Another criticism of globalization is that it leads to the **outsourcing** of jobs. Companies in the developed world can increase their profits by using the much cheaper labor available in developing countries, where millions of people are desperate for jobs. For example, a U.S. worker at a technology software company might earn a salary of $60,000 a year and receive health and vacation benefits, while the same job could be done in India by a worker earning only $20,000 a year with no benefits. This discrepancy tends to encourage companies to maximize their profits by sending those jobs overseas. [52]

It is estimated that between 1992 and 2002, American companies outsourced 1.5 million jobs. Increasingly, many U.S. high-tech companies are outsourcing better-paying work, such as writing software code. Between 2000 and 2003, about 240,000 high-tech jobs were outsourced from the United States abroad.[53]

The Case for Globalization— Creating Income and Growth through Free Trade

Supporters of economic globalization argue that the tremendous power of free trade can bring both income and economic development to poorer nations. According to them, any attempt to restrict the profits, investments, or operations of regional or multinational business will hinder the economic growth that poorer nations so desperately need. Supporters of globalization say that economic opportunity can only come with economic freedom. They contend that although economic freedom may result in some degree of inequality, at least it allows the opportunity for income generation to exist.

The defense of globalization has been based on the following four ideas:[54]
1. Worldwide, poverty and inequality have fallen over the past two decades for the first time in more than a century and a half.
2. The governments of poorer countries should make integration into the world economy their top development objective.
3. The spread of manufacturing to developing countries is a force that can eliminate the structural divide between rich and poor countries.
4. The process of globalization could be used to equalize the distribution of power and wealth, thus undermining the root causes of conflicts.[55]

According to this argument, if poverty reduction is the goal, free trade and access to foreign markets are necessary to inspire economic growth in the developing world. This position claims that there is a systematic relationship between economic growth and poverty reduction and that if corporations and business are over-regulated, they will cease to be productive and profitable. If allowed to flourish freely in developing countries in accord with market forces, business can maximize profits and have more *capital* (money) to reinvest in these new economies, thus creating more jobs and more economic growth.

Youths in Vietnam learn to use a sewing machine.

Photo © 1999 Pham Hong Long, courtesy of Photoshare

Proponents of outsourcing, such as the Information Technology Association of America, believe that outsourcing dramatically reduces labor costs, allowing companies to sell goods ranging from software to tax-preparation services at lower costs or higher profit margins.[56] These greater profits theoretically allow companies to buy new equipment, employ more people, or expand their operations, which in turn will benefit workers in the United States. These proponents argue that continued outsourcing of white-collar jobs will lead to lower prices for consumers, keep inflation down, boost productivity, and eventually create more jobs at home.

Globalization will continue to be a hotly debated topic for many years to come. A question to consider in this debate is how an increasingly globalized economy can balance the desire and need for profit while providing people in both the developed and developing world with humane and equitable livelihoods.

The Heart of the Globalization Controversy: Debts, Profit, and Trade

Focal points of the controversy over globalized economic growth are the International Monetary Fund (IMF), the World Bank, and the World Trade Organization (WTO).

The IMF, founded in 1944, is an international organization of 184 member countries. It was established to promote international monetary cooperation, economic stability, and orderly exchange arrangements; to foster economic growth and high levels of employment; and to provide temporary financial assistance to countries in need. The IMF addresses these goals by monitoring countries' economic activities and lending money to nations to enable conditions for strong economic growth. The IMF does not lend money for specific development projects.

The World Bank is another international financial organization that makes loans to developing countries. It is a specialized agency of the United Nations that provides loans, policy advice, technical assistance, and information to low- and middle-income countries in order to reduce poverty and improve living standards. As of 2004, the World Bank had lent its support to more than 1,800 projects in the developing world. These included providing **microcredit** loans, raising AIDS awareness, supporting education of girls, and improving health-care delivery.

Critics of the IMF and World Bank claim that these institutions actually perpetuate poverty, debt, and inequality in poorer countries. The critics assert that the borrowing countries have trouble paying back the loan debts and that, in order to help poorer countries reach economic stability, these debts should be canceled.

Some have argued that, if it used just 5 percent of its money, the IMF would have more than enough financial resources for the total cancellation of debt for developing countries.[57]

The World Trade Organization (WTO) is at the center of controversy over gobalized trade. The WTO was founded in 1995 during a General Agreement on Tariffs and Trade (GATT) meeting to oversee a wide range of trade agreements and rules between nations. The WTO is the primary international body that helps promote free and open trade between nations.

Critics of the WTO say that the organization favors the participation of large corporations over smaller companies, poorer nations, and the general public. Due to these charges, the WTO has become the focus of widespread controversy and a catalyst for the antiglobalization movement that began in earnest in the 1990s.[58] WTO critics claim that free-trade policies lead to low-wage jobs and poor employment conditions that perpetuate poverty in developing countries. They maintain that opening global markets to speculative, short-term infusions of capital actually produces economic insecurity rather than growth. Critics cite the cases of China and other East Asian countries that experienced economic growth and concurrent reductions in poverty while maintaining trade barriers in opposition to the United State's free-trade policies.[59]

Young farmers in Senegal bag cotton for sale.
Photo by Elizabeth Benedict Huttman

It is important to remember that globalization and trade are themselves not "the enemy," unless they foster inequity and poverty. The UN suggests that in determining what type of economic development is good for **human development**, the focus should be on the appropriateness of particular policies for particular countries. It suggests that there should be rules for how globalization occurs and a focus on international economic institutions that can help promote growth and reduce poverty in the developing world.[60]

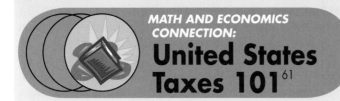

MATH AND ECONOMICS CONNECTION:
United States Taxes 101[61]

Taxes (money taken by the government from people and businesses to pay for government services) can be a critical but confusing piece of a country's economic picture. To meet their expenses, governments need income, or "revenue," which is usually raised through taxes.

The U.S. economy is based on a free-enterprise system in which private businesses produce goods and services that the public can buy. Since a free-enterprise system does not produce all the services needed by society, some services are provided by government agencies. Two examples of government-provided services are national defense (the military) and law enforcement (police). Other examples are the management of natural resources, such as water supplies or publicly owned land, and the development of infrastructure, such as schools or highways. Taxes are collected to pay for these services and to finance their construction or maintenance.

Generating Revenue: What Gets Taxed?

The U.S. government imposes different types of taxes on individuals and businesses, as explained below.

- **Income Tax:** The federal government relies mainly on income taxes for its revenue. The earnings of both individuals and corporations are subject to income taxes. Personal income tax produces about five times as much revenue as corporate income tax.
- **Sales and Excise (consumption) Tax:** Sales taxes usually are paid on most goods and services but are sometimes excluded from basic needs such as food. State governments depend on income, sales, and excise taxes for their revenue. Sales taxes are also an important source of revenue for some large cities and counties. The tax rate varies from state to state, and the list of taxable goods or services also varies from one state to the next. Excise taxes, sometimes called "luxury taxes," are used by both state and federal governments. Examples of items subject to federal excise taxes are airplane tickets, gasoline, alcohol, firearms, and cigarettes.
- **Property and Wealth Tax:** Most county and city governments use property and wealth taxes to raise their revenue. Private homes, land, and business properties are taxed based on the property's value. Some state and local governments also impose taxes on the value of certain types of expensive personal property. Examples

are some cars, boats, recreational vehicles, and livestock. Property taxes account for more than three-fourths of the revenue raised through taxes on wealth. Other taxes imposed on wealth include inheritance, estate, and gift taxes.

Some people in the United States believe that the government takes too much tax from its citizens, while others believe that the government doesn't take enough to adequately fund needed public services. Still others believe that the tax structure (who and what gets taxed) should be restructured to better serve all of society. Some questions to ask when considering taxation are:

What would happen if the government didn't collect taxes? How would vital services such as roads, fire departments, and schools be funded?

How could the tax structure be altered to better serve society's needs?

Cartoon © Andy Singer

Chapter 7. Sustainable Solutions: Strategies for Economic Development

Economic growth without social progress lets the great majority of the people remain in poverty, while a privileged few reap the benefits of rising abundance.

—John F. Kennedy
(fortieth president of the United States)

The goal of economic development is to increase the material and financial well-being of a country's people. An economic development project can take a variety of forms, from the development of a large-scale water project that allows for increased agricultural production to the construction of a furniture manufacturing plant that provides jobs and goods. Economic development can be undertaken by governments and by organizations, large and small. It often involves co-ordinated international efforts by large intergovernmental organizations such as the United Nations Development Programme (UNDP).

Economic development is not desirable in itself unless it results in *human development*.[62] It is important to consider economic growth in the context of the health, education, and social well-being of people. People are the real "wealth" of nations, as stated by the UNDP:

> *The basic purpose of development is to enlarge people's choices. People often value achievements that do not show up at all, or not immediately, in income or growth figures: greater access to knowledge, better nutrition and health services, more secure livelihoods, security against crime and physical violence, satisfying leisure hours, political and cultural freedoms, and sense of participation in community activities. The objective of development is to create an enabling environment for people to enjoy long, healthy, and creative lives.*[63]

Human development is about much more than the rise or fall of the gross domestic product. It is about creating a world in which people can develop their full potential and lead productive, creative lives according to their needs and interests. The most basic requirements for human development are long and healthy lives, education, access to the resources needed for a decent standard of living, and the ability to make personal life decisions and participate in the life of the community. Without these aspects of human development, many opportunities in life are simply not available.

Young school boys in Kenya.
Photo © 2002 Mark Mason,
courtesy of CARE

Development thus attempts to expand the choices people have to lead lives that they value. Together, economic and human development can result in sustainable solutions to many global issues. This chapter explores the transformational power of economic development, focusing on strategies for sustainable development, including both personal and **structural solutions** for overcoming the devastating effects of poverty.

Breaking the Cycle of Poverty

Economic growth is a tremendous force for global change because it directly affects quality of life. With rising incomes, families are able to spend money on health and education. The cycle of structural poverty can be broken as children who benefit from health and education are themselves much less likely to lead a life of poverty. Instead, they are more able to improve their own children's standard of living.[64]

At very low income levels, families must spend all their limited money on the basic needs of food, water, and shelter—and in the case of an emergency, health care. Only when incomes rise above the survival threshold can families afford other things that improve the quality of their lives. For example, with even minor increases in earnings, low-income families in the developing world are able to improve their lives by making their homes safer with bed netting or window screens to keep out disease-bearing mosquitoes or by purchasing clean-burning propane stoves to replace dangerously polluting wood fires.[65]

Sustainable economic and human development can break the cyclical and structural character of poverty, which, when left unattended, tends to reproduce itself across generations. Also, higher incomes provide the added benefit of stabilizing population growth through lower **fertility rates**. Households with higher income and education levels tend to have fewer children, which means that they will be more likely to afford education and health care for their children. These children will in turn be less likely to live in poverty themselves.[66]

Young boys carry bricks at a construction site in New Delhi, India. For poor families, having many children sometimes makes economic sense. Children help support their families by producing food, hauling water, and begging on the streets.

Photo courtesy of the UN

Alleviating Poverty— a World of Solutions, Large and Small

In addition to the major international organizations that impact economic development, such as the IMF, World Bank, and WTO, a wide variety of governments, organizations, and programs have specialized strategies to accomplish sustainable economic growth. A range of solutions is presented in the sections below, from government legislation to corporate reform to strategies for responsible personal investing.

Governmental Solutions

Eliminating global poverty is an issue that bears heavily on the economic and security interests of the United States and the world. If global poverty persists, the international community will likely shoulder the increasing costs of regional conflicts, public health challenges, humanitarian crises, and environmental degradation. The pressures of poverty, disease, debt, lack of quality education, rising population, and conflict that developing countries experience can breed hopelessness and despair—providing fertile ground for the growth of terrorism, extremism, and instability. Governments can improve global security and promote economic growth by helping developing countries stave off these pressures.[67]

Although all developing countries must pursue policies that are suited to their own particular geography, population, and needs, the United Nations suggests a few key benchmarks for desirable economic growth. First, *exports* (goods or materials that are traded out of a country) in low-income countries should emphasize manufactured products, such as electronics and clothing, rather than **commodities** or raw materials such as oil, timber, minerals, or agricultural products. This is because countries focusing on exporting manufactured goods rather than commodities generally enjoy much higher economic growth. Also, to ensure that economic development will benefit those who need it most, economic growth should be *labor intensive*, creating the maximum number of wage-earning jobs for people, rather than *capital intensive*, which relies on technology and machinery in place of labor.[68] This strategy tries to ensure that economic development supports, rather than undermines, human development.

Private Sector Solutions: Corporate Transparency, Responsibility, and Democracy

An emerging example of how economic growth can serve human development is found in the private sector, wherein corporations are increasingly being asked to consider the needs of people in the communities where they operate.

A shareholder or stockholder legally owns one or more shares of stock in a company; but what about *stakeholders*, people who do not necessarily own stock in a company, but who may be impacted, positively or negatively, by a corporation's actions?

More than 200 years ago, corporations were created to serve the public interests. Investors could pursue profits, but they had to consider stakeholders. However, in 1930 the U.S. Congress made corporations' accountability to investors *more important* than their accountability to the public.[69] Today it is acceptable in many circles for corporations to maximize the wealth of their executives and shareholders rather than to promote the interests of the communities where they obtain that wealth. There is a growing movement, though, to consider the interests of everyone with a stake in a corporation's actions. This includes not only a corporation's employees and customers but also members of a community where its offices or factory may affect the local economy or environment.

For stakeholder interests to gain a greater voice, corporations need to develop greater transparency by freely, openly, and completely disclosing to stakeholders and shareholders the facts and figures of their operations. Only with this transparency can all shareholders and stakeholders, including the public, hold corporations responsible. Transparency would also serve to reduce the corruption, such as the numerous scandals involving falsified accounting and illegal "insider trading" of stocks, that has compromised corporations during recent decades of deregulation.

The Interfaith Center for Corporate Responsibility (ICCR) tackles issues of corporate transparency and social responsibility through a blending of religious ethics and corporate values.[70] ICCR priorities include eliminating sweatshops and corporate investment in human rights abuses, reversing global warming, halting the spread of **genetically modified foods**, and forgiving the international debt of the poorest countries. The ICCR influences companies to engage in **corporate social responsibility (CSR)**, which requires that corporations be accountable to community stakeholders. ICCR contends that, in the expanding global economy, businesses that can operate effectively without compromising the environment or quality of life may stand a better chance of being financially sustainable in the long run.

The UN Global Compact provides another example of an organization confronting issues of corporate responsibility. The compact brings together companies, UN agencies, and civic organizations to support human rights, labor laws, and the environment and to counter corruption. Rather than policing organizations, the UN Global Compact achieves these goals by engaging participants in policy dialogues, education, and projects to directly alleviate global poverty.[71]

A wide range of inventive programs have also emerged from the private sector in recent years. The Coca-Cola Company, for example, has embarked on research and development efforts to produce a drink to provide micronutrients to help prevent diseases of **malnutrition**. Hewlett-Packard has partnered with international nongovernmental organizations and the Grameen Bank in Bangladesh to provide HP products and services to bridge the "digital divide." Pharmaceutical companies and biomedical institutes are researching new drugs that could prevent diseases common to poor countries, such as malaria, rotavirus (the most common cause of severe diarrhea among children), and even HIV/AIDS. In recent years, businesses have considered direct marketing efforts toward the 3 billion people living on less than $2 a day. This radical idea requires changes in thinking, pricing, product development, and possibly new measurements of profitability to include social and human investments.[72]

Nongovernmental Organization Solutions: Microcredit

Microcredit is also a powerful tool for helping break the cycle of poverty. Microlending is the practice of providing very poor people, especially women, with access to credit that allows them to start small businesses. The resulting income transforms their own and their families' lives, enabling better nutrition, education, housing, and health. In impoverished parts of the world, very small loans—of $150 or less—for starting or expanding a self-employment venture, provided at competitive interest rates, can allow people to rapidly become self-sufficient.[73]

A woman feeds pigs purchased through a community microcredit program in Rwanda. The animals now provide food and livelihoods for 24 women and their families.
Photo courtesy of CARE

A microcredit borrower might buy the materials to open a small store selling basic cooking and household supplies or buy a pot and bulk ingredients for selling simple baked goods or snack foods on the street. Some borrowers take out additional loans to expand their businesses—buying a second cow to sell even more milk in their village or building a simple hut with a tin roof to house their store. Successful microcredit programs not only improve the financial health of individuals but also improve the economic health of whole communities, from the bottom up. Women, who receive the majority of these loans, later reinvest their profits in their families.

Studies show that microcredit works. Since its inception in Bangladesh in the early 1980s, microcredit has become popular among donor agencies and those undertaking development work, both because of its impressive success rate and because it is financially sustainable (since loans are small and repaid with interest). In a 1998 study, the World Bank found that extreme poverty fell 70 percent within five years among borrowers of the Grameen Bank's microcredit program in Bangladesh.[74] Microcredit programs have branched out to reach rural and urban borrowers on nearly every continent, as well as in the United States.

Personal Solutions: Natural Investing

Natural investing is a relatively new movement that addresses the ethics of personal investment decisions, by promoting alternatives to mainstream investing.[75] Research has shown that natural investors, who guide their investments according to their personal values, do not suffer from underperforming stock. For example, during the U.S. stock boom from 1990 through 1998, the Domini 400 Social Index, which tracks those companies screened for sound social and ethical investment, did significantly better than the unscreened Standard and Poor's 500 Index. The Social Investment Forum estimated that in 1999, $1 trillion—about one-tenth of all investment dollars—was invested according to ethical criteria.

Natural investing can be a positive force in protecting the environment.
Photo courtesy of the U.S. National Parks Service

According to one survey, 83 percent of all investors would prefer that their social and environmental values be reflected in their financial portfolio. With natural investing, people can merge their personal and financial values through three proven steps. First, with *avoidance screening*, they can choose not to invest in industries or corporations that do not fit their values. Second, with *affirmative screening*, they can actively seek out socially responsible corporations or small, cutting-edge companies in emerging fields such as alternative energy. Finally, with *community investing*, they can invest in grassroots organizations and poor people, locally or globally, through programs that address issues such as affordable housing and small business development and through targeting investment in urban and rural areas where those with the greatest need can benefit from economic development.

The Way Ahead: Economics in the Service of Human Development

Throughout recent history, developed nations have waged campaigns against poverty both within and outside their own borders, often looking for simple answers to complex problems. In fact, the problems of the world are so intertwined that their interconnections demand attention. This is especially true with poverty, which is fundamentally linked to other global issues such as health, education, and economic development. Togeth-er, human and economic development are the keys to dealing with poverty, poor health, environmental decline, and security concerns. Effective governance that encourages a standard of sustainability can guide development by blending the forces of the state, civic organizations, individuals, and the private sector.

A variety of innovative, productive, and ethical solutions to poverty already exist. People can begin accounting for the true costs of business by phasing out subsidies that mask those costs, damage the environment, and hurt small producers. Shifting taxation away from things that are good for people (like income and investment) to things that aren't (like resource depletion and pollution) can move businesses toward sustainability and stimulate employment, which in turn will help alleviate poverty and protect the environment. Closed-loop and **lifecycle design** using **cradle-to-grave** and **cradle-to-cradle** models can build sustainability into economic development, reducing the large ecological footprint of developed countries and allowing developing nations to leapfrog to sustainability.

Changing economic indicators to reflect human and ecological well-being is also important, since current indicators such as gross domestic product measure only the *quantity* of economic activity—not the *quality* of that activity. New indicators can offer a genuine marker for progress by reflecting human and **ecosystem** health through such benchmarks as infant mortality, education, gender equality, water and air quality, volunteerism, and biological diversity.

Advocating corporate transparency and responsibility can help companies consider stakeholder interests as well as shareholder returns. By following guidelines such as those offered in natural investing, individuals with enough capital to invest can obtain not only secure futures for themselves and their families but also socially responsible results. People in wealthy countries can also aim to reduce their ecological footprints and the stressors related to overwork and overconsumption—with a net gain in environmental sustainability for the Earth as well as greater personal happiness.

Finally, international development efforts—both intergovernmental (such as the UN, IMF, and WTO) and nongovernmental (such as the ICCR) can emphasize sustainable economic development, pursuing the UN strategy for joint human and economic development.

Economic Solutions for Sustainable Development

Decentralized Solutions—
Tajik Groups Set Their Own Agenda[76]

Increasingly, local or decentralized economic development is preferred to large-scale, top-down economic development. After the United Nations brokered a peace accord in 1997, Rustam and Jalol Ibragimov, former fighters in Tajikistan's civil war, returned home to a region where 80 percent of the people lived below the poverty line. Fortunately for the Ibragimov brothers, the local Jamaot Development Committee (JDC) provided them with a loan to purchase a shop, equipment, and materials so they could start a successful business making chimneys for heating stoves.

Working with former opposition commanders, the United Nations Development Programme (UNDP) assisted in the formation of the JDC, a local, representative organization of village farmers, elders, and civic leaders that provides reintegration for war veterans, war widows, the elderly, and single-income families through training and employment. The JDC secures loans for a wide range of *microenterprises* (small businesses) and funds as well as plans for essential infrastructure, including local health clinics and schools. These local planning committees provide a much-needed link between the state, civic organizations, and a renewed private sector, bringing both resources and decision-making power to the local level.

Serving the Poorest of the Poor—
Trickle-Up Economics[77]

The Trickle Up Program is an NGO whose mission is to help the lowest-income people worldwide take the first steps out of poverty. In partnership with local agencies, Trickle Up pursues a microenterprise strategy of providing basic business training and seed capital in the form of conditional grants, usually of US$100 distributed in two installments of $50 each, to families or groups of three or more people. Trickle Up entrepreneurs receive the first grant installment after preparing a Trickle Up Business Plan; then after three months or the first business cycle, they complete a Trickle

Photo courtesy of Trickle Up

Up Business Report showing they have established a viable business and then can receive the second grant installment. Trickle Up Program encourages entrepreneurs to build their assets by saving individually or in groups.

Through Trickle Up's philosophy of "alleviating poverty, one business at a time," its microgrants have had a major impact on people such as Sampa Turay, a married woman with seven children. Several years ago, rebels attacked her village of Rokupr, in northern Sierra Leone, forcing Sampa and her family to flee. When Sampa and her family returned to begin life again, Sampa found it difficult to provide for her family. She was selected for a Trickle Up grant, which she used to start a business buying and selling fish. However, Sampa found it tiring to walk around the market and decided to open a small restaurant instead. She used the rest of her grant to buy raw materials and benches for her clients. Since then, her weekly profit has quadrupled. She can now buy food and clothes, pay her medical expenses, and send four of her children to school.

Personal Solutions for Poverty Reduction and Equity

Individuals can have a big impact on creating sustainable economies, reducing poverty, and increasing equity. Here are a few actions you can take:

- Vote with your dollars. Support businesses that are environmentally sustainable and that build equity through good wages, employment conditions, and benefits.
- Become familiar with the Millennium Development Goals and support organizations that work toward reducing poverty, locally and worldwide.
- Volunteer with homeless shelters, food banks, and other social service organizations that work to reduce the impact of poverty locally.

Chapter 8. The Evolution and Impacts of Conflict

Never has there been a good war or a bad peace.

—Benjamin Franklin
(United States statesman,
printer, and scientist)

Peace, like human rights, is an essential condition for maintaining a sustainable world and for enjoying a good quality of life. Good health, universal education, and economic well-being mean little without peace. Only in conditions of stability and security can we protect human rights, guarantee food and water security, implement sustainable economic development, and protect the environment. This chapter explores the history, types, interconnections, and impacts of conflict.

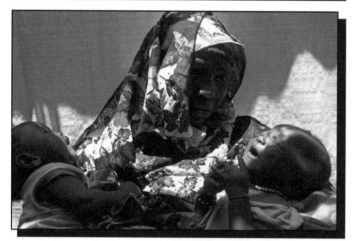

A refugee cradles her daughter and the daughter of her sister, who was killed during the 2004 civil conflict in Sudan. Photo courtesy of the U.S. State Department

Defining Conflict

The United States Department of Defense generally classifies military conflicts as "low-," "medium-," or "high-intensity," depending on the types of weapons used, involvement of outsiders, and number of deaths. World Wars I and II are examples of high-intensity conflicts, and the Vietnam and Korean Wars are examples of medium-intensity conflicts. The U.S. invasion of Grenada in 1983 is an example of a low-intensity conflict.[78]

Interstate wars occur between countries, whereas **intrastate** or **civil wars** occur within countries between antagonists with particular political, religious, or ethnic differences.[79] **Genocide** is the planned, systematic extermination of an entire ethnic, national, political, or religious population; **ethnic cleansing** is a term sometimes used to describe a program of genocide carried out by one ethnic group against another.[80]

Terrorism is a tactic of violence or threat that targets civilians, with the objective of creating fear or political disruption in the attacked population.[81] Terrorism is also called *asymmetric warfare* because it allows a weaker opponent to gain advantage over a stronger one through unconventional means such as suicide bombing and hostage taking.[82] Terrorist acts are, by definition, nonstate actions (not connected to a particular country or nation), even though terrorists may be supported by countries that do so for their own purposes. Countries sometime commit acts of terror in their pursuit of policy, but such acts are not defined as terrorism. Countries may also sponsor and equip proxy or substitute groups that commit terrorist acts.

A Tanzanian soldier.
Photo © Paul Taggart, courtesy of CARE

The History and Evolution of Conflict

Written human history, it has been argued, is largely the history of warfare. The great empires and civilizations of the past, such as the Romans, Greeks, Aztecs, and Chinese, were created, maintained, and often terminated by the wars they fought. Some of the most memorable and famous figures in history—including Alexander the Great of Macedonia (Greece), Julius Caesar of Rome, William the Conqueror of England, George Washington of the United States, and Mao Zedong of China—are those who led or launched armies into battle.

From the end of World War II in 1945 through the 1990s, the number of intrastate (within nations) armed conflicts grew. The majority of these wars were low-intensity, and many of them were fought in sub-Saharan Africa and the Middle East. During the last decade of the twentieth century, civil wars, ethnic cleansing, and acts of genocide claimed approximately 5 million lives, the majority of whom were civilians. In World War II, civilian casualties accounted for only 50 percent of the total deaths; since then, civilian casualties during times of conflict have increased to an average of 90 percent.[83]

Following the end of the Cold War (1945–89), a period marked by political tension and a nuclear arms race between the Soviet Union and the United States, prospects for a more peaceful world seemed good. There were a growing number of peace agreements, arms control treaties, and responses to interstate aggression. For example, in 1992 a United Nations Conference on Environment and Development, held in Rio de Janeiro, Brazil, was attended by 172 governments. Participants recognized the importance of addressing the role of conflict in the global picture of human development and sustainability. The conference spurred other political discussions and ideas promoting interdependence between nations, a global community, and new thinking about **sustainable development**. Democracy was expanding to places such as South Africa, where the institutionalized racism of **apartheid** had been dismantled under the leadership of Nelson Mandela.[84]

Unfortunately, a new global order of peace did not come about. By the beginning of the twenty-first century, there were numerous low- and medium-intensity wars raging around the planet—even more than during the Cold War. The rise of intrastate, rather than interstate, clashes has come to mark the character of twenty-first-century conflicts. Concurrently, the nature of war and the concept of security have been redefined by the threat of *weapons of mass destruction* (biological, chemical, and nuclear weapons) and the rise of ethnic nationalism, religious fundamentalism, international terrorism, **transnational** crime organizations, and increasing hostility toward the United States and other wealthy nations.[85]

Technology has changed the nature of conflict in the twenty-first century. Conventional weapons, which do not carry a nuclear, biological, or chemical capacity (guns, missiles, tanks, etc.), have become increasingly accurate and deadly. **Biological warfare** and **chemical weapons** may be more useful to terrorists than to state military forces because of difficulties in hitting targets accurately with them.[86]

There have been some positive trends in the last few years. The number of people killed in recent wars has fallen to its lowest point in the post–World War II period. For example, nineteen major armed conflicts were underway worldwide in 2003, a significant drop from the thirty-three wars counted in 1991. Meanwhile, peacemaking missions, in which organizations such the UN intervene in potential conflicts before they erupt into wars, are growing in number. [87]

Economic Impacts of Conflict

A nation's economy suffers during conflict, and the country's poor population almost always suffers the most. World War II is often regarded as having ended the Great Depression in America, but although the military draft in World War II ended unemployment by bringing 16 million people into the U.S. armed forces, the increase in gross domestic product consisted almost entirely of military goods and services rather than services that benefited the general public, such as schools, hospitals, and roads. The idea that war boosts economic prosperity does not make a distinction between government war expenditures and the kinds of economic production that serve society and create genuine economic prosperity.

Although there have been no high-intensity wars for decades, low-intensity conflicts in the last thirty years have had a devastating effect on human and economic development in poorer countries and on the planet as a whole. In addition to military and civilian casualties, regional economies have been disrupted and local ecosystems have been destroyed as a result of conflict. During these times, rather than invest in public welfare, nations invest in military equipment and defense. Money that could have been spent on public services such as education, health care, and police and fire protection goes to taking care of people whose lives have been disrupted by conflict. In developing countries, the economic impacts of conflict can linger for years if infrastructure, farmland, and industries that people depend on for jobs are destroyed.

Impacts of Conflict on Global Issues

Conflict threatens the future of both developing and developed countries and also affects many other global issues. Conventional armed conflicts can damage the environment, disrupt economies, and greatly diminish quality of life for the inhabitants of the warring countries. Terrorism, amplified by the increasing power of conventional weapons and the potential use of weapons of mass destruction, threatens not only massive civilian death in both developing and developed regions but also destruction of the financial and technological systems that support modern societies.

An Afghani man stands before his destroyed house.
Photo © Jason Sangster, courtesy of CARE

Social, Cultural, and Human Rights Impacts of Conflict

War and conflict are destructive to society and culture. The regular activities of society, including school, work, recreation, and artistic and spiritual pursuits, are greatly disrupted by war. People may be forced into military service, driven from their homes and businesses by fighting, or unable to cultivate land because of land mines and unexploded bombs. Masses of people may become refugees who flee into bordering nations or may be internally displaced within their own war-torn homeland. For example, by the summer of 2004, after eighteen months of ethnic conflict in the Darfur region of western Sudan, 1.4 million people had fled from their homeland.[88]

Kosovar refugees forced to flee from their homeland.
Photo courtesy of the UN

Sometimes cultural institutions or treasures are lost during conflict. The Iraqi National Museum was looted following the fall of Baghdad in the Iraq war that began in 2003. In another example, a massive cliff sculpture of Buddha in Afghanistan was destroyed after the removal of the Taliban regime in 2001. These important cultural and religious relics were lost forever.

Conflict can also lead to losses or abuses of human rights. In the interest of increasing security, governments facing conflict may deny basic freedoms of speech and assembly, as well as other economic, civil, and political freedoms. Even in the democracies of Western Europe and North America, civil liberties and personal freedoms have been reduced to combat terrorist groups such as Italy's Red Brigades, the Irish Republican Army, and al Qaeda. One example of this is the controversial U.S. Patriot Act, passed by the federal government following the attacks of September 11, 2001, in an effort to ensure the safety and security of the nation. Some people feel that the act went too far, restricting civil liberties and legal rights in the interest of national security.[89]

Impacts of Conflict on Health Care, Food, and Water

At the beginning of the twenty-first century, more than 14 million people faced hunger due to military conflict in their homelands. Rates of malnutrition and infant and maternal mortality are higher during times of war. AIDS and other diseases often run rampant in areas facing conflict, because medical care may be disrupted. Also, water supplies often become contaminated and water delivery systems disrupted, resulting in drastic increases of water-borne illnesses.[90]

In poorer countries with internal conflict, local money and foreign assistance that could be used for education, health care, and economic development are often diverted to military uses. In some cases, fuel and energy are used to serve the war effort and are denied to citizens. Basic infrastructure for food production, transportation, and communication can be destroyed or appropriated by soldiers, often causing severe food and water shortages for citizens.

View of a makeshift refugee camp on the border between Kosovo and the Former Yugoslav Republic of Macedonia. Up to 65,000 Kosovar refugees lived here during the internal conflict of 1999.
Photo courtesy of the UN

Environmental Impacts of Conflict

Violent conflict often leads to environmental destruction. *Scorched earth tactics* may leave an area completely destroyed, and other direct attacks on natural resources and ecosystems may occur during war. Animal species, while not directly targeted, are often killed by soldiers for food or for valuable hides, ivory, or other trophies, which can be sold to support the ongoing violence. This has recently been the case in the civil wars of equatorial Africa, where soldiers in tropical jungles rely on gorillas or chimpanzees as a food source or for income by illegally *poaching* (killing and selling) the animals. Mass **migrations** of people fleeing conflict can increase environmental damage as people cut and burn firewood and hunt wild animals in efforts to survive.[91]

Chapter 9. Sustainable Solutions: Halting Conflict at its Roots

Balance and stability in the world will require the commitment of all nations, rich and poor, and a global development compact to extend the wealth of possibilities to all people.

—United Nations Human Development Report, 2003

A focus on the root causes of conflict points the way toward solutions that help protect human rights, improve food and water security, foster sustainable economic development, and protect and restore the environment. This chapter addresses the question of how the world can shift from reactive peacekeeping, in which nations try to halt existing or developing conflicts, to the proactive, long-term task of peace building.

What kind of worldview shift might this require?

Understanding the Root Causes of Conflict

The underlying conditions of different conflicts are often the same: resource scarcity; lack of economic and human development; political instability with weak systems of governance; social divisions based on class, race, ethnicity, or religion; rapid population growth; and ready availability of lethal weapons.[92]

Resource Scarcity

Resource scarcity is frequently the underlying cause of conflict. In the twenty-first century, wars are primarily expected to be fought over access to or control of water supplies, farmland, forests, **fisheries**, or valuable commodities including coffee, diamonds, gold, oil, or narcotics.[93] Resource scarcity was linked to modern-era conflicts in Rwanda, Somalia, and Chiapas, Mexico.[94] Control of fresh water for drinking and irrigation is one issue contributing to the ongoing conflict in the Middle East between Israelis and Palestinians, where the Israelis control most of the water in the region.[95] Further conflict looms in the Middle East as Turkey moves forward with major dams in the headwaters of two of the region's most important rivers, the Tigris and Euphrates.

Desertification can lead to resource scarcity and conflict.
Photo courtesy of the UN

Low Economic and Human Development

When people don't have the economic means for a good quality of life, they are more likely to try to improve their situation with violent action. Economic situations that may indicate a potential for conflict include low levels of per capita income, slow or negative economic growth, high levels of external debt, and a widening rich-poor gap. Human development indicators for potential conflict include poor health and low levels of education. Together, lack of economic opportunities, poor health, and illiteracy can also breed hopelessness. In some cases this hopelessness creates fertile ground for terrorism.[96]

Ineffective Governance

Political causes of conflict often revolve around weak governance. When the important elements of citizen involvement and government responsiveness are missing in the relationship of the state, civic organizations, and the private sector, an imbalance exists that can result in conflict within the country. When governance is weak, the state may be overrun by its own military or by militias formed by rebel groups or private interests. This was the case in Somalia, where warlords were the primary power brokers. In this impoverished country that lacks effective governance, these warlords rule by force.

Social Division

Social divisions—whether based on class, caste, ethnicity, region, or religion—often provide the sparks that ignite conflicts. The twentieth century was filled with examples of low-intensity wars characterized and created by such social divisions. Perhaps the most chronic and well-known of such conflicts is the Arab-Israeli (Muslim-Jewish) conflict in the Middle East. Many other social, ethnic, and religious divisions contributed to armed conflicts at the end of the twentieth century, including Muslim versus Christian in Sudan's civil war, Serbian versus Croatian during the Bosnian war, and the Protestant versus Catholic conflict within Ireland and between Ireland and England.

High Population Growth and Density

Rapid population growth and high population density contribute to resource depletion, scarcity, and environmental degradation. Also, high fertility rates create young populations (half the world's people are presently under the age of twenty-five). This means that there is a large pool of fifteen- to twenty-nine-year-olds in developing nations—without education, employment, or hope for a better future—who may be easily recruited into the military or militia groups. Many regions, including India, Africa, the Middle East, Central Asia, and Latin America, now face the dangerous combination of high population growth and resource scarcity.

One example of how population growth and resource scarcity combine to cause conflict can be seen in Rwanda. In the early 1990s, there arose a severe gap between the Rwandan food supply and the food needs of the population.[97] The growing population also began to overharvest firewood, resulting in deforestation and erosion of the soil, which in turn resulted in a steep decline in food production. This severe resource scarcity and collapse of food sources set the stage for the genocidal conflict that eventually claimed more than 800,000 lives.

Access to Lethal Weapons

Deadly conflict cannot occur without lethal weapons. Easy access to arms is a major factor contributing to many of the low-intensity wars currently being fought around the world. These conflicts have the potential to become medium- and high-intensity wars, because of the proliferation of small arms throughout the world.[98]

Nuclear Arms Race

In the early twenty-first century, the U.S. Department of Defense identified twenty-five states that were pursuing the development of nuclear weapons and other weapons of mass destruction.[99] The United States, Russia, and China collectively hold more than 30,000 nuclear weapons. In a number of places in the world, countries with long-standing feuds have, or are suspected of having, nuclear weapons. These feuding countries include India and Pakistan, Israel and Iran, and North and South Korea. Their disputes, coupled with their potential for nuclear weapons, raise concern for the possibility of a high-intensity war.

Structural Solutions: Reversing the Cycle of Conflict— Strategies for Peace

The causes of conflict provide both lessons and solutions for peace and sustainability. A global focus on alleviating poverty and supporting social health, good governance, human rights, and environmental protection holds the potential to counter many social, economic, and political causes of conflict.

Postconflict Opportunities

The period following violent conflict offers an opportunity for the international community to become peacekeepers by helping to rebuild societies impacted by war and remove the causes of future wars.[100] Steps in this process include removing the number of arms available, negotiating treaties, providing people with livelihoods, monitoring to ensure human rights are respected after conflicts, and implementing "truth and reconciliation" commissions that review and resolve historical reasons for conflict. The removal of land mines, postwar reconstruction, and prosecution of war criminals through international courts are also effective postconflict steps.

Reprioritizing Budgets

Reducing inequality within and between nations lessens conflict at all levels. Numerous international conferences and organizations have called on nations to reprioritize their budgets, reduce military spending, and to increase funding for education and anti-poverty programs. For this to occur, industrialized nations, with their strong economies and technical expertise, could also help finance and facilitate these transitions by reprioritizing their own budgets to support sustainable development in poor countries.

International Debt Relief

Another strategy to address conflict is for major debtor (borrower) nations of the developing world to be given debt relief. This enables poorer nations to devote more resources to health care, education, and the provision of adequate food and fresh water—key elements for avoiding conflict and building peace.

Universal Primary Education and Adult Literacy

Adult literacy and universal primary education—especially for girls and women—can reduce conflict by fueling economic development, helping stabilize population growth, and increasing civic participation. From basic human rights lessons in primary grades to development of leaders and professionals in colleges and universities, the educational process leads to increased social capacity, tolerance, and a willingness to seek peaceful rather than violent solutions to conflicts.

Universal Health Care

The battle against illness and disease is another important factor in reducing conflict. The World Health Organization, in cooperation with numerous international NGOs, is making significant strides in immunization and the prevention of deadly diseases such as polio, as well as better access to fresh water.[101] A similar approach could provide hope in the fight against HIV/AIDS, malaria, and other communicable diseases that are destabilizing to societies and economies in the developing world.

Photo courtesy of the UN

Human Rights and War Crime Courts

The UN Commission of Human Rights and the International Criminal Court are essential elements in conflict prevention. Citizen activists in both developed and developing countries, human rights organizations, and court systems all contribute to creating and maintaining just societies. These entities are important in creating peaceful societies because they can help assure that citizens will have the freedom to organize and voice their opinions without fearing violence or intimidation from corrupt leaders or from groups holding different views.

Photo by Djordje Zlatanovic
WAGE PEACE

Environmental Protection and Conservation

The examples of Sudan and Rwanda show that environmental destruction was a root cause of conflict when deforestation impacted food production. Protection and conservation of the environment can contribute to a more stable society. These efforts may include reforestation, sustainable agriculture, renewable energy sources, and ecotourism. Progress in these areas can reduce conflict related to environmental destruction and its resulting resource scarcity.

Peace has to be created in order to be maintained.
—Dorothy Thompson
(twentieth-century American journalist)

Peace Building—
A New Role for Armies and Peacekeepers?

Historically, armies have been used to wage war. Many experts believe that modern-day armies can be used to wage peace. These experts point out that the military forces of the developed world already possess the skills, infrastructure, and logistical and technical abilities to build peace. In addition to the primary responsibility of national defense, military forces could be redirected and mobilized for peacekeeping, peace building, disaster relief, and environmental security. Military force could thus be a powerful tool for building sustainable peace. There is a growing consensus that peace building is an idea whose time has come. Can the army fashion a new role for itself and for a more peaceful future?

Personal Solutions: Citizenship and Investment for a Global Culture of Peace

Both personal and structural solutions can help build a more peaceful world. At the local level, emphasis on education about and awareness and respect of other cultures can help people overcome discrimination and social divisions that sometimes lead to conflict. Here are a few strategies that individuals can take to create a more peaceful world:

- Try to resolve disagreements with friends and family peaceably.
- Become skilled in mediating conflict. Many schools and community groups offer conflict mediation training.
- Support or volunteer with organizations that work to alleviate domestic violence.
- Support international peacekeeping efforts with letters to government officials and advocate for diplomacy and policies that build peace. Consider a career in international peacekeeping.

Creating a more peaceful world will require the commitment of individuals, organizations, and governments to understand the nature of conflict and to build societies and economies that promote mediation and peace rather than war. In particular, what is needed is a commitment to erase the root causes of the small-scale, mostly intrastate conflicts that plague the world in the twenty-first century.

Calmer Waters—
Nile Basin Water Sharing[102]

Photo © Stephen Eric Wood

The Nile Basin, a region that includes ten countries in central and northern Africa, supplies the fresh water for agricultural, industrial, and household uses for more than 300 million people. With the growing population of this region, the competition for scarce water resources has been significant. Nowhere is the threat of diminishing water supplies more real—or more political. Fortunately, progress in this region is also tangible.

Beginning in the late 1990s, the nations of the Nile Basin reached agreements over sustainable and equitable water use. These agreements included compromises from Sudan and Egypt, nations that had traditionally dominated decisions about and use of the water there. The spirit of decentralized water management inspired the treaty participants, who declared, "We are living in a world where **transboundary** waters have to be shared. ...[T]he Nile River is not the property of any one state."

Under the new treaty, projects have already begun to improve agricultural irrigation and water delivery systems. Secure water sources will mean secure agricultural production and drinking water, economic growth, and a greatly improved climate for peace in the Nile Basin.

The Nile Basin treaty breathes new hope into reducing hunger and poverty in the region and improving the quality of life there. These are all factors that can reduce conflict. A peaceful future depends on the equitable distribution of resources today. Many regions and resources around the world would benefit greatly from collaborative solutions such as the Nile Basin water-sharing initiatives.

Seeds of Peace—
Arab-Israeli Youth Peace Camp[103]

Treaties are negotiated by governments.
Peace is made by people.
Seeds of Peace is doing what no government can.
It is sowing the seeds of peace among children who have
grown up with the horror of war.
By teaching teenagers to develop trust and empathy for one another,
Seeds of Peace is changing the landscape of conflict.
It is enabling people blinded by hatred
to see the human face of their enemies.
It is equipping the next generation with the tools
to end the violence and become the leaders of tomorrow.
(from Seeds of Peace website)

Seeds of Peace is a nonprofit, nonpolitical organization that provides teenagers from areas of conflict around the world with the leadership skills to promote coexistence and peace. A group of forty-six Israeli, Palestinian, and Egyptian teenagers met for the first Seeds of Peace International Camp in 1993 to bring together future leaders, selected by their governments, "to reveal the human face of those they were raised to hate."

Photo by Seeds of Peace

The starting point for the Seeds of Peace program is its international camp in Maine, where teenagers from the Middle East, the Balkans, South Asia, and Cyprus all participate in a wide variety of activities designed to help young people overcome social divisions and gain respect for other cultures. Follow-up programs take place year-round in the United States and in other countries to strengthen and broaden the initial experiences from the summer camp.

In response to the attacks on America on September 11, 2001, Seeds of Peace convened the International Youth Summit on Uprooting Hatred and Terrorism, held at the United Nations in November 2001. At the conference, Seeds of Peace brought together 120 "Seeds" (delegates) from twenty-two nations to address the roots of terror, hatred, and violence. Delegates met with visiting heads of state, renowned academics, business leaders, and media personalities to develop their Charter on Uprooting Hatred and Terror, which begins:

We, Seeds of Peace, young people representing twenty-two war-ravaged
nations, hereby declare that we are tired of hatred, violence, and
terror. ... Do not dismiss this as youthful idealism. Many of us live in
places where killing and humiliation, poverty and homeless refugees
are commonplace. At Seeds of Peace, we have experienced real equity,
understanding, and joy. ... We now refuse to accept what is, when
we know what can be. ... We know it is possible to redirect human
passions toward the positive goal for creating peace.

Seeds of Peace empowers youth living in war-impacted countries to break down social divisions that are often at the root cause of conflict. In doing so, Seeds of Peace ensures that the future of peace is in the hands of friends rather than enemies.

UNIT 6
FACING THE FUTURE
ACTIVITIES

- **When the Chips Are Down**
  (models interconnections of environment, population, and conflict)

- **Deep Space 3000**
  (experiments with creating a sustainable world addressing human needs, governance, and quality of life)

To download activities visit http://www.facingthefuture.org

UNIT 6
FURTHER INFORMATION

For information on colonization and decolonization: United Nations, "The United Nations and Decoloniza-tion," 2000–2004, http://www.un.org/Depts/dpi/decolo-nization/history.htm.

For an exploration of definitions of governance: Tufts University, "Governance and Accountability," April 19, 2004, http://www.tufts.edu/~kregan02/index.htm. Also, go to http://www.un.org and use the search feature for key words, such as "governance," to view a wide range of documents and articles on this topic.

For a history of the United Nations: United Nations, "About the United Nations—History," 2004, http://www.un.org/aboutun/history.htm.

For a comprehensive treatment of economic and human development issues and strategies before the UN: United Nations Human Development Reports visit: http://hdr.undp.org.

For the changes that development can bring: Ancient Futures: Learning from Ladakh, a documentary video on the changes (starting with just a paved road) brought to Ladakh, the world's highest inhabited city in northern India. This culture, with Tibetan Buddhism and sustain-able agricultural practices, struggled with the coming of television, drugs, consumerism, and industry. Available from The International Society for Ecology & Culture at: http://www.isec.org.uk/.

For interesting new ideas and strategies concerning peace, conflict, and development: Peace, Conflict and Development—An Interdisciplinary Journal, June 2003, http://www.peacestudiesjournal.org.uk.

For information on policy making at the United Na-tions, accountability of global decisions, global citizen participation, and international peace and justice: Global Policy Forum monitors the UN, educates and mobilizes for citizen participation, and advocates on vital issues, http://www.globalpolicy.org.

UNIT 7
POSSIBLE FUTURES AND SUSTAINABLE SOLUTIONS

Be the change that you want to see in the world.

—Mahatma Gandhi (pacifist and founding father of modern India, 1869–1948)

Essential Questions

• **How can people begin to address global issues, and why should they?**

• **What personal solutions will have the greatest impact on global issues?**

• **What role can individuals have in helping to address structural solutions to global issues?**

Chapter 1. Introduction

We face a world in which unprecedented population growth, resource **scarcity** (especially water), and environmental degradation have converged in a relatively short period of time. The basic needs of growing populations in the developing world and the larger **ecological footprints** of citizens in the developed world have begun to impact the planet. Although people have been slow to react to this deepening threat, there is a growing world consensus about the major problems facing humanity, as well as previously unimaginable solutions. Compelling strategies and proven technologies for sustaining people and the planet are within our reach.

This book on global issues features an inspiring array of individuals, organizations, and **governments** that are working toward solutions for a more sustainable existence. Now it is your chance to join this worldwide effort. This unit presents some rules of the road for **sustainability** and ways to check whether a potential solution is appropriate. The unit concludes with an activity in which you will be guided through a road test for a particular global issue and region, making use of some of the **personal** and **structural solutions** explored in this book. In taking a test drive with a global issue, you may be surprised by how quickly interconnected solutions can combine to create prospects for a better future.

Youth in Action!
Gaining Global Vision through Travel and Service[1]

Global Visionaries is a nonprofit organization that provides opportunities for U.S. students with diverse racial and economic backgrounds to have a global experience through education and travel to Guatemala. There they help improve the well-being of people from another culture and learn a great deal about themselves in the process. The philosophy of this work is summed up in this quote attributed to an indigenous woman: "If you have come here to help me, you are wasting your time; but if you understand that your liberation is tied to mine—let's work together." The mission of Global Visionaries is to educate and empower youth to become active leaders and global citizens who promote social and environmental justice through community service at home and abroad.

Photo courtesy of Global Visionaries

In preparation for the trip, students study global issues starting from their local perspective. For example, they study the impact of the U.S. ecological footprint on the rest of the world. Then they travel to Guatemala, where they see firsthand the small size of a Guatemalan's ecological footprint. The students are able to see that many Guatemalans work long hours yet are able to remain socially connected, polite, and at peace with themselves. This exposure to the Guatemalan people's lifestyle of simplicity and hard work leaves students more aware of how young people in the United States often take for granted the privileges and luxuries available to people in the developed world.

Students who participate in the Global Visionaries experience report that they have become richer in global vision through their service abroad. Global Visionaries urges young people who want to make a global difference to start locally by involving students in a variety of environmental and social justice volunteer work teams that help local disenfranchised communities. To learn more about Global Visionaries visit **www.global-visionaries.org**.

Chapter 2. On the Road With Global Issues: Sustainable Solutions Close to Home

If you think your actions are too small to make a difference, you've never been in bed with a mosquito.
—Anonymous

People wishing to make a difference need not be discouraged by the vast scope of global issues. Some of the most crucial global issues can be effectively addressed by the actions of individuals, especially in the developed world. As we've seen throughout this book, many **developed countries** have large ecological impacts. Therefore, steps taken by individuals in industrialized nations to reduce their ecological footprints can result in measurable progress toward sustainability.[2]

For sustainability to become a reality, **economies** should focus on developing the best products and services with minimal social risk and low resource use.[3] For this strategy to work, individuals will have to shrink their ecological footprints by consuming fewer **nonrenewable resources** and shifting demand to more sustainable goods and services. There are some basic actions that individuals can do to help achieve a more sustainable world.

A Tanzanian woman heats water on a solar cooker.
Photo © Sarah Bones, courtesy of CARE

Rules of the Road for Personal Action

Below are some *rules of the road* for effectively addressing global issues with personal action.

- *Learn more about global issues and basic scientific concepts.* Your decision-making and progress with **personal solutions** will be enhanced according to your level of knowledge about global issues. Read newspapers, especially the international pages and foreign news websites. Visit websites of governments, **nongovernmental organizations**, and religions and cultural groups that address global issues. Inform yourself with **media** that provide a variety of perspectives and opposing viewpoints. Check out the list of references at the end of each unit in this book for websites, books, and videos to help increase your global **literacy**. In addition to studying global issues, it is equally important to educate yourself in the basic concepts of disciplines such as physics, chemistry, economics, geography, and ecology.

- *Be a wise and critical consumer of goods and services.* Transportation and food production are the main contributors to large ecological footprints. Individuals can reduce transportation and energy impacts. Learn about organic foods, fair trade products, and industries and companies that have sustainable practices, such as sustainable **fisheries** or logging companies. Buy recycled and recyclable products, taking into consideration **lifecycle design** factors. Be aware of which industries and brands have unhealthy and unfair work environments, such as **sweatshop** labor.

- *Build your connections with the world.* The world is only more "interconnected" for you if you make it that way by taking advantage of opportunities to know the world better. Learn a foreign language. Get involved with **immigrant** and ethnic communities in your own city or region to build your cultural literacy and appreciation for diversity. Travel abroad as a student, volunteer, or visitor. Help your family to host an exchange student.

- *Your voice counts, so make it heard.* Active citizenship is your right in a **democracy** and a privilege that not all people in the world enjoy. Share your ideas in meetings, write letters and E-mails to elected officials and businesses, join organizations, and volunteer your time and money for causes you care about. Communicate your views to newspapers and magazines. Contact elected officials about your ideas, concerns, and expectations. Last but not least, when you are old enough, vote!

What other rules of the road for being an active citizen in a global world can you think of?

Chapter 3. Going Global: Sustainable Structural Solutions

When you change the way you look at things, the things you look at change.

—Max Planck (German Nobel Laureate in physics, 1918)

People in the developed world can take immediate steps toward a more sustainable future by reducing their ecological footprint and pursuing the strategies outlined in the previous chapter. As they do so, they may become more motivated to participate in long-term structural solutions to global issues.

Global Issues and Global Goals

Faced with the immensity of global issues, some people in the developed world tend to dismiss global problems as either insurmountable or simply a factor of geographical fate. They believe that some areas in the world just have it rough or that geography defines destiny. This thinking promotes the acceptance that some people are lucky enough to be born in a wealthier country that offers opportunity, while others are born into poverty. They believe that poverty is simply a fact of life on Earth.

Many people believe that geography is *not* destiny. Development policy, **governance**, and appropriate technology can be tailored to meet regional challenges such as providing food, water, energy, health, education, and **human rights**. For example, by increasing the productivity of poor farmers and transitioning from extraction-based economies to mixed economies that promote sustainable manufacturing, families can devote more income to education. Combined with programs that promote **primary health care**, nutrition, universal primary education (especially targeting girls and women), and literacy, the cycle of poverty, hunger, and poor health can be broken.[4]

A young Kosovar man with two cows.
Photo © 2002 Alan Gignoux, courtesy of CARE

So how does a person "go global" in the pursuit of sustainable solutions? How can an individual prioritize global issues? Setting goals is a useful first step, and important work has already been undertaken toward defining goals for global issues. At the turn of the twenty-first century, the United Nations prioritized steps toward attaining a sustainable future by identifying eight Millennium Development Goals (MDGs) for humankind. All 191 member states of the UN (including the United States) pledged to meet these goals by the year 2015:

United Nations Millennium Development Goals
(to be met by 2015)[5]

1. Eradicate Extreme Hunger and Poverty
- Reduce by half the proportion of people who suffer from hunger and who live on less than $1 a day.

2. Achieve Universal Primary Education
- Ensure that all boys and girls complete a full course of primary schooling.

3. Promote Gender Equality and Promote Women
- Eliminate gender disparity in primary and secondary education, preferably by 2005 and at all levels by 2015.

4. Reduce Child Mortality
- Reduce by two-thirds the mortality rate among children under five years old.

5. Improve Maternal Health
- Reduce by three-quarters the maternal mortality rate.

6. Combat HIV/AIDS, Malaria, and Other Diseases
- Halt, and begin to reverse, the spread of HIV/AIDS and the incidence of malaria and other major diseases.

7. Ensure Environmental Sustainability
- Integrate the principles of sustainable development into country policies and programs; reverse loss of environmental resources.
- Reduce by half the proportion of people without sustainable access to potable water.
- Achieve significant improvement in the lives of at least 100 million slum dwellers by 2020.

8. Develop a Global Partnership for Development
- Develop an open trading and financial system that is rule-based, predictable, and nondiscriminatory, including a commitment to good governance, development, and poverty reduction.
- Address the least developed countries' special needs. This includes tariff- and quota-free access to their exports, enhanced debt relief, debt cancellation, and more generous development assistance for countries committed to poverty reduction.
- Address the special needs of landlocked and small-island developing nations.
- Deal comprehensively with developing countries' debt problems through national and international measures to make debt sustainable in the long term.
- In cooperation with developing countries, create decent and productive work for youth.
- In cooperation with pharmaceutical companies, provide access to affordable, essential drugs in developing countries.
- In cooperation with the private sector, make available the benefits of leapfrog technologies, especially information and communications technologies.

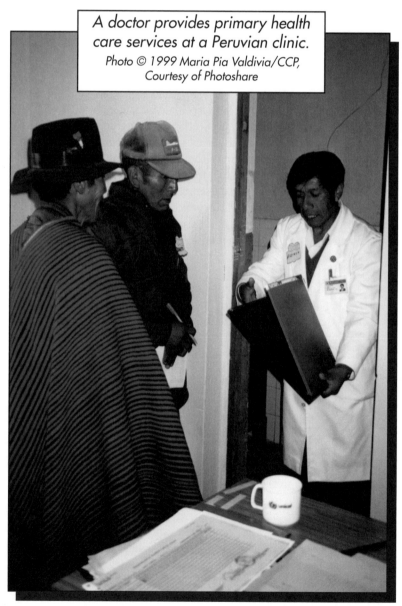

A doctor provides primary health care services at a Peruvian clinic.
Photo © 1999 Maria Pia Valdivia/CCP, Courtesy of Photoshare

Individuals can play an important role in helping to meet these global goals by understanding the issues, connections, underlying causes, and **leverage points**.

Leverage Points for Systems Thinking

By now, you may have decided that you want to start addressing some of the structural solutions to global problems. As described in Unit 1, **systems thinking** offers insight and tools for dealing with the complexity of global issues.

The late systems thinker Donnella Meadows proposed specific leverage points for change. Leverage points are optimal places to intervene in a complex system (such as a business, a city, a state, or an **ecosystem**), where small shifts can produce significant results.[6] In the same way that using a lever makes it easier to move a large and heavy object, leverage points can make it easier to change a situation with just a little effort. Although global issues by their nature are complex and challenging and require the cooperation of many parts of society, from scientists to governments to community groups to individuals, taking advantage of these leverage points when working on global issues can help achieve greater structural change.[7]

Photo by Elizabeth Benedict Huttman

Let's take the example of the Daillos, a poor family living in Senegal, Africa, and apply leverage points to their situation. The Daillos' main source of food and livelihood comes from a small plot of land on which they grow corn and peanuts. Mr. and Mrs. Daillo have three boys (ages five, twelve, and seventeen) and two girls (ages one and eight). The father and the oldest son spend most of their days in a distant city looking for work. The younger boys attend school in the nearby village for about three hours a day. This leaves the mother, Assitou, and her eight-year-old daughter with the bulk of the farming and household work. In the last few years, the Daillos' plot of land has been much less productive because of poor soil quality and a lack of water. This has left the family in a serious state of **malnutrition** and poor health. Assitou would like to limit the size of her family, but she doesn't have the money to buy contraceptives and there is no health-care clinic in their village.

The Diallo family is a small system that is part of a larger system of poverty in the country of Senegal. How and where could one intervene in this system of poverty and scarcity? Using the steps below, let's see how a systems thinking approach might guide someone in deciding how to help.

12 Leverage Points for Systems Thinking

1. **Know how the system behaves.** One of the first systems thinking steps is to take the time to simply understand how the Diallo family system functions. It would probably be a mistake to walk in and make big changes in this family's situation without understanding the complexities and nuances of their family. A systems approach would look at how each part of the family system affects each other part. For example, what happens to the family when the boys go to school? What happens when Assitou has another child?

2. **Understand what's working well.** It's important to pay attention to the value of what is already happening in the system. The Diallos do have a plot of land on which they are able to grow some food, even if it's not enough to sustain their growing family. Also, in spite of their lack of money and food, the boys spend time every day playing soccer, and the family spends regular evenings listening to their radio and playing games. Whatever new solution might help this family survive, it would be important not to disturb the good things that are happening in their lives.

3. **Check your assumptions.** We cannot assume that the Diallos do not already know what they need to survive and thrive or that there is only one answer to the Diallo family's poverty. There may be a multitude of possible solutions, some that haven't even been thought of yet. Check what other people and organizations are doing to help alleviate poverty. Instead of becoming fixated on one possible explanation or hypothesis, collect as many ideas as possible and think critically about each one.

4. **Be a learner**. What else can be learned about this family and their community, village, or country that might help you figure out what to do? Systems are dynamic and changing, so it is important to continue to learn even after you have begun to address the issue.

5. **Present clear and direct information.**
For the Diallo family, it would be important for an organization working on the issue of poverty in Senegal to understand and present information on why the water source is going dry and the soil is being depleted. The Diallos, along with other people in their village, have noticed in recent years that there has been less rainfall in their region. That is important information because it could indicate a root cause of the low levels of water and depleted soil. Often what goes wrong in a system goes wrong because of faulty or missing information. It's important to present clear and direct information so people can make informed decisions.

6. **Locate responsibility in the system**.
Try to find out where responsibilities are for the problems or flaws in this family's system of poverty. The Diallos are part of a larger system of poverty in which families who want to limit their growth cannot because they do not have access to **reproductive health care**. Some questions then might be, "Why is reproductive health care not available, and how could it be made available?"

7. **Make feedback policies for feedback systems**. If a main cause of the low productivity of the Diallos' plot of land is insufficient water, a systems thinking approach might be to monitor the well throughout the year to track when the water levels are dropping. People in the village could then respond to these lower levels before the wells run completely dry.

8. **Pay attention to what is important, not just what is quantifiable.** It's important to consider not only the numbers and statistics associated with the Diallo family but also those factors that are not quantifiable but are also important. These could be characteristics such as the time that the family spends together, the music and art that people in the village create, and the traditions and ceremonies passed down from generation to generation. If systems are not designed to produce these unquantifiable but valuable qualities, such benefits may cease to exist.

9. **Consider the whole system.** The long-term health of the Diallo family depends on the health of each member of the family as well as on the health of the soil and water. A solution should address the whole system, not just a part.

10. **Expand time frames**. The time frame of a solution to address this family's situation should extend beyond their generation. It should consider the future generations that may have to live off the same plot of land and use the same source of water. How can a system be designed that takes into account the future effects?

11. **Understand systems complexity.**
The Diallo family system, like all systems, is complex. By their very nature, systems are complex. Often, the solutions to systems' problems also require a degree of complexity.

12. **Look for the good.** Last, it is important to focus on good things that are happening in the world. Even though the Diallos are a family in Senegal living a hard life, there are numerous individuals and organizations committed to alleviating poverty in the Diallos' country of Senegal and around the world. Examples of negative human behavior are often magnified by the media. More numerous examples of human goodness are barely noticed, so notice and celebrate them. Turn off network television newscasts that dwell on violence and destruction, and instead read poetry and literature of hope, tell funny stories with friends, and listen to music. Surf the web for stories of success and inspiration.

There is much to be hopeful about in the world today. Leverage points such as these can turn hopes into realities. There are governments, organizations, and individuals working to create a sustainable world so that today's citizens and future generations can make choices and enjoy a good **quality of life**. You are also a part of creating a sustainable world. What choices will you make? What actions will you take?

A group of Kenyan boys with a home-made soccer ball.

Photo © Jenny Matthews, courtesy of CARE

The Earth Charter —From Vision to Principles and Practice

Español | Français

Values and Principles for a Sustainable Future

The Earth Charter is a close relative of the Universal Declaration of Human Rights, but with a broader focus on sustainability and governance in addition to human rights. The Earth Charter was officially launched by the United Nations in 2000 to establish a sound ethical foundation for the emerging global society and to help build a sustainable world based on respect for nature, universal human rights, economic **justice**, and a culture of peace.[8]

The Earth Charter begins with this statement, followed by sixteen specific principles under four areas:

We stand at a critical moment in Earth's history, a time when humanity must choose its future. As the world becomes increasingly interdependent and fragile, the future at once holds great peril and great promise.
To move forward we must recognize that in the midst of a magnificent diversity of cultures and life forms we are one human family and one Earth community with a common destiny.

I. Respect and Care for the Community of Life
1. Respect Earth and life in all its diversity.
2. Care for the community of life with understanding, compassion, and love.
3. Build democratic societies that are just, participatory, sustainable, and peaceful.
4. Secure Earth's bounty and beauty for present and future generations.

II. Ecological Integrity
5. Protect and restore the integrity of Earth's ecological systems, with special concern for biological diversity and the natural processes that sustain life.
6. Prevent harm as the best method of environmental protection, and when knowledge is limited, apply a precautionary approach.
7. Adopt patterns of production, consumption, and reproduction that safeguard Earth's regenerative capacities, human rights, and community well-being.
8. Advance the study of ecological sustainability and promote the open exchange and wide application of the knowledge acquired.

III. Social and Economic Justice
9. Eradicate poverty as an ethical, social, and environmental imperative.
10. Ensure that economic activities and institutions at all levels promote human development in an equitable and sustainable manner.
11. Affirm gender equality and equity as prerequisites to sustainable development, and ensure universal access to education, health care, and economic opportunity.
12. Uphold the right of all people, without discrimination, to a natural and social environment supportive of human dignity, bodily health, and spiritual well-being, with special attention to the rights of indigenous peoples and minorities.

IV. Democracy, Nonviolence, and Peace
13. Strengthen democratic institutions at all levels, and provide transparency and accountability in governance, inclusive participation in decision making, and access to justice.
14. Integrate into formal education and lifelong learning the knowledge, values, and skills needed for a sustainable way of life.
15. Treat all living beings with respect and consideration.
16. Promote a culture of tolerance, nonviolence, and peace.

The Earth Charter presents an impressive vision of sustainability that can inspire nations, **civic organizations** and the **private sector** to create a better—and lasting—world.

**GLOBAL STUDIES
CURRICULUM CONNECTION:
My Footprint and
My World—Take a Test
Drive in Global Action**

Here is a chance to apply what you have learned about global issues and sustainable solutions. In this activity you will:

- *Compare* your own ecological footprint to that of a person in a developing country and *analyze* some component parts of your ecological footprint, such as water use and carbon emissions.
- *Identify* and *understand* factors limiting quality of life in a developing nation through **demographic** and geographic information.
- *Evaluate* alternatives for effective governance around a particular global issue in a developing country.
- *Propose* a menu of sustainable personal and structural solutions for a particular global issue in a developing country.
- *Reflect* on your use of systems thinking during this global issues exercise.

Time and Resources for Completing Activity

Working either individually or with a partner, you can complete the activity informally on your own time or in two or three one-hour classroom sessions. You will need Internet access at school and/or at home.

Before Getting Started

Ideally, you have read all or most of this book along with supplemental activities and readings. Before getting started, read though all the steps of the activity below and make sure that you recall and understand the concepts covered in this book.

Let's Get Global!

1.   Review the UN Millennium Development Goals (MDGs) in this unit. Choose one issue or MDG that interests you, or pick a specific issue treated elsewhere in this book, such as **refugees** or the state of the oceans or forests.

2.   Choose a developing nation in Central or South America, Africa, or Asia that you want to learn more about.

3.   Calculate your ecological footprint using the on-line footprint calculator at Redefining Progress's website: www.redefiningprogress.org.

4.   Compare the average size of your country's footprint to that of your chosen developing country in the "Footprints of Nations" section of Redefining Progress's website www.redefiningprogress.org (Table 2 on page 12 of "Footprint of Nations"). Study the pie charts in Illustrations 5–8 to compare the global "Footprint Sources" to richer and poorer nations' footprint sources.

A mother and daughter from Bangladesh.
Photo © 2000 Billy Howard, courtesy of CARE

5.   Look up the average home water use for Americans on the "Residential Water Use Summary" page http://www.aquacraft. com/Publications/resident.htm of the American Water Works Association Research Foundation. Then go to the International Red Cross Water and Sanitation Centre website http://www.irc.nl/. Enter your developing country in the "Search" window to view articles on its water issues.

6.   Calculate your personal greenhouse gas and carbon dioxide emissions with the Environmental Protection Agency's on-line calculators:

- greenhouse gas calculator: http://yosemite.epa.gov/ oar/globalwarming.nsf/content/ResourceCenterToolsGH-GCalculator.html)
- carbon dioxide emission calculator: http://globalwarm-ing.enviroweb.org/games/yourscore/yourscore2.html

7.   Get to know and understand your developing country:

- Go to National Geographic's MapMachine website: http:// plasma.nationalgeographic.com/mapmachine/. Do a "Quick Map Search" from this homepage to get a basic map of your country. Then, keeping your chosen topic or goal in mind, find one map each from the "Conservation and Ecology" and "Educators and Students" links.
- Go to the CIA World Factbook website: http://www.odci. gov/cia/publications/factbook/index.html. Select your

developing country's name from the pull-down window, "Select a Country." What important background information can you locate for your particular issue or goal?

• Read the Earth Charter feature in this unit. Go to the Human Rights Watch website http://www.hrw.org/ and check the "Info by Country" link. Using the standards in the Earth Charter, evaluate your chosen country's record on human rights.

• Go to the U.S. Committee for Refugees website http://www.refugees.org/ and check the "Search by Country" link. How many refugees does your country produce or host? Why?

• Go to the Population Reference Bureau website: http://www.prb.org/. From the "Data Finder" link on the homepage, select your developing country and then scroll through the "variable" options. Study a few different variables that relate to your chosen topic or goal. Compare this data with similar variables for your own country.

• Go to the United Nations website: http://www.un.org/english/. Click on the "Search" link and enter the name of your developing country. Scan the list of articles, and skim one article that addresses your particular topic/goal.

8. Using the "Internet User Guidelines" in Unit 1 of this book, do a key word search to identify the mission and program for one of each of these participants in governance (for your chosen country):
  • government or intergovernmental agency
  • business or business association
  • nongovernmental (nonprofit) organization

Write a three-paragraph summary, one paragraph for the mission and program offered by each player in governance listed above. Choose one of the participants, and in a fourth paragraph evaluate how successfully it meets the standards of *involvement, responsiveness,* and *decentralization.*

9. Write a Sustainability Statement that summarizes what you think can be done to build a sustainable future for your chosen topic and region. Include:
  • *Personal Change*: What could you do to contribute to a positive future on this topic? *Structural Change*: What could each of the participants in governance (the state, civic organizations, and private/business sector) do to implement your solution?
  • *Sustainability*: Do these solutions aim at the deeper causes of problems and not just symptoms? How will these actions build sustainability and create a positive future?

10. Write a reflective journal entry on your experience during this test drive of a global issue. Consider the Twelve Leverage Points for Systems Thinking to guide your own research, thinking, and writing process during this exercise.

UNIT 7
FACING THE FUTURE ACTIVITIES

• **Metaphors for the Future**
  (use different metaphors to explore how our worldviews influence and shape our actions)

• **Creating Our Future**
  (visualize and create a plan of action using an action planning tool)

• **Bears in the Air**
  (redesign a system and identify assumptions)

To download activities visit **http://www.facingthefuture.org**

UNIT 7
FURTHER INFORMATION

For information and resources for taking action on global issues, go to the website for Facing the Future: People and the Planet (www.http://facingthefuture.org). The link for "Creative Action" offers "Fast Facts and Quick Action," "Service Learning Projects," "Games and Quizzes," and more.

The National Service-Learning Clearing House offers extensive, nationwide resources on service learning projects. From the homepage, http://www.servicelearning.org/, go to the "K–12" link and search for the type of service projects that interest you (e.g., "environment" or "hunger").

Explore two diametrically opposed perspectives on global issues. Visit the website of the "Skeptical Environmentalist" Bjørn Lomborg (http://www.lomborg.com/), where you can learn more about his thesis that the state of the environment is actually improving and that economic growth is the key to further progress. For a position that is critical of the globalized economy and transnational corporations, read How to Succeed at Globalization (New York: Metropolitan Books, 2002), with leftist politics and cartoons, by El Fisgón, a well-known Mexican activist and cartoonist.

For a magazine that profiles stories of hope and human innovation across global issues: Yes—A Journal of Positive Futures, Positive Futures Network: http://www.yesmagazine.org.

Mindwalk (Paramount Home Video) is a movie by Bernt Capra. Mindwalk explores the scientific, social, and ecological questions about the nature of perception.

GLOSSARY

acid rain—precipitation containing harmful amounts of sulfuric, nitric, and other acids, which arise from emissions released during the burning of fossil fuels. Acid rain is widely considered responsible for damaging forests, crops, and human-made structures and for killing aquatic life.

AIDS (Acquired Immunodeficiency Syndrome)—a disease caused by the Human Immunodeficiency Virus (HIV) in which the immune system is weakened and therefore less able to fight infections and diseases; AIDS is transmitted through contaminated body fluids, especially via sexual contact or contaminated needles.

apartheid—an official policy (ended in 1991) of racial segregation and white supremacy enforced by the South African government. *Apartheid* means "apartness," separation of the people according to their race. In South Africa, it was used to limit the governing power and places of residence of nonwhite people.

aquaculture—the farming of plants and animals that live in water, such as fish, shellfish, and algae.

aquifer—a naturally occurring underground geologic formation that stores a significant amount of fresh water.

arable land—land fit to be cultivated or farmed productively.

asylum—protection and immunity from extradition granted by a government to a political refugee from another country.

BCE (Before Common Era)—a nonreligious term used in place of BC (before Christ) to describe the period of time before the year 1.

biodiesel—a clean-burning fuel for diesel engines that can be made from renewable resources such as vegetable oil, animal fat, and even used cooking oil, an abundant waste product.

biodiversity—the variety of life in all its forms, levels, and combinations, including ecosystem diversity, species diversity, and genetic diversity.

biological warfare—the intentional use of viruses, bacteria, other microorganisms, or toxins derived from living organisms to cause death or disease in humans, animals, or plants.

biomass fuel—a renewable fuel derived from a living organism or the byproduct of a living organism. Biomass fuels include wood, animal dung, methane gas, and grain alcohol.

carbon dioxide—a colorless, odorless, non-combustible gas with one carbon and two oxygen atoms (CO_2) present in the atmosphere. Carbon dioxide is produced when any substance containing carbon is burned. It is also a product of breathing and fermentation. It is the principal greenhouse gas. Carbon dioxide is removed from the atmosphere through ocean absorption and photosynthesis.

carbon sink—a natural environment that absorbs and stores more carbon dioxide from the atmosphere than it releases.

carrying capacity—the maximum population that an environment can support.

cash crops—crops grown mainly for sale and usually for export rather than for feeding local populations.

CE (Common Era)—a nonreligious term used in place of AD (*Anno Domini*, Latin for "in the year of the Lord") to describe the period of time after the year 1.

chemical weapons—chemical substances that can be delivered using munitions and dispersal devices to cause death or severe harm to people, animals, or plants.

civic engagement—individual or community participation in governance through influencing and sharing government responsibilities, such as policy making, resource allocation, and access to public goods and services.

civic organizations—community groups and nongovernmental organizations such as the Sierra Club, Amnesty International, and the Boy Scouts.

clear-cut logging—the process of cutting all trees from an area with little regard for the long-term health of the forest or sustainability of the area.

colonization—the establishment of a population in a place formerly unoccupied by that group.

commodity—an article of trade or commerce, especially an agricultural or mining product that can be processed and resold.

commons—those resources, such as land for grazing livestock, that all members of a community may use without payment.

community or **ecological biodiversity**—the variety of habitats and ecosystems that exist on Earth.

consumption—the process of using natural resources, materials, or finished products to satisfy human wants or needs.

conventional weapons—weapons customarily used in warfare, such as guns, bombs, and missiles; in contrast to nonconventional weapons such as nuclear, biological, and chemical weapons.

corporate social responsibility (CSR)—the decision-making and implementation process that guides all company activities in its protection and promotion of labor standards, international human rights, and environmental standards and in its compliance with legal requirements within its operations and in its relations to the societies and communities where it operates.

cradle-to-cradle design—a strategy for developing ecologically intelligent products that generate economic, social, and environmental benefits at every phase of their use, while removing disposal (products' "graves") from their lifecycle.

cradle-to-grave design—a strategy for developing products that tries to anticipate consequences of their ecological footprints through their entire "lives"—from the extraction of raw materials to their disposal and from energy used in their production and operation to their transportation to market.

critical thinking—the ability to acquire information, analyze and evaluate it, and reach a conclusion or answer by using logic and reasoning skills.

culture—the totality of socially transmitted behavior patterns, arts, beliefs, institutions, and all other products of human work and thought.

decentralized state—a government whose power or function is dispersed from a central to local authorities.

democracy—a form of government in which ordinary citizens take part in governing, in contrast with a monarchy (rule by kings) or oligarchy (rule by the wealthy or powerful).

demographics—the characteristics of a human population (for example, age, gender, religion, ethnic background, or education level).

desertification—the transformation of arable or habitable land to desert, as by a change in climate or destructive land use.

developed countries—the United Nations' term for those countries with a high average per-person income. Developed countries include Japan, Canada, the United States, Australia, New Zealand, and countries in Western Europe. *See also* the sidebar "What's in a Name?" in Unit 1 for a detailed discussion of this and other terms used to describe different countries.

developing countries—the United Nations' term for those countries with a low average per-person income. Developing countries include all countries except those in the former Soviet Union and Eastern Europe and those countries that are considered developed. *See also* the sidebar "What's in a Name?" in Unit 1 for a detailed discussion of this and other terms used to describe different countries.

ecological footprint—the area of the Earth's productive surface that it takes to produce the goods and services necessary to support a particular lifestyle.

ecology—the science that studies the distribution and abundance of living organisms, their habitats, and the interactions between organisms and their environment.

economic development—the process of raising the level of prosperity and material living in a society through increasing per capita income, reducing poverty, and enhancing individual economic opportunities.

economy—originally, the "management of a household." More commonly today, the system of production, distribution, and consumption of goods and services.

ecosystem—a community of organisms (plant, animal, and other living organisms) together with their environment, functioning as a unit.

emigrant—a person who leaves one country to settle in another.

environmental justice—the equitable treatment of all people, regardless of race, income, culture, or social class, with respect to the development, implementation, and enforcement of environmental laws, regulations, and policies.

environmental scarcity—insufficiency of amount or supply of a natural resource. *See also* structural scarcity.

equality—a condition in which certain different people have the same social status and rights according to a particular social situation or standard.

equity—the state, quality, or ideal of being just, impartial, and fair.

ethnic cleansing—the systematic elimination of an ethnic group or groups from a region or society, as by deportation, forced emigration, or genocide.

exponential growth—a constant rate of growth applied to a continuously growing base over a period of time.

famine—a severe shortage of food (as through crop failure) resulting in violent hunger, starvation, and death.

fertility or **birth rate**—the ratio of live births in an area to the population of that area; expressed per 1,000 population per year.

fishery—an organized fishing effort centered on either a particular marine region or a particular species or type of fish or aquatic animal.

fish polyculture—the production of two or more fish species within a particular aquaculture environment.

fossil fuel—a fuel, such as coal, oil, and natural gas, produced by the decomposition of prehistoric plants and animals.

free market—an economic system that operates according to the principle of supply and demand without government involvement.

fuel cell—a device that converts chemical energy into electricity and hot water through an electrochemical process rather than through the combustion of a fuel source.

genetic biodiversity—the range of genetic variation within a single species, such as in size, coloration, and behavior, evolved to allow the species to survive in its own particular ecosystem.

genetically modified (GM) foods—foods whose genetic makeup is altered by combining their genes with genes from other organisms.

genetically modified organisms (GMOs)—animals, plants, or bacteria whose genetic makeup is altered by combining their genes with genes from other organisms.

genocide—the systematic and deliberate extermination of an entire national, racial, political, or ethnic group.

genuine progress indicator (GPI)—a measurement of quality of life that combines economic measures with indicators of social well-being.

globalization—(1) The closer integration of the countries of the world, especially the increased level of trade and movements of capital. (2) The expansion of global linkages and the organization of social life on a global scale.

global warming—the phenomenon of a rise in the temperature of the Earth's climate, which occurs as greenhouse gases such as carbon dioxide build up in the atmosphere and trap heat radiated from the sun.

governance—the traditions, institutions, and processes that determine how power is exercised, how citizens are given a voice, and how decisions are made on issues of public concern; it is not the sole domain of government but transcends government to encompass the business sector and civil society.

government—the official governing organization that has the power to make and enforce laws for a certain territory.

greenhouse gases—Specific gases and chemicals, including carbon dioxide, that accumulate in the atmosphere and lead to global warming.

green power—electricity generated from renewable sources such as solar energy, wind power, geothermal power, biomass, and small hydroelectric sources.

Green Revolution—agricultural practices and technologies started in the 1950s to increase food production through the use of machines, fertilizer, pesticides, irrigation, and the growth of hybrid varieties of rice, wheat, and corn.

gross domestic product (GDP)—the total value of goods and services produced by and within a country.

habitat—the environment in which an organism or biological population lives or grows.

HIV (Human Immunodeficiency Virus)—a retrovirus that causes Acquired Immunodeficiency Syndrome (AIDS) by infecting helper T cells of the immune system.

human development—the creation of an environment in which people can develop their full potential and lead productive lives in accord with their needs and interests; the most basic objectives for human development are to promote long and healthy lives, knowledge, access to the resources needed for a decent standard of living, and participation in the life of the community.

human rights—the basic rights and freedoms to which all humans are entitled, often held to include the right to life and liberty, freedom of thought and expression, and equality before the law.

hybrid vehicle—a motorized vehicle such as an automobile that is propelled by two or more sources of power, usually a battery and an internal combustion engine.

hydrologic cycle—the cycle of evaporation and condensation that controls the distribution of the Earth's water as it evaporates from bodies of water, condenses, precipitates, and returns to those bodies of water.

immigrants—people who move into one country from another for political, economic, or social reasons.

immigration—movement of people into a country from another country.

indigenous people—populations that are native to a particular country or area.

infrastructure—the basic facilities, services, and installations needed for the functioning of a community or society, such as transportation and communications systems, water and power lines, and public institutions including schools, post offices, and prisons.

internally displaced persons—people who are forced to leave their homes because of conflict, food scarcity, or other crisis but who remain within their country.

interstate war—a state of open, armed, and often prolonged combat between the regular military forces of two or more state members of the international system.

intrastate or **civil war**—a state of sustained armed combat between factions or regions within the same country.

justice—the concept involving the fair and moral treatment of all persons, especially in law.

Kyoto Protocol—an international agreement reached in 1997 in Kyoto, Japan, that extends the commitments of the United Nations Framework Convention on Climate Change. In particular, it sets targets for future carbon dioxide emissions by developed countries.

leapfrog technology—sustainable technology designed in developed countries and transferred to developing nations, allowing them to raise their standards of living while "jumping over" unsustainable technology previously used by developed countries.

legislature—an officially elected or otherwise selected body of people vested with the responsibility and power to make laws for a political unit, such as a state or nation.

leverage points—places within a complex system (e.g., a corporation, an economy, a living body, a city, or an ecosystem) where a small change in one part can produce big changes in the whole system.

lifecycle design—strategies for developing products that take into consideration the environmental effects of the entire cycle of their manufacture, use, and disposal.

literacy—the ability to read and write.

malnutrition—a state of poor nutrition; can result from insufficient, excessive, or unbalanced diet or from inability to absorb foods.

mass media—those means of communication, especially newspapers, popular magazines, Internet, radio, and television, that reach and influence large numbers of people.

media—means of communication.

microcredit or **microlending**—the business or policy of making small loans to poor people for entrepreneurial (business) projects.

migrant—a person who moves from one region to another by chance, instinct, or plan.

migration—movement of people or animals.

mortality or **death rate**—the ratio of deaths in an area to the population of that area; expressed per 1,000 per year.

multiple perspectives—different ways of looking at the same event based on different knowledge and experiences.

nongovernmental organization (NGO)—any organization that is neither part of government or business, generally referring to those involved in environmental or social issues, whether they have a domestic or international focus.

nonpoint source pollution—pollution whose source is not specific in location; generally occurs when rainfall, snowmelt, or irrigation runs over land or through the ground, picks up pollutants, and deposits them into rivers, lakes, and coastal waters or introduces them into ground water.

nonprofit organization—an organization whose primary objective is something other than returning a profit to its owners, such as for educational or charitable reasons.

nonrenewable resource—a resource, such as coal or oil, that cannot be replaced as it is used.

nutrient—any substance taken in by organisms that produces growth.

outsourcing—paying another company to provide services that a company might otherwise have employed its own staff to perform, in order to cut costs.

ozone holes—gaps in the ozone layer caused by emissions from paints, solvents, pesticides, gasoline, and other petroleum-based chemicals that vaporize directly into the atmosphere; ozone holes can allow harmful sun rays to reach the Earth's surface.

ozone layer—a layer in the upper atmosphere (at approximately 20 miles) that contains a concentration of ozone sufficient to block most ultraviolet radiation from the sun.

pandemic—a widespread disease outbreak affecting the population of an extensive area of the world.

pathogen—a disease-causing organism such as a bacterium or virus.

peace building—the process of restoring normal relations between people after a dispute or conflict.

personal solution—a way in which an individual can act to alleviate a problem.

plague—a highly infectious, usually fatal, epidemic disease.

political injustice—the violation of individual liberties, including the denial of voting rights or due process, infringements on rights to freedom of speech or religion, and inadequate protection from cruel and unusual punishment.

potable water—water that is safe to drink.

primary health care—the principal vehicle for the delivery of health care at the most local level of a country's health system; services, including family planning, clean water supply, sanitation, immunization, and nutrition education, are designed to be affordable for both the poor people who receive the services and the governments that provide them.

private sector—the part of the economy consisting of business, companies, and professionals who trade products and services for income and profit.

quality of life—the level of well-being and physical conditions in which people live.

quality-of-life indicators—comprehensive statistics of national well-being that go beyond traditional economic indicators to include social and environmental factors.

refugees—people who have fled their country because they have a well-founded fear of persecution for reasons of race, religion, nationality, membership in a particular social group, or political opinion.

renewable resource—a resource, such as wind, trees, or fish, that can be replaced as it is consumed.

representative government—a form of government in which the citizens delegate authority to elected representatives.

reproductive health care—health-care services that include family planning, contraception, fertility treatment, abortion, and prevention and treatment of sexually transmitted diseases and other sexual afflictions.

S

sanitation—methods for solving basic public health problems, such as drainage, water and sewage treatment, and waste removal.

scarcity—insufficiency of amount or supply; shortage.

selective harvesting—the process of gathering a renewable resource, such as logging a forest or fishing for salmon, in which only a portion of the resource is harvested each year.

self-sufficiency—the ability to provide for oneself without the help of others; independence.

shareholder or **stockholder**—owner of one or more shares of stock in a company.

smog—heavy air pollution that can persist for an extended period of time, especially in warmer climates in geologic basins surrounded by hills or mountains and densely populated cities. (Generated from the words "smoke" and "fog.")

species biodiversity—the variety of living creatures found within a habitat or region.

stakeholder—any party that has an interest in an organization. Stakeholders of a company include stockholders, bondholders, customers, suppliers, employees, and so forth.

structural poverty—a situation in which the poor are unable to accumulate the resources required to move out of poverty.

structural scarcity—an unequal social distribution of resources; an imbalance in the distribution of wealth and power.

structural solution—a way in which a component of a system can be changed in order to alleviate a problem.

subsidy—direct or indirect payment from government to businesses, citizens, or institutions to encourage people do something the government believes is desirable.

subsistence—the means of obtaining food, water, and other items necessary for basic existence.

sustainability—meeting current needs without limiting the ability of future generations to meet their needs.

sustainable development—practices in agriculture, economic development, health care, and education that lead to progress and meet the needs and desires of the current generation without decreasing the ability of future generations to meet their needs.

sustainable yield—the highest rate at which a renewable resource, such as trees or fish, can be harvested without reducing its available supply locally, regionally, or globally.

sweatshop—a shop or factory in which employees work long hours at low wages under poor conditions.

systems thinking—the ability to see the structures that underlie complex situations and to think and act based on an understanding of how a system functions.

T

terrestrial—living or growing on land; not aquatic.

terrorism—the calculated use of violence (or threat of violence) against civilians in order to attain goals that are political, religious, or ideological in nature; this is done through intimindation or instilling fear.

thermohaline circulation—the flow of water in the world's oceans induced by differences in temperature (*thermo-*) and salinity (*haline*).

tragedy of the commons—the concept of the overuse of a common resource in a society to the point where the resource is damaged or destroyed.

transnational or **transboundary**—involving several nations without regard for national boundaries.

transparency—the full, accurate, and timely disclosure of information.

U, W

urbanization—he expansion of cities into rural regions because of population growth.

worldview—a set of assumptions, perspectives, and beliefs held by individuals, cultures, and societies through which we make sense of our lives and our world.

UNIT 1 ENDNOTES

1 Environmental Protection Agency, "Global Warming," 2002, http://yosemite.epa.gov/oar/global-warming.nsf/content/index.html.

2 Total fertility rate estimates for Darfur 5.9 (Sudan DHS 1989/1990); Northern/Southern Darfur, 7.2; and Western Darfur, 6.5 (Safe Motherhood Survey, 1999).

3 William Upski Wimsatt, "Young, Righteous—and Voting," YES! magazine, (fall 2003), pp. 17–20.

4 "The Message: Rhythmic Forward Movement of Hip-Hop Jolts Young Voters into Political Action," Marc Ramirez, Seattle Times, July 18, 2004.

5 United Nations Statistics Division's definition of developed and developing countries, http://millenniumindicators.un.org/unsd/mi/mi_dict_xrxx.asp?def_code=491.

6 World Bank country classifications, http://www.worldbank.org/data/countryclass/countryclass.html, based on 2002 per capita gross national income.

7 PBS website, "Additional Resources Glossary," 2004, http://www.pbs.org/warrior/content/resource/glossary.html.

8 From the 1987 United Nations Brundtland Report's definition of sustainable development. G. Brundtland, Our Common Future, World Commission on Environment and Development (London: Oxford University Press, 1987).

9 Environmental Research and Studies Centre, "Definitions of a Few Environmental Concepts," April 2004, http://www.ualberta.ca/~ersc/Handbook/section3/def.htm#sude.

10 World Bank, glossary, 2004, http://youthink.worldbank.org/glossary.php.

11 Jared Diamond, "Easter Island's End," Discovery Magazine, 1995, http://www.hartford-hwp.com/archives/24/042.html.

12 National Council of Economic Educators, EconEdLink, "A Case Study: Gross Domestic Product—April 29, 2004," June 17, 2004, http://www.econedlink.org/lessons/index.cfm?lesson=EM225.

13 Redefining Progress, "Genuine Progress Indicator," http://www.redefiningprogress.org/projects/gpi/.

14 Daniel H. Kim, "Introduction to Systems Thinking," Waltham, Maine, Pegasus Communications, Inc., 1999, pp. 4–5.

15 U.S. in the World—Talking Global Issues with Americans: A Practical Guide, Rockefeller Brothers Fund and the Aspen Institute, 2004, pp. 22, 32, http://www.usintheworld.org/index.php?flash=yes.

UNIT 2 ENDNOTES

1 Population Reference Bureau, "2004 World Population Data Sheet," www.prb.org/wpds.

2 Germany's population in 2003: 82,000,000 (U.S. Census Bureau, http://www.census.gov). San Francisco's population in 2003: 764,000 (U.S. Census Bureau, http://quickfacts.census.gov/qfd/states/06/06075.html).

3 Population Reference Bureau, "2003 World Population Data Sheet."

4 United State Agency for International Development, "Telling Our Story," http://www.usaid.gov/stories/egypt/ss_egypt_family.html.

5 International Rescue Committee, "IRC Seattle Programs and Services," March 2004, http://www.theirc.org/index.cfm/programs/show/wwwID/494/locationID/33.

6 International Rescue Committee, February 29, 2004, http://www.volunteersolutions.org/uwkc/org/583146.html.

7 U.S. Committee for Refugees, "Worldwide Refugee Information," http://www.refugees.org/world/worldmain.htm.

8 U.S. Committee for Refugees, "Glossary," 2004, http://www.refugees.org/world/glossary.htm.

9 http://www.prb.org/Template.cfm?Section=PRB&template=/ContentManagement/ContentDisplay.cfm&ContentID=7421.

10 Jared Diamond, Guns, Germs and Steel: The Fates of Human Societies (New York: W. W. Norton and Co., 1999), p. 411.

11 William Hardy McNeill, Plagues and Peoples (New York: Bantam Doubleday Dell, 1977), http://www.globalterrorism101.com/JustiniansPlague.html.

12 Fact Index, "Black Plague," Wikipedia, http://www.fact-index.com/b/bl/black_death.html.

13 Wikipedia—the Free Encyclopedia, http://en.wikipedia.org/wiki/Viking.

14 Agency for Healthcare Research and Quality, "History of Smallpox," University of Alabama School of Medicine website, 2001, http://www.bioterrorism.uab.edu/EIPBA/Smallpox/history.html.

15 GeoHive, "Regional Population from 1750 to 2050," 2003, http://www.xist.org/global/linkg.php?xml=hist1&xsl=hist1. Data taken from United Nations, The Determinants and Consequences of Population Trends, vol. 1 (New York: United Nations, 1973).

16 Osamu Saito, "The Postwar Population Explosion and Asia," Asian Historical Statistics Project, 1996, http://www.ier.hit-u.ac.jp/COE/Japanese/Newsletter/No.3.english/saitoe.htm.

17 The medium scenario in United Nations, World Population Prospects: The 1998 Revision.

18 Ecofuture.org, "Exponential Growth and the Rule of 70," 2002, http://www.ecofuture.org/pop/facts/exponential70.html.

19 Linda Booth Sweeney, When a Butterfly Sneezes: Systems Thinking for Kids, Big and Small (Maine, Pegasus Communications, Inc., 2001), pp. 69–70.

20 Population Reference Bureau, "Data Finder," http://www.prb.org/datafind/datafinder.htm. Based on birth rate of 22 per 1,000 and death rate of 9 per 1,000.

21 The actual replacement-rate fertility is 2.1 children per couple, which takes into account deaths before children reach adulthood. In addition, even if the average number of children per couple dropped to 2.1 tomorrow, the population would continue to grow. This is because there are 1.8 billion people under age fifteen—nearly a third of the global population. Even if this group averaged only 2.1 children per couple, they would add almost 2 billion people over time, and an equivalent number of people are not expected to die during that time. Thus, the total population would expand for some time even if the rate of growth was at replacement levels. For more information, see the section "Momentum for Population Change" in Population Reference Bureau, "Transitions in World Population," Population Bulletin, March 2004, p. 15, http://www.prb.org/Template.cfm?Section=PRB&template=/ContentManagement/ContentDisplay.cfm&ContentID=10110, and "Population Momentum," facts in Audubon website, http://www.audubon.org/campaign/population_habitat/momentum.html.

22 "World in Balance," NOVA (video), WGBH Boston, http://www.wgbh.org.

23 GeoHive, "Regional Population from 1750 to 2050," 2003, http://www.xist.org/global/linkg.php?xml=hist1&xsl=hist1. Data taken from United Nations, The Determinants and Consequences of Population Trends, vol. 1.

24 World Population Projections, Research Note 9, 1999–2000, October 19, 1999, from Parliament of Australia website, http://www.aph.gov.au/library/pubs/rn/1999-2000/2000rn09.htm.

25 "Use of family planning worldwide rose from less than 10 percent of married women in 1960 to about 60 percent in 2003," according to Population Reference Bureau, "Transitions in World Population," Population Bulletin, March 2004, p. 10, http://www.prb.org/Template.cfm?Section=PRB&template=/ContentManagement/ContentDisplay.cfm&ContentID=10110.

26 Ibid.

27 United Nations Family Planning Association, "The State of World Population 2001," http://www.unfpa.org/swp/2001/english/ch01.html.

28 Riverdeep, "Global Population Trends," 2004, http://www.riverdeep.net/current/2001/06/061101_population.jhtml.

29 Acton Institute for the Study of Religion and Liberty, "Population Growth Benefits the Environment," interview with Julian Simon, 5, No. 2 (March–April 1995), http://www.acton.org/publicat/randl/interview.php?id=144.

30 Redefining Progress, "Ecological Footprint Analysis," 2004, http://www.redefiningprogress.org/footprint/.

31 Based on 2000 data on footprint size. By hectares: India, 0.77; Mexico, 2.52; France, 5.26; United States, 9.7. From Redefining Progress, "Ecological Footprint of Nations 2004," http://www.redefiningprogress.org/publications/footprintnations2004.pdf.

32 U.S. Committee for Refugees, "Worldwide Refugee Information," 2004, http://www.refugees.org/who/faq.htm.

33 U.S. Committee for Refugees, "Worldwide Refugee Information," 2004, http://www.refugees.org/who/faq.htm.

34 Ashley Hamilton, "Resource Wars and the Politics of Abundance and Scarcity," University of Queensland, Australia, School of Political Science and International Studies, http://www.polsis.uq.edu.au/dialogue/vol-1-3-5.pdf; Jenny Goldie, "Natural Resource Scarcity and Violent Conflict," presented at In Search of Sustainability Conference, http://www.isosconference.org.au/papers/Goldie.pdf; and Future Harvest, "Four Million Killed in Post-Cold War Conflicts: Prospects for Peace Increase, Even in Poorest Countries, with Investments in Agricultural Research and Technology," 1999, http://www.futureharvest.org/news/02161999.shtml.

35 Seattle Times, "Refugee Numbers Lowest in a Decade," June 17, 2004.

36 Michael Brower and Warren Leon, The Consumer Guide to Effective Environmental Choices: Practical Advice from the Union of Concerned Scientists (New York: Three Rivers Press, 1999), p. 85.

37 International Conference on Population and Development, Cairo, Egypt, September 1994, http://www.un.org/popin/icpd2.htm.

38 Population Reference Bureau, "Iran's Family Planning Program: Responding to a Nation's Need," MENA Policy Brief, 2002, http://www.prb.org/pdf/IransFamPlanProg_Eng.pdf, and Janet Larsen, "Iran's Birth Rate Plummeting at Record Pace: Success Provides a Model for Other Developing Countries," Earth Policy Institute, December 28, 2001, www.earth-policy.org/Updates/Update4ss.htm.

UNIT 3 ENDNOTES

1 "Remote Farm Town Is Test Case for Anti-hunger Campaign Introduced by Brazil's President," 2003, PlanetSave.com http://www.planetsave.com/ViewStory.asp?ID=3881.

2 "Brazil's Zero Hunger International Gets Wide Backing," Brazzil Magazine, 2004, http://www.brazzil.com/mag/index.php?option=content&task=view&id=82.

3 "The Lake and the 'Hood," Jane Braxton Little, YES! magazine, No. 28 (Winter 2004), pp. 22–25, www.yesmagazine.org.

4 United Nations World Food Programme, http://www.wfp.org/.

5 United Nations Food and Agriculture Organization (UNFAO), 2002, ftp://ftp.fao.org/docrep/

fao/003/y6265E/Y6265E.pdf.

6 UNFAO, Towards 2015/30 (New York: UNFAO, Economic and Social Department, 2003), http://www.fao.org/english/newsroom/news/2003/14640-en.html.

7 United Nations Development Programme, "As World Food Production Increases, So Does the Number of Hungry," Choices—The Human Development Magazine, March 2004, p. 28.

8 UNFAO, "The State of Food Insecurity in the World 2003," ftp://ftp.fao.org/docrep/fao/006/j0083e/j0494e00.pdf.

9 Lester R. Brown, Plan B: Rescuing a Planet under Stress and a Civilization in Trouble (New York: W. W. Norton & Company, with Earth Policy Institute, 2003), www.Earth-policy.org/Books/PlanB_ch5_socialdivide.pdf.

10 World Health Organization, http://www.who.int/en/.

11 UNFAO, "The State of Food Insecurity in the World 2002," http://www.fao.org/docrep/005/y7352e/y7352e00.htm.

12 Bread for the World Institute, "Domestic Hunger and Poverty Facts," 2004, http://www.bread.org/hungerbasics/domestic.html.

13 National Academy of Sciences of the United States of America website, "New Consumers: The Influence of Affluence on the Environment," Table 3—meat, 2003, http://www.pnas.org/cgi/content/full/100/8/4963/T3.

14 United Nations, Climate Change 2001: Impacts, Adaptation, and Vulnerability, Intergovernmental Panel on Climate Change, 2001, http://www.grida.no/climate/ipcc_tar/wg2/057.htm#1212.

15 Ibid.

16 World Health Organization, 2003, http://www.who.int/nut/nutrition3.htm.

17 Brown, Rescuing a Planet.

18 Rosie Mestel, "One-Third of Calories Consumed Are Junk," Los Angeles Times, June 20, 2004.

19 Northwestern University, "Nutrition Fact Sheet," http://www.feinberg.northwestern.edu/nutrition/factsheets/fad-diets.html, and Center for Disease Control,"Physical Activity and Good Nutrition: Essential Elements to Prevent Chronic Diseases and Obesity," 2004, http://www.cdc.gov/nccdphp/aag/aag_dnpa.htm.

20 In 1968, when the administrator for the U.S. Agency for International Development (USAID) wrote in his annual report that there was a big improvement in Pakistan and India, he said, "It looks like a Green Revolution." ActionBioscience.org, "Biotechnology and the Green Revolution Interview with Norman Borlaug," 2002, http://www.actionbioscience.org/biotech/borlaug.html.

21 Wikipedia Encyclopedia, June 21, 2004, http://en.wikipedia.org/wiki/Green_revolution.

22 "Green Revolution Curse or Blessing?" International Food Policy Research Institute, 2002, http://www.ifpri.org/pubs/ib/ib11.pdf.

23 British Medical Association, Board of Science and Education, "The Impact of Genetic Modification on Agriculture, Food and Health—An Interim Statement," May 1999, http://www.twnside.org.sg/title/genmo-cn.htm, and United States Environmental Protection Agency, "Terms of the Environment," http://www.epa.gov/OCEPAterms/gterms.html.

24 World Health Organization, "Food Safety," 2004, http://www.who.int/foodsafety/publications/biotech/20questions/en/.

25 Wikipedia Encyclopedia, June 21, 2004, http://en.wikipedia.org/wiki/Green_revolution.

26 World Health Organization, "Food Safety," 2004.

27 Matthew Rousu and Wallace Huffman, "GM Food Labeling Policies of the U.S. and Its Trading Partners," 2001, http://www.biotech.iastate.edu/publications/IFAFS/gmtrade.pdf.

28 Pew Initiative on Food and Biology, "Genetically Modified Crops in the United States," 2004, http://pewagbiotech.org/resources/factsheets/display.php3?FactsheetID=2.

29 UNFAO, Towards 2015/30.

30 United Nations, "International Year for Fresh Water," UN initiative, 2003, http://www.un.org/works/sustainable/freshwater.html.

31 Ibid.

32 Population Action International, "People in the Balance: Population and Natural Resources at the Turn of the Millennium," update, 2003, http://www.populationaction.org/resources/publications/peopleinthebalance/pb_water.shtml.

33 Ismael Serageldin, World Bank vice president, quoted in "A Warning of Water Wars," People and the Planet 3, no. 5 (1996), http://www.oneworld.org/patp/vol5_3/intro.html.

34 Robert S. Boyd, "Ancient History Threatens to Repeat Itself," The San Diego Union—Tribune, March 21, 2001, http://www.carryingcapacity.org/ancienthistory.html.

35 Robert F. Service, "As the West Goes Dry," Science, February 20, 2004.

36 The International Panel on Climate Change (IPCC), Third Annual Assessment on Climate Change offers four comprehensive reports: The Scientific Basis; Impacts, Adaptation, and Vulnerability; Mitigation; and Synthesis Report, http://www.ipcc.ch/. See also Brown, Rescuing a Planet.

37 The World Watch Institute, State of the World 2004 (New York: W. W. Norton & Co., 2004), p. 55.

38 WaterPartners International, "Water Facts," 2004, http://water.org/crisis/waterfacts.html.

39 Brown, Rescuing a Planet, pp. 7–19.

40 Ibid., pp. 113–30.

41 Ibid., pp. 131–50, 190–92.

42 United Nations Development Programme, "New Technologies and New Business Outlook for Sri Lankan Farmers," Choices: The Human Development Magazine, June 2004, pp. 15–16.

43 WaterPartners International, 2004, http://water.org/crisis/waterfacts.html.

44 World Food Programme, 2004, http://www.wfp.org/index.asp?section=1.

45 Heifer Project International, 2004, http://www.heifer.org/Our_Work/Our_Approach/Cornerstones.shtml.

46 Janet L. Sawin, "Making Better Energy Choices," The State of the World—2004 (Washington, D.C.: The World Watch Institute, 2004), p. 25.

47 Tim Appenzeller, "The End of Cheap Oil," National Geographic Magazine, June 2004, p. 88.

48 George F. Will, "Oil: How Bad Do You Want It?" The Washington Post, June 2004, http://www.progressforamerica.com/pfa/wrapper.jsp?PID=1101-134&CID=1101-061404C.

49 Sawin, "Making Better Energy Choices," p.28.

50 Brown, Rescuing a Planet, pp. 60–61.

51 United Nations, Climate Change 2001: Impacts, Adaptation, and Vulnerability, Intergovernmental Panel on Climate Change, 2001, http://www.grida.no/climate/ipcc_tar/wg2/057.htm#1212.

52 "The Oil Industry," Do or Die, No. 7, pp. 59–67, http://www.eco-action.org/dod/no7/59-65.html, and "Environmentalists and the Oil Companies," Artic Circle, http://arcticcircle.uconn.edu/ANWR/anwrenv-oil.html.

53"Ibid.

54 U.S. Department of Energy, Energy and Renewable Energy, "Contribution of Renewable Energy to the U.S. Energy Supply," July 1, 2004, http://www.eere.energy.gov/consumerinfo/factsheets/da8.html.

55 C. J. Cleveland, R. Costanza, C. A. S. Hall, and R. Kaufmann, "Energy and the United States Economy: A Biophysical Perspective," Science 225, pp. 890–97.

56 California Energy Commission, "Selected World Gasoline Prices Average Prices for February 2004," http://www.energy.ca.gov/gasoline/statistics/world_gasoline_prices.html.

57 Appenzeller, "End of Cheap Oil," p. 897.

58 The World Watch Institute, Vital Signs 2003 (New York: W. W. Norton & Co., 2002), p. 34.

59 Ibid., p. 56.

60 Taxpayers for Common Sense, "Fossil Fuel Subsidies: A Taxpayer Perspective," http://www.taxpayer.net/TCS/fuelsubfact.htm.

61 Molly Farneth, "Powering Foreign Policy, the Role of Oil in Diplomacy and Conflict," Physicians for Social Responsibility, 2004, http://www.psrenergysecurity.org/PoweringForeignPolicy.pdf.

62 Ibid.

63 Brown, Rescuing a Planet, pp.151–75.

65 Alternative Fuel Vehicle Group, Alexander Communications Group, Inc., 2004, http://www.altfuels.com/glossary1.php.

66 Ibid., http://www.altfuels.com/glossary2.php#F.

67 Sawin, "Making Better Energy Choices," p.34.

68 Ibid.

69 U.S. Department of Energy, Energy and Renewable Energy, "Contribution of Renewable Energy to the U.S. Energy Supply," July 1, 2004, http://www.eere.energy.gov/consumerinfo/factsheets/da8.html.

70 Ibid.

71 Brown, Rescuing a Planet, pp. 151-53.

72 International Council for Local Environmental Initiatives, Local Governments for Sustainability, "Case Study—Spirit Lake, Iowa," 2004, http://www.greenpowergovs.org/wind/Spirit%20Lake%20case%20study.html.

73 International Institute for Sustainable Development, 2004, http://www.iisd.org/, and Climate Change Knowledge Network, "Decentralized Renewable Energy," 2003, http://www.cckn.net/dre.asp.

74 Craig Morris, "Are Wind Turbines Actually Bird Blenders?" Telepolis, April 24, 2003. In AlterNet, http://www.alternet.org/story/15900.

75 Audubon—New York, "Position on Wind Power Development," June 22, 2004, http://ny.audubon.org/wind_power.htm.

UNIT 4 ENDNOTES

1 E. O. Wilson, The Diversity of Life (New York: W. W. Norton & Co., 1999).

2 U.S. Environmental Protection Agency, "U.S. Climate Action Report 2002," p. 4, http://yosemite. epa.gov/oar/globalwarming.nsf/UniqueKeyLookup/SHSU5BNPYJ/$File/ch1.pdf.

3 Wilson, Diversity of Life.

4 Wikipedia—The Free Encyclopedia, "Ecosystem," 2004, http://en.wikipedia.org/wiki/Ecosystem.

5 Ibid., "Biodiversity," http://en.wikipedia.org/wiki/Biodiversity.

6 David Suzuki Foundation—Web of Life, "What Is biodiversity?"2004, http://www.davidsuzuki. org/WOL/Biodiversity/default.asp.

7 Wilson, Diversity of Life.

8 Thirty-four percent of scientists surveyed believe that 20 percent to 50 percent of species will be extinct in thirty years, and 69 percent of scientists surveyed believe we are in a period of mass extinction. Louis Harris and Associates, "Biodiversity in the Next Millennium," 1998 poll conducted on behalf of the U.S. Citizen Museum of Natural History, http://research.amnh.org/biodiversity/ crisis/crisis.html.

9 Story by Kim Rakow Bernier, based on interviews and personal experience in Solomon Islands, 1999–2000.

10 Greenaction for Health and Environmental Justice, http://www.greenaction.org/features/index. shtml

11 World Resources Institute, World Resources Report 2000–2001.

12 International Union for Conservation of Nature and Natural Resources, "2003 IUCN Red List of Endangered Species," http://www.redlist.org/.

13 Tropical Forest New European Commission Guidelines for Cooperation with Developing Countries, 1997, http://www.euforic.org/spp/97238_gb.htm.

14 R. DeFries, "Past and Future Sensitivity of Primary Production to Human Modification to the Landscape," Geophysical Research Letters 29, no. 7, Department of Geography and Earth Systems Science Interdisciplinary Center, University of Maryland, College Park, 2002; World Resources Institute, "Forests and Land Cover: Introduction," 2004, http://pubs.wri.org/pubs_content_text. cfm?ContentID=873; and Theodore Panayotou, "Environmental Regulation and Sustainable Development," April 5, 2005, http://www.caf.com/attach/4/default/EnvironmentalRegulationandSustainableDevelop_Panaetal.pdf.

15 David Suzuki Foundation, Web of Life, "What Is biodiversity?" 2004, http://www.davidsuzuki. org/WOL/Biodiversity/default.asp.

16 U.S. Fish and Wildlife Service, "Bald Eagle Biologue," USFWS Region 3, 2004, http://midwest. fws.gov/eagle/success/biologue.html.

17 Brooklyn Botanical Garden, "Vanishing Plants," 2004, http://www.bbg.org/gar2/topics/botany/ con_vanishing.html.

18 "Carbon Sequestration: Position of the Soil Science Society of America," Soil Society of America, 2001, http://www.soils.org/carbseq.html.

19 "Living with Risk: A Global Review of Disaster Reduction Initiatives," International Strategy for Disaster Reduction, 2004, http://www.unisdr.org/eng/about_isdr/basic_docs/LwR2004/ ch1%20Section%201.pdf.

20 Earth Trends World Resources Institute, country profile, United States, http://earthtrends.wri. org/pdf_library/country_profiles/For_cou_840.pdf.

21 Dirk Bryant, Daniel Nielsen, and Laura Tangley, "Last Frontier Forests: Ecosystems and Economies on the Edge," World Resources Institute, 1997, http://forests.wri.org/pubs_description. cfm?PubID=2619.

22 "Survey of Energy Resources," World Energy Council, 2004, http://www.worldenergy.org/wec-geis/publications/reports/ser/wood/wood.asp.

23 Musokotwane Environment Resource Centre for Southern Africa, "CEO Factsheet Series 12: Energy Sources and Uses," http://www.sardc.net/Imercsa/Programs/CEP/Pubs/CEPFS/CEPFS12.htm.

24 Lester R. Brown, Plan B: Rescuing a Planet under Stress and a Civilization in Trouble, New York: Earth Policy Institute, 2003), pp. 104–5.

25 World Watch Institute, "Accelerating Demand for Land, Wood, and Paper Pushing World's Forests to the Brink," April 1998, http://www.worldwatch.org/press/news/1998/04/04/.

26 National Association of Homebuilders, "Resources," 2004, http://www.nahb.org/page.aspx/ landing/sectionID=87.

27 Wulf Killmann, Gary Q. Bull, Olaf Schwab, and Reino E. Pulkki, "Reduced Impact Logging: Does It Cost or Does It Pay?" an academic review of 266 studies in Applying Reduced Impact Logging to Advance Sustainable Forest Management, United Nations Food and Agriculture Organization International Conference 2002, http://www.fao.org/DOCREP/005/AC805E/ac805e0f.htm#bm15.

28 Cost based on the report's average cost of 390 rupees (exchange rate in 2000 was 43.64 rupees to the U.S. dollar). United Nations Educational, Scientific and Cultural Organization, "Best Practice on Renewable Energy: India—Programme on Improved Smokeless Chulas," published sometime after 2001, http://www.unesco.or.id/apgest/pdf/india/india-bp-re.pdf.

29 Popular Gentle, Women's Participation in Community Forestry and Decision Making Process in Forestry Partnership Project, 8(1) CARE Nepal Newsletter, 2003.

30 "Grief as Haitians and Dominicans Tally Flood Toll," New York Times, May 28, 2004, http://www. worldrevolution.org/article/1410.

31 Brown, Rescuing a Planet, p. 209.

32 John de Graaf, David Wann, and Thomas H. Naylor, Affluenza: The All-Consuming Epidemic (San Francisco: Berrett-Koehler Publisher, 2001), pp. 90–91.

33 Global Exchange, "Fair Trade," July 13, 2004, http://www.globalexchange.org/campaigns/ fairtrade/coffee/.

34 International Institute for Sustainable Development, "IISD Brews Up Sustainable Coffee Report," September 18, 2003, http://www.iisd.org/media/2003/sept_18_2003.asp.

35 Starbucks, "Environmental Activities from Bean to Cup," 2004, http://www.starbucks.com/ aboutus/beantocup.asp.

36 Starbucks, "Coffee, Tea, and Paper Sourcing," 2004, http://www.starbucks.com/aboutus/sourcing.asp.

37 The Natural Step, 2003, http://www.naturalstep.org/.

38 "The Natural Step: The Science of Sustainability," interview with Dr. Karl-Henrik Robert, in YES! magazine no. 7 (fall 1998), Positive Futures Network.

39 World Watch Institute, State of the World 2004 (New York: W. W. Norton & Co., 2004), p. 132.

40 World Watch Institute, Vital Signs 2003 (New York: W. W. Norton & Co., 2002), p. 74.

41 International Development Research Center, "Taking Control of Air Pollution in Mexico City," August 12, 2003, http://web.idrc.ca/en/ev-31594-201-1-DO_TOPIC.html.

42 World Health Organization, "Bronchial Asthma," 2000, http://www.who.int/mediacentre/factsheets/fs206/en/.

43 National Institutes of Health, "Asthma Statistics," data fact sheet, 1999, http://www.nhlbi.nih. gov/health/prof/lung/asthma/asthstat.pdf.

44 U.S. Environmental Protection Agency website, "'Clean Air Markets—Environmental Issues," 2005, http://www.epa.gov/airmarkets/acidrain/index.html.

45 Australian Academy of Science website, 2004, http://www.science.org.au/nova/004/004key. htm.

46 Disaster Relief, "It's Official: 1998 Ranks as the Warmest Year on Record," January 14, 1999, http://www.disasterrelief.org/Disasters/990113Temps/; and Daniel Glick, "The Big Thaw," National Geographic Magazine, September 2004, p. 27.

47 Fen Montaigne, "No Room to Run," National Geographic Magazine, September 2004, p. 72.

48 U.S. Environmental Protection Agency, "U.S. Climate Action Report 2002," p. 4, http://yosemite. epa.gov/oar/globalwarming.nsf/UniqueKeyLookup/SHSU5BNPYJ/$File/ch1.pdf.

49 Arni Isaksson, of the Directorate of Freshwater Fisheries, Iceland, E-mail to Devin Hibbard, April 1, 2004.

50 World Watch Institute, Vital Signs 2003, p. 88.

51 International Institute for Sustainable Development, "An Ozone-Friendly Future: Full Restoration Possible by 2050," 2003, http://www.iisd.org/briefcase/ten+ten_success1.asp; and Wikipedia—the Free Encyclopedia, "ozone layer," 2004, http://en.wikipedia.org/wiki/Ozone_layer.

52 Climate Change Knowledge Network, 2003, http://www.cckn.net/.

53 Virginia Morrell, "Way Down Deep," National Geographic Magazine, June 2004, pp. 43–44.

54 World Wildlife Fund International, "Endangered Seas," January 2004, http://www.panda.org/ about_wwf/what_we_do/marine/problems.cfm; and Glick, "The Big Thaw," National Geographic Magazine, pp. 27–28.

55 Ibid.

56 Bruce McKay, Kieran Mulvaney, and Boyce Thorne-Miller, "Danger at Sea: Our Changing Oceans," SeaWeb, 2004, http://www.seaweb.org/campaigns/danger/.

57 World Wildlife Fund International, "Endangered Seas."

58 Ibid.

59 Dayton L. Alverson, et al., "A Global Assessment of Fisheries Bycatch and Discards," United Nations Food and Agriculture Organization, 1996, http://www.fao.org/DOCREP/003/T4890E/

T4890E00.HTM.

60 Glick, "The Big Thaw," National Geographic Magazine, p. 27.

61 McKay, Mulvaney, and Thorne-Miller, "Danger at Sea."

62 National Research Council, Research to Protect, Restore and Manage the Environment (Washington, D.C.: National Academy Press, 1993).

63 For further information on the use of the precautionary approach see the website of North Atlantic Salmon Conservation Organization, www.nasco.int.

64 "U.S. Commission on Oceans Policy," Executive Summary, April 2004, http://oceancommission. gov/documents/prelimreport/overview_summary.pdf.

65 John Pickrell, "New Marine Conservation Area to Span Four Nations," National Geographic News, February 26, 2004, http://news.nationalgeographic.com/news/2004/02/0226_040226_oceanpark. html#main.

66 Brown, Rescuing a Planet, pp. 139–40.

67 Ibid.

68 Data from the New Internationalist Magazine, no. 325, www.newint.org; United Nations Food and Agriculture Organization's website, www.fao.org; Environmental News Service, February 2002, www.enn.com; and Terry Leitzell, interview with author, 2004.

69 First articulated by Garrett Hardin in 1968. For Hardin's original article, see http://www.garretthardinsociety.org/articles/art_tragedy_of_the_commons.html.

70 Anne Platt McGinn, "From Rio to Johannesburg: Healthy Oceans Key to Fighting Poverty," World Watch Institute World Summit Policy Brief No. 5, May 21, 2002, http://www.worldwatch. org/press/news/2002/05/21/.

71 Gunnar Knapp, "Alaska's Seafood Industry: Changes, Challenges and Current Issues," Institute of Social and Economic Research, University of Alaska, Anchorage, presentation to Commonwealth North, November 13, 2003, http://www.commonwealthnorth.org/transcripts/KnappPresentation. pdf.

72 Ibid.

73 United States Environmental Protection Agency, "Environmental Justice," June 2004, http:// www.epa.gov/compliance/environmentaljustice/.

74 Dr. Robert Bullard, "New Civil Rights Battlegrounds," Blue Ridge Press, November 2, 2002, http://www.blueridgepress.com/index.ws4d.

75 Timothy Begany, "Poverty, Youth, and Minority Ethnicity Raise Risk of Asthma Hospitalizations," Pulmonary Reviews.Com 4, No. 9 (November-December 1999), http://www.pulmonaryreviews. com/novdec99/pr_novdec99_PovAsthma.html.

76 Daniel Carroll and Steven Weber, "EPA Needs to Consistently Implement the Intent of the Executive Order on Environmental Justice," EPA Office of the Inspector General Evaluation Report, March 1, 2004, http://www.epa.gov/oig/reports/2004/20040301-2004-P-00007.pdf.

77 There are numerous excellent examples of organizations concerned with environmental health and justice in the United States: Center for Community Action and Environmental Justice, http://www.ccaej.org/; Center for Environmental Health and Justice, http://www.chej.org/; Environmental Justice Research Center, http://www.ejrc.cau.edu/; and Green Action for Health and Environmental Justice, http://greenaction.org/.

78 "Pipelines to Power," New Internationalist, No. 361 (October 2003), pp. 10, 18.

79 Ibid.

80 "Kyoto Protocol to the United Nations Framework Convention on Climate Change," May 2002, http://unfccc.int/resource/docs/convkp/kpeng.html.

81 Environmental Justice Foundation, http://www.ejfoundation.org/index.html.

82 World Watch Institute, State of the World 2004 (New York: W. W. Norton & Co., 2004), p. 93.

UNIT 5 ENDNOTES

1 The American Heritage Dictionary (New York: Houghton Mifflin Company, 2001).

2 Gary Gardner and Erik Assadourian, "Rethinking the Good Life," in The State of the World 2004 (New York: Worldwatch Institute, 2004), p. 165.

3 Sherry Salway Black, "Indigenous Economics," YES! magazine, spring-summer 1996, pp. 33–36.

4 Ricardo Chavez, "Talking Back: Media for the People," YES! magazine, winter 2003, p. 32.

5 Gary Gardner, Erik Assadourian, and Radhika Sarin, "The State of Consumption Today," in The State of the World 2004 (New York: Worldwatch Institute, 2004), p. 18.

6 Five weeks of additional work is based on a forty-hour week. Juliet Schor, "The (Even More)

Overworked U.S. Citizen," in Take Back Your Time, ed. John DeGraaf (San Francisco, Calif.: Berrett-Koehler Publishers, 2003), p. 7.

7 Joe Robinson, "The Incredible Shrinking Vacation," in Take Back Your Time, ed. John DeGraaf, p. 21.

8 Economist.com, "Europe's Workplace Revolution," 2004, http://www.economist.com/business/ displayStory.cfm?story_id=2967451.

9 David G. Myers, "Happiness," in Psychology, 7th ed. (New York: Worth Publishers, 2004); also see Chart 3 at http://www.davidmyers.org/happiness/Excerpt.html.

10 Gardner, Assadourian, and Sarin, "State of Consumption," p. 18.

11 David G. Myers, "What Is the Good Life?" YES! magazine, No. 30, summer 2004), p. 15.

12 Ibid.

13 William Dietrich, "From American Ethic to Global Imperative—the World of Work Turns," The Seattle Times, July 25, 2004, pp. 20–21.

14 Gardner, Assadourian, and Sarin, "State of Consumption," pp. 18–19.

15 Ibid, p. 9.

16 Ibid.

17 Gardner and Assadourian, "Rethinking the Good Life," pp. 165–66.

18 Ibid., p. 174.

19 Gardner, Assadourian, and Sarin, "State of Consumption," p. 8.

20 Gardner and Assadourian, "Rethinking the Good Life," p. 164.

21 Ibid., p. 169.

22 Myers, "What Is Good Life?" p. 16.

23 New Road Map Foundation, "All-Consuming Passion: Waking Up from the U.S. Citizen Dream," 1995, http://www.ecofuture.org/pk/pkar9506.html#acp-foot.

24 Gardner and Assadourian, "Rethinking the Good Life," p. 21.

25 "Take Back Your Time," http://www.simpleliving.net/timeday/, and John de Graaf, "Take Back Your Time Day," both in YES! A Journal of Positive Futures, No. 27 (fall 2003), Positive Futures Network.

26 John de Graaf, ed., Take Back Your Time: Fighting Overwork and Time Poverty in America San Francisco: Berrett-Koehler Publishers, Inc., 2003.

27 Michael Renner, "Moving Toward a Less Consumptive Economy," The State of the World 2004 (New York: Worldwatch Institute, 2004), pp. 98–99.

28 Lester R. Brown, Plan B: Rescuing a Planet under Stress and a Civilization in Trouble (New York: Earth Policy Institute, 2003), pp. 78–79.

29 Lisa Mastny, "Purchasing for People and the Planet," in The State of the World 2004 (New York: Worldwatch Institute, 2004), p. 125.

30 Renner, "Less Consumptive Economy," p. 99–100.

31 Gardner, Assadourian, and Sarin, "State of Consumption Today," pp. 20–21.

32 Mastny, "Purchasing for People and Planet," p. 131.

33 Ibid.

34 Renner, "Less Consumptive Economy," pp. 100–101.

35 Adapted from work by McDonough Braungart Design Chemistry and from William McDonough and Michael Brangart, Cradle to Cradle: Remaking the Way We Make Things (New York: North Point Press, 2002).

36 MBDC, "News and Announcements," 2001–2004, http://www.mbdc.com/news.htm.

37 Tom Sorel, "The Life Cycle Continuum," U.S. Department of Transportation, July-August 2004, http://www.tfhrc.gov/pubrds/04jul/04.htm; and "Life-cycle Planning Solves Distance, Information Problems," Design Intelligence 10, No. 2 (February 2004), Greenway Communications International, http://www.di.net/article.php?article_id=306.

38 Yang Jianxin, Hao Fu, Rusong Wang, and Yuichi Moriguchi, "Issues and the Future of Ecocities," 2003, http://www.ias.unu.edu/proceedings/icibs/ecocity03/papers/yangjianxin/; and " Life Cycle Planning Module," U.S. Department of Energy, March 12, 2004, http://www.id.doe.gov/DOEID/RF-PSharedLibrary/PDF/Integrated_Planning/chp04_vol1.pdf.

39 Wikipedia—the Free Encyclopedia, July 2, 2004, http://en.wikipedia.org/wiki/Culture.

40 United Nations Development Project, Civil Society Organizations and Participation Programme,

"Indigenous Peoples," http://www.un.org/issues/m-indig.asp#, 2005.

41 South and Meso American Indian Rights Center website, 2004, David Rothschild, Protecting What's Ours: Indigenous Peoples and Biodiversity, http://saiic.nativeweb.org/biodiver.html.

42 Eduardo Galeano, "Sheltering Hope," in Rethinking Globalization: Teaching for Justice in an Unjust World (Milwaukee: Rethinking Schools, Ltd., 2002), p. 341.

43 Andrew Kimbrell, "Technology: Who Chooses?" YES! magazine, fall 2001, p. 14, Positive Futures Network.

44 Ibid.

45 "Technology Gap Seen as a Barrier to Easing Poverty," Seattle Post-Intelligencer, June 18, 2004.

46 Ibid.

47 Ibid.

48 Jasmina Sopova, "Africa: Cell Phones for Citizenship," interview with Ibrahima N'Diaye in The Unesco Courier, June 2002.

49 Jame Hall, "Good to Talk," New Internationalist, No. 365 (March 2004), p. 7.

50 Robert W. McChesney, "The New Global Media: It's a Small World of Big Conglomerates," The Nation, November 11, 1999, http://www.thenation.com/doc.mhtml?i=19991129&c=1&s=mcchesney.

51 World Information.Org, "Centralization of the Content Industry," 2003, http://world-information.org/wio/infostructure/100437611795/100438659096?opmode=contents.

52 McChesney, "New Global Media."

53 Cultural Survival, 2003, http://www.culturalsurvival.org/.

54 Cultural Survival, "Media Autonomy in the Third World," No. 7.2, June 30, 1983, http://www.culturalsurvival.org/publications/csq/csq_article.cfm?id=00000085-0000-0000-0000-000000000000&region_id=0&subregion_id=1&issue_id=27.

55 Sue Schardt, "Public Radio—A Short History," Christian Science Monitor, 1996, http://www.wsvh.org/pubradiohist.htm.

56 "NeoRadio Succeeds by Cutting the Noise," All Things Considered, National Public Radio, June 30, 2004.

57 UNDP website, 2005, http://www.undp.org/dpa/pressrelease/releases/2005/january/2-MP-FastFacts-E.pdf.

58 UNDP website, 2005, http://www.undp.org/dpa/pressrelease/releases/2005/january/7-TF5c-malaria-E.pdf.

59 UNDP website, 2005, http://www.undp.org/dpa/pressrelease/releases/2005/january/8-TF5d-tuberculosis-E.pdf.

60 UNDP website, 2005, http://www.undp.org/dpa/pressrelease/releases/2005/january/4-TF4-women-E.pdf.

61 World Health Organization website, 2005, http://www.who.int/tobacco/en/.

62 David Suzuki, "Human Activities Give Rise to New Diseases," Environmental News Network, June 3, 2003, http://www.enn.com/news/2003-06-03/s_4695.asp.

63 Ibid.

64 National Intelligence Council, "The Global Infectious Disease Threat and Its Implications for the United States," report, 2000, http://www.cia.gov/cia/reports/nie/report/nie99-17d.html.

65 Dr. Stephen Bezruchka, "The (Bigger) Picture of Health," Take Back Your Time: Fighting Overwork and Time Poverty in America, ed. John de Graaf (San Francisco: Berrett-Koehler Publishers, Inc., 2001), p. 78.

66 Uwe E. Reinhardt, Peter S. Hussey, and Gerard F. Anderson, "U.S. Health Care Spending in an International Context," Health Affairs 23, No. 3, pp. 10–25, http://content.healthaffairs.org/cgi/content/full/23/3/10, copyright © 2004 by Project HOPE.

67 Bezruchka, "Picture of Health," p. 78.

68 Brown, Rescuing a Planet, p. 81.

69 United Joint Nations Programme on HIV/AIDS, "Questions and Answers," 2004, http://www.unaids.org/EN/resources/questions_answers.asp.

70 Ibid.

71 United Nations Program on HIV/AIDS, Report on the Global AIDS Epidemic, 2004, http://www.unaids.org/bangkok2004/report.html.

72 Centers for Disease Control and Prevention, "Division of HIV/AIDS Prevention," June 2, 2004, http://www.cdc.gov/hiv/pubs/facts.htm; and AIDS.org website, 2004, http://www.aids.org/index.

html.

73 UNESCO website, "UNESCO'S Strategy for HIV/AIDS Prevention Education," 2005, http://unesdoc.unesco.org/images/0013/001345/134572e.pdf.

74 World Health Organization website, "700,000 People Living with AIDS in Developing Countries Now Receiving Treatment," 2005, http://www.who.int/mediacentre/news/releases/2005/pr07/en/index.html.

75 Steve Sternberg, "Condoms and Comedy to the Rescue in Thailand," USA Today, July 11, 2004, http://www.usatoday.com/news/health/2004-07-11-thailand-condom-king_x.htm.

76 Brown, Rescuing a Planet, pp. 185–86.

77 The National Community of Women Living with HIV/AIDS in Uganda (NACWOLA), http://www.wougnet.org/Profiles/nacwola.html.

78 Ibid, p. 186; and United Nations Human Development, "Millennium Development Goals: A Compact Among Nations to End Poverty, report 2003, p. 85, http://hdr.undp.org/reports/global/2003/.

79 Kathy George, "Drawn to Help Society's Poorest," Seattle Post-Intelligencer, July 12, 2004.

80 United Nations Millennium Development Goals 2000, http://www.un.org/millenniumgoals/.

81 Ibid.

82 World Health Organization, "Macroeconomics and Health: Investing in Health for Economic Development," report on the Commission of Macroeconomics and Health, December 20, 2001, http://www3.who.int/whosis/menu.cfm?path=whosis,cmh&language=english.

83 Wikipedia—the Free Encyclopedia, "Morbidity," 2004, http://en.wikipedia.org/wiki/Morbidity.

84 WHO, "Macroeconomics and Health."

85 Ibid.

86 Ibid.

87 Ibid.

88 Educations statistics and arguments for the link between education, poverty, and health from United Nations Human Development Report 2003, "Millennium Development Goals: A Compact Among Nations to End Poverty, p. 85, http://hdr.undp.org/reports/global/2003/; and Brown, Rescuing a Planet, pp. 89–91, 181–86.

89 Ibid.

90 United Nations Development Program, Human Development Indicators, 2003, http://www.undp.org/hdr2003/indicator/indic_2_1_1.html.

91 Brown, Rescuing a Planet, pp.181–82.

92 Ibid, pp. 89–90.

93 Ibid., pp. 183–84, 190–93.

94 Ibid.

95 United Nations Human Development Report 2003, "Millennium Development Goals," p. 85.

96 Ibid.

97 Ibid.

98 Ibid.

99 Interaction—American Council for Voluntary International Action, "Educating Girls Gives Them a Healthier Future," 2004, http://www.interaction.org/campaign/success%20stories/WE_educ.html; and World Education, June 18, 2004, http://www.worlded.org/.

100 David Sobel, "Beyond Ecophobia," YES! magazine, No. 8 (winter 1998–1999), pp. 19–23.

101 David W. Orr, "Breaking Ground," YES! magazine, No. 8 (Winter 1998–1999), pp. 24–25.

102 United Nations Information System, Amnesty International 2003 press report, May 26, 2004, http://domino.un.org/UNISPAL.NSF/0/4440633426888f5d85256ea000630554?OpenDocument.

103 Amnesty International, "Campaign—Stop Violence Against Women," 2004, http://web.amnesty.org/actforwomen/scandal-index-eng.

104 Office of the United Nations High Commissioner for Human Rights, "International Law," 2004, http://www.ohchr.org/english/law/.

105 Office of the United Nations High Commissioner for Human Rights, "About OHCRC," 2004, http://www.ohchr.org/english/about/.

106 Society of Professional Journalists, "Reference Guide to the Geneva Conventions," 2002, http://www.genevaconventions.org/.

107 International Criminal Tribunal for Rwanda, "About the Tribunal," 2004, http://www.ictr. org/default.htm.

108 Helen Vesperini, "Rwanda's Parliament Now Leads World in Gender Parity," in Choices for the 21st Century, United Nations Development Program, March 2004, p. 11.

109 International Court of Justice, 2004, http://www.icj-cij.org/icjwww/icjhome.htm.

110 Human Rights Watch, "About HRW," 2004, http://www.hrw.org/about/; and Amnesty International, "About Amnesty International," 2004, http://web.amnesty.org/pages/aboutai-index-eng.

111 International Committee of the Red Cross, "The ICRC's Mandate," 2004, http://www.icrc. org/web/eng/siteeng0.nsf/iwpList2/About_the_ICRC:Mandate.

112 Office of the High Commissioner for Human Rights, "Universal Declaration of Human Rights," United Nations, 2004, http://www.unhchr.ch/udhr/.

113 United Nations Development Fund for Women (UNIFEM), WomenWatch website, 1997, http:// www.un.org/womenwatch/asp/user/list.asp?ParentID=3001.

114 Ibid., 2000, http://unstats.un.org/unsd/demographic/ww2000/edu2000.htm.

115 United Nations Development Fund for Women (UNIFEM), "The World's Women 2000: Trends and Statistics," WomenWatch website, http://unstats.un.org/unsd/demographic/ww2000/overview. htm.

116 Janice G. Raymond, executive director of the Coalition Against Trafficking of Women, "The Ongoing Tragedy of International Slavery and Human Trafficking: An Overview," hearings before the Subcommittee on Human Rights and Wellness of the Committee on Government Reform, U.S. House of Representatives, October 29, 2003, http://action.web.ca/home/catw/readingroom. shtml?sh_itm=68f9a02ebd640b77783e0b2cb0e7684c.

UNIT 6 ENDNOTES

1 United States Agency for International Development, "Telling Our Story," 2004, http://www. usaid.gov/stories/sierraleone/ss_sierraleone_listening.html.

2 Desiree Evans, "Digital Storytellers," YES! magazine, No. 24 (winter 2003), p. 33.

3 Tufts University, "Governance and Accountability," April 19, 2004, http://www.tufts. edu/~kregan02/index.htm.

4 Robertson Work, "Overview of Decentralisation Worldwide: A Stepping Stone to Improved Governance and Human Development," United Nations Development Program, 2002, http://www.undp. org/governance/docsdecentral/overview-decentralisation-worldwide-paper.pdf.

5 Office of the High Commissioner for Human Rights, "Universal Declaration of Human Rights," United Nations, 2004, http://www.unhchr.ch/udhr/.

6 Philippine European Solidarity Centre website, "Campaign Against the Coal-fired Power Plant in Negros Occidental: A Project Brief," http://www.philsol.nl/A99b/NACP-brief-aug99.htm; and Green Peace South East Asia website, http://www.greenpeacesoutheastasia.org/en/pr/pr_ce/ pr_ce_20010328.html.

7 Vote for America, 2004, www.voteforamerica.org.

8 United Nations Development Program, "Mobilizing Grassroots Support for the Goals," ch. 7 in "Millennium Development Goals: A Compact Among Nations to End Poverty," Human Development Report 2003, http://hdr.undp.org/reports/global/2003/pdf/hdr03_chapter_7.pdf.

9 Ibid.

10 Ibid., pp. 134–37.

11 Roy Madron and John Jopling, "The Web of Democracy," New Internationalist, No. 360 (September 2003), pp. 16–18.

12 United Nations Development Program, "Mobilizing Grassroots Support," pp. 134–37.

13 United Nations, "The United Nations and Decolonization," 2000–2004, http://www.un.org/ Depts/dpi/decolonization/history.htm.

14 OGIEK.org website, "About the Maasai," 2004, http://www.ogiek.org/faq/maasai.htm.

15 TexacoRainforest.org website, 2004, http://www.texacorainforest.org/, and T. Christian Miller, "Ecuador: Texaco Leaves Trail of Destruction," Global Policy Forum, 2003, http://www.globalpolicy. org/socecon/tncs/2003/1130texacoecuador.htm.

16 GlobalIssues.org website, Anup Shah, "Human Rights for All," 2004, http://www.globalissues. org/HumanRights/Abuses/Myanmar.asp.

17 The Struggle Site, 2004, "Chiapas and the Zapatista Rebellion," http://flag.blackened.net/revolt/mexico.html, and University of Texas Department of Economics website, 2004, "Basta! Land and the Zapatista Rebellion in Chiapas: A Review," 2004 http://www.eco.utexas.edu/Homepages/ Faculty/Cleaver/collier.html.

18 U.S. Department of Labor, "Youth and Labor," 2004, http://www.dol.gov/dol/topic/youthlabor/.

19 U.S. Environmental Protection Agency, "Timeline," 2004, http://www.epa.gov/history/timeline/index.htm.

20 John de Graaf, David Wann, and Thomas H. Naylor, eds., "Political Prescriptions," ch. 8 in Affluenza: the All-Consuming Epidemic, (San Francisco: Barrett-Koehler Publishers, Inc., 2001) pp. 215–23.

21 Open Secrets, "Campaign Finance Reform—What's the Issue?" December 31, 2003, http://www. opensecrets.org/news/campaignfinance/index.asp.

22 Ibid.

23 David Lewit, "Porto Alegre's Budget—Of, By, and For the People," YES! magazine, No. 24 (winter 2003), pp. 21–22.

24 United Nations, "About the United Nations—History," 2004, http://www.un.org/aboutun/history.htm.

25 Ibid.

26 United Nations Development Program, "The Millennium Development Goals," p. 31.

27 United Nations Millennium Goals, 2004, http://www.un.org/millenniumgoals/.

28 United Nations Development Program, "The Millennium Development Goals," p. 31.

29 United Nations Development Program, "Overcoming Structural Barriers to Growth," ch. 3 in "Millennium Development Goals: A Compact Among Nations to End Poverty," UN Human Development Report 2003, p. 69, http://hdr.undp.org/reports/global/2003/pdf/hdr03_chapter_3.pdf.

30 Diogo Freitas do Amaral, "The United Nations at the Crossroads," Yale University Library, May 2, 1996, http://www.library.yale.edu/un/un3d2.htm.

31 Joan Lawson and Richard B. Blankney, "U.N. Has Major Role in Foreign Policy," Seattle Post-Intelligencer, July 16, 2004.

32 United Nations website, "Is the UN Good Value for the Money?" http://www.un.org/geninfo/ ir/ch5/ch5.htm.

33 Freitas do Amaral, "United Nations at the Crossroads"; Anup Shat, "The United Nations on Development Issues," GlobalIssues.org, July 25, 2001, http://www.globalissues.org/TradeRelated/ UNAndDevelopment.asp; and "United Nations," Microsoft® Encarta® Online Encyclopedia, 2004, http://encarta.msn.com.

34 The American Heritage Dictionary (New York: Houghton Mifflin, 2002).

35 Robert Guisepi, "The Rise of Civilization in the Middle East and Africa Civilization: Drawbacks and Limits," 1989, http://ragz-international.com/civilization%20drawbacks.htm.

36 Luis Angeles, "Income Inequality and Colonialism: How Much Does History matter?" University of Lausanne, February 2004, http://www.hec.unil.ch/langeles/ineq_fev04.pdf.

37 U.S. Census Bureau, "Income and Poverty 2002," September 26, 2003, http://www.census. gov/hhes/poverty/poverty02/pov02hi.html.

38 United Nations Development Program, "Human Development Report 2002," p 17.

39 Ibid., p 19.

40 United Nations Development Program, United Nations Human Development Report 1998 (New York: Oxford University Press, 1998), cited by the Shared Capitalism Institute, http://www.shared-capitalism.org/scfacts.html#Call54.

41 Ibid.

42 U.S. Census Bureau, "Income and Poverty 2002," September 26, 2003, http://www.census. gov/hhes/poverty/poverty02/pov02hi.html.

43 Dr. Stephen Bezruchka, "The (Bigger) Picture of Health," in Take Back Your Time: Fighting Overwork and Time Poverty in America, edited by John de Graaf (San Francisco: Berrett-Koehler Publishers, Inc., 2001), p. 78.

44 World Watch Institute, Vital Signs 2003 (New York: W. W. Norton & Co., 2002), p. 88.

45 United Nations Development Project, Overcoming Structural Barriers to Growth," p. 1.

46 Edward S. Herman, "The Threat of Globalization," Global Policy Forum website, 1999, http:// www.globalpolicy.org/globaliz/define/hermantk.htm.

47 Ibid.

48 Ksenia Yudaeva, "Globalization and Inequality in CIS Countries: Role of Institutions," Centre for Economic and Financial Research website, December 28, 2002, http://www.cefir.org/Papers/ cefwp22.pdf.

49 Jeremy Brecher and Tim Costello, Global Village or Global Pillage: Economic Reconstruction from the Bottom Up (Cambridge, Mass.: South End Press, 1994).

50 Domini Social Investments, "Spotlight on Sweatshops," 2004, http://www.domini.com/share-holder-advocacy/Issue-Spotlight/.

51 Seattle Initiative for Global Development, "Building a Better World: A New Global Development Strategy to End Extreme Poverty," 2004, pp. 5, 8, http://www.seattleinitiative.org/SIPolicyBrief.pdf.

52 Brier Dudley, "From Redmond to India: High Tech's Global Families," Seattle Times, August 8, 2004.

53 Ibid.

54 Robert Hunter Wade, "Globalization, Poverty, and Income Distribution: Does the Liberal Argument Hold?" The Brookings Institution, Economic Studies, June 17, 2002, http://www.brookings.edu/gs/research/projects/glig/worldshortinequalityjune02.pdf.

55 Herfried Münkler, "The Wars of the 21st Century," International Review of the Red Cross, No. 849 (March 31, 2003), pp. 7–22, http://www.icrc.org/Web/Eng/siteeng0.nsf/iwpList553/0B15A195650D60C3C1256D0B00435D32.

56 Tech News World website, "ITAA Report: IT Outsourcing Benefits Economy," 2004, http://www.technewsworld.com/story/33261.html.

57 U.S. House of Representatives, "International Financial Institution Advisory Commission (Meltzer Commission), Final Report," March 2000, www.house.gov/jec/imf/meltzer.htm.

58 Wikipedia, "World Trade Organization," 2004, http://en.wikipedia.org/wiki/World_Trade_Organization.

59 United Nations Development Program, "Overcoming Structural Barriers to Growth," p. 80.

60 Ibid.

61 U.S. Department of Treasury, "Fact Sheet: Taxes," 2004, http://www.treas.gov/education/fact-sheets/taxes/economics.html#income.

62 United Nations Development Program, "Overcoming Structural Barriers to Growth," pp. 77–78, http://hdr.undp.org/reports/global/2003/pdf/hdr03_chapter_3.pdf.

63 "What Is Human Development?" Human Development Reports, United Nations Human Development Programme, 2004, http://hdr.undp.org/hd/default.cfm.

64 United Nations Development Program, "Overcoming Structural Barriers to Growth," pp. 67–69

65 Ibid.

66 Ibid., p. 75.

67 "Building a Better World: A New Global Development Strategy to End Extreme Poverty", Seattle Initiative for Global Development, January 2004. http://www.seattleinitiative.org/SIPolicyBrief.pdf.

68 United Nations Development Program, "Overcoming Structural Barriers to Growth," p. 78.

69 Ralph Estes, "Let the Sun Shine In," YES! magazine, No. 23 (fall 2002), p. 19.

70 Interfaith Center for Corporate Responsibility, 2004, http://www.iccr.org/.

71 UN Global Compact, 2004, www.unglobalcompact.org.

72 "Building a Better World," .

73 Results website, "Microcredit," 2002, http://www.results.org/website/article.asp?id=244.

74 Ibid.

75 Hal Brill, Jack Brill, and Cliff Feigenbaum, "Natural Investing," YES! magazine, No. 11 (fall 1999), pp. 48–49.

76 Gulchehra Namsurova, "A Harbinger of Decentralization: Local Tajik Groups Set Their Own Agenda," Choices: The Human Development Magazine, United Nations Development Programme, March 2004.

77 Trickle UP Website, Success Stories, 2004, http://www.trickleup.org/MediaKit/mk_success.pdf.

78 Jochen Hippler, "Low-intensity Warfare and Its Implications for NATO," 1988, http://www.jochen-hippler.de/Aufsatze/low-intensity_conflict/low-intensity_conflict.html.

79 E. A. Stepanova, "Military Operations Other than War: The U.S. View," Military Thought, March-April 2002, in Looksmart, http://www.findarticles.com/p/articles/mi_m0JAP/is_2_11/ai_89021711.

80 Wikipedia—the Free Encyclopedia, "genocide," 2004, http://en.wikipedia.org/wiki/Genocide.

81 Ibid, "terrorism," 2004, http://en.wikipedia.org/wiki/Terrorism.

82 Ibid, "asymmetrical warfare," 2004, http://en.wikipedia.org/wiki/Asymmetrical_warfare.

83 Ibid.

84 Ibid.

85 Herfried Münkler, "The Wars of the 21st Century," International Review of the Red Cross, No. 849 (March 31, 2003), pp. 7–22, http://www.icrc.org/Web/Eng/siteeng0.nsf/iwpList553/0B15A195650D60C3C1256D0B00435D32.

86 J. S. Dewar, "Revolution in Military Affairs: the Divergence between the Most Dangerous and the Most Likely," War, Peace and Security, 1998, http://wps.cfc.forces.gc.ca/papers/amsc1/008.html.

87 Stockholm International Peace Research Institute, "Yearbook 2004, Armaments, Disarmament and International Security," pp. 10, http://editors.sipri.se/pubs/yb04/pr04.pdf.

88 Ed Johnson, "Red Cross to Airlift Supplies," Seattle Post-Intelligencer, August 25, 2004.

89 Human Rights Watch, World Report 2002, http://www.hrw.org/wr2k2/us.html.

90 United Nations Development Program, "Overcoming Structural Barriers to Growth," p.77.

91 John Sewell, "The Realpolitik of Poverty," Environmental Change and Security Project, 2003, http://www.wilsoncenter.org/topics/pubs/commentaries_povsec_27-39.pdf.

92 Ibid.

93 Ashley Hamilton, "Resource Wars and the Politics of Abundance and Scarcity," University of Queensland, Australia, School of Political Science and International Studies,2003, http://www.polsis.uq.edu.au/dialogue/vol-1-3-5.pdf; and Jenny Goldie, "Natural Resource Scarcity and Violent Conflict," In Search of Sustainability Conference, http://www.isosconference.org.au/papers/Goldie.pdf.

94 Future Harvest, "Four Million Killed in Post–Cold War Conflicts: Prospects for Peace Increase, Even in Poorest Countries, with Investments in Agricultural Research and Technology," 1999, http://www.futureharvest.org/news/02161999.shtml.

95 Population Action International, "Water Scarce Countries," in Sustaining Water, 1993 http://www.cnie.org/pop/pai/water-14.html.

96 Seattle Initiative for Global Development, "Building a Better World: A New Global Development Strategy to End Extreme Poverty," 2004, http://www.seattleinitiative.org/SIPolicyBrief.pdf.

97 Lester R. Brown, Plan B: Rescuing a Planet under Stress and a Civilization in Trouble (New York: Earth Policy Institute, 2003), p. 104.

98 Amnesty International, "Control Arms," 2003–2004, http://www.controlarms.org/the_issues/index.htm.

99 Nuclear Weapons Archive, "Nuclear Weapons Nations and Arsenals," January 2004, http://nuclearweaponarchive.org/Nwfaq/Nfaq7.html.

100 "Post-conflict Peace-building," United Nations, Report of the Secretary General, 1995, http://www.un.org/Docs/SG/SG-Rpt/ch4h.htm.

101 "World Health Report 2003," overview and chapters 2 and 4, http://www.who.int/whr/2003/en/overview_en.pdf.

102 Joyce Mulama, "Calmer Waters," New Internationalist, No. 367 (May 2004), p. 6; and "Nile Initiative," United Nations Development Programme—Sustainable Water Management, June 2001, http://www.undp.org/seed/water/region/nile.htm.

103 Seeds of Peace, "Empowering Children of War to Break the Cycle of Violence," 2004, http://www.seedsofpeace.org/Display.cfm?id=2.

UNIT 7 ENDNOTES

1 Anthony Guess, "Guatemalans Provide New Definition of Wealth," Mockingbird Times, August 2004.

2 William E. Rees, "Area-Based Indicators of Sustainability," Population and Environment: A Journal of Interdisciplinary Studies 17, No. 3 (January 1996).

3 The Earth Council, "Rethinking Economics," March 13–19, 1997, Rio + 5 Forum, Ecological Footprints of Nations, http://www.ecouncil.ac.cr/rio/focus/report/english/footprint/economics.htm.

4 United Nations Human Development Report 2003, "Overcoming Structural Barriers to Growth," chapter 3 in "Millennium Development Goals: A Compact Among Nations to End Poverty," pp. 74–78, http://hdr.undp.org/reports/global/2003/pdf/hdr03_chapter_3.pdf.

5 United Nations Millennium Goals, http://www.un.org/millenniumgoals/.

6 "Donnella Meadows' twelve leverage points to intervene in a system," Wikipedia—the Free Encyclopedia, http://en.wikipedia.org/wiki/Donnella_Meadows'_twelve_leverage_points_to_intervene_in_a_system.

7 Donnella Meadows, "Dancing with Systems," Whole Earth, winter 2001, http://www.wholeearthmag.com/ArticleBin/447.html.

8 Earth Charter USA website, 2004, http://www.earthcharterusa.org/earth_charter.html.